Dr Anita Heiss is the author of non-fiction, historical fiction, commercial women's fiction, poetry, social commentary and travel articles. Her books include *Tiddas*, *Am I Black Enough for You?* and *Barbed Wire and Cherry Blossoms*. She is a regular guest at writers' festivals and travels internationally performing her work and lecturing on Aboriginal literature. She is a proud member of the Wiradjuri nation of central NSW, a Lifetime Ambassador of the Indigenous Literacy Foundation and manages the Epic Good Foundation. Anita was a finalist in the 2012 Human Rights Awards and the 2013 Australian of the Year Awards.

Growing Up Aboriginal in Australia

EDITED BY **ANITA HEISS**

Published by Black Inc.,
an imprint of Schwartz Publishing Pty Ltd
Level 1, 221 Drummond Street
Carlton VIC 3053, Australia
enquiries@blackincbooks.com
www.blackincbooks.com

9781863959810 (paperback)
9781743820421 (ebook)

A catalogue record for this
book is available from the
National Library of Australia

Cover, text design and typesetting by Tristan Main

Printed in Australia by McPherson's Printing Group.

MIX
Paper from
responsible sources
FSC® C001695

In memory of Alice Eather (1988–2017)
and so many others who were lost too soon

Contents

Introduction

Anita Heiss

There is no single or simple way to define what it means to grow up Aboriginal in Australia, but this anthology is an attempt to showcase as many of the diverse voices, experiences and stories together as possible.

We received more than 120 original submissions from Aboriginal people nationally as a result of the callout for contributions, each with an important story to tell, proving that many want mainstream Australia to understand what it's like to 'grow up Aboriginal'.

Each account reveals, to some degree, the impacts of invasion and colonisation – on language, on country, on ways of life, on how people are treated daily in the community, the education system, the workplace and in friendship groups.

The stories cover country from Nukunu to Noongar, Wiradjuri to Western Arrernte, Ku Ku Yalinji to Kunibídji, Gunditjamara to Gumbaynggirr and many places in between.

Experiences span coastal and desert regions, cities and remote communities, and all of them speak to the heart – sometimes calling for empathy, oftentimes challenging stereotypes, always demanding respect.

We did not place any boundaries on the collection, other than that the pieces had to be non-fiction and so we have life stories written from all around the country, including from boarding schools and even from inside prison; and from schoolchildren, university students and grandparents. We also have recollections of growing up Aboriginal in Australia by opera singers, actors, journalists, academics and activists. In many ways, this anthology will also serve to demonstrate how we contribute to, and participate in, many varied aspects of society every day.

While lives have been lived and expressed individually, there are numerous communal connections and shared experiences that frame common themes, including the importance and influence of identity, the stolen generations, family and kinship, education, concepts of country and place, and sport.

This collection mirrors the society that Aboriginal people live in and engage with every day, so there are motivational and uplifting stories alongside those on suicide; words on feminism and sexuality, as well as football and theatre. Role models and religion and road trips. We are diverse peoples and that's exactly what growing up Aboriginal means today in Australia.

Many contributors are being published for the first time. All have generously and courageously bared their personal and family histories, their pain and heartache, their experiences of racism so that others can learn about what it means to grow up as a First Nations person in a country where they are often viewed and treated as second-class citizens, and sometimes even worse than that.

But this anthology is not one of victimhood: it is one of strength and resilience, of pride and inspiration, demonstrating the will to survive and the capacity to thrive against the odds. *Growing Up Aboriginal in Australia* paints a landscape of a country that has created leaders who form strong communities, with a generous heart and passion for change. That is why this anthology matters. The goal is to break down stereotypes – many of which are identified within these pages – and to create a new dialogue with and about Aboriginal Australians.

There are over fifty contributors to this collection. One deserves special mention, not only for her work as a poet and community role model, but because during the process of compiling this book she took her own life at the age of twenty-eight. Alice Eather was a devoted and passionate bilingual primary school teacher, and in recent years she was widely recognised for her performance poetry, her work as an activist, and a dynamic member of her community. Alice had an unswerving commitment to sustaining her language, people and homeland. Alice's family and all those involved in the production of the anthology hope her work and messages will remain as a legacy to inspire others.

Reading through the submissions for *Growing Up Aboriginal in Australia*, I saw elements of myself as a child and as an adult, still on a journey of learning and discovery. I felt the same sting of racism as described by some contributors, as well as the strength and resilience expressed by others. I was fortunate as a child growing up Aboriginal in Australia: although I wasn't surrounded by my extended Wiradjuri family in the Sydney suburb of Matraville, my close-knit immediate family provided all the support, guidance and the protection I sometimes needed to become a strong, proud, urban Koori who knows how to assert her rightful place in this country, and the world. Here's hoping this collection proves that many Aboriginal Australians feel similarly, that it goes some way to enabling those who don't to do so, and inspires all Australians to allow that to happen.

Two tiddas

Susie (27) and Alice (21) Anderson

S: What did it mean to you, when we were younger, that we're Aboriginal?

A: Well, I don't ever really remember being sat down and told, 'Hey, Alice, guess what, you're Aboriginal.' For some reason it was an unspoken understanding. It was as much of an understanding to me that I had ten fingers and ten toes or the fact that I only had one parent. I guess when you're a kid you just don't question the *why* so much. Things just *are*.

In primary school things were simpler. Not so much in my world around me, but in my mind at the time. Those were my glory days in terms of sport, and I wanted to be the next Cathy Freeman. Life was confusing, but in the way that it can be for kids.

Now I'm twenty-two and somewhat of an 'adult', I like to reflect on the things that were said or happened around me and think about how they affected me and what seeped into my sponge-like child brain.

S: Yeah, to me it honestly didn't *mean* something: it was just a lived experience. I didn't second-guess it until I became a teenager, I think. It wasn't a conspicuous part of my identity, just normal, as most things seem when you're a kid. Our second cousins called us Aunty as a joke. We had to respect our elders; we had to call distant

5

relatives Aunty and if we didn't the consequences were dire. There was one time at someone's birthday party that I didn't hug Aunty Trudy hello (frankly because she scared me, but I was also being a terrible preteen) and there was much disapproval. Needless to say, I learnt my lesson: I went to hug Aunty when we were leaving and it was a tacit apology. She still brings it up every time I see her, and another time she said she'd always known I had something about me. Basically, I take this to mean that Aunty Trudy is in tune with the ancestors and blak magic is real.

A: Firstly, blak magic is totally real. And I always remember that. Around family I knew and understood who I was, I think. Especially looking to our aunties as idols. But at school it was like all of that was taken away from me. No one really knew I was Aboriginal. In fact, a lot of people didn't know until high school. I guess because I didn't walk around with it written on my forehead. I wanted people to know. But I didn't want to do the telling. But neither my face nor my skin did that for me. This was something that I would go on to learn – and am still learning – how to own. And carry. Always.

It felt like we spent a lot more time around family then too. I think of Aunty Nor's house and her possum-skin cloak hanging proudly on a mannequin in a room. I knew it was significant because it felt like it was. I knew my background was significant because I could feel that it was.

S: I know. All my memories of specifically 'growing up Aboriginal' are within our family context. Like listening to Yothu Yindi and Tiddas in the car, and knowing it as a part of who we were but none of the implications. Going along with kids in my year level when we talked about fractions of ancestry. Looking back on it now, those socialised things probably contribute to the imposter syndrome I have when I think about being 'black', but I wasn't to know then, just a child.

Were there times at school where you felt really aware of it?

A: ALL. THE. TIME. But it almost never felt celebrated. It always seemed to be followed by questions. People just questioning me rather than accepting me. Even my teachers would sort of tilt their head and require some sort of mathematical equation or diagram so they could compute 'what fraction Aboriginal' I was. As if being fifteen and angsty and having an identity crisis every other day wasn't fun enough ...

I remember Australian history lessons being taught as if it only began in 1788. I remember finding that weird but 'kid Alice' hadn't yet become as antagonistic and outspoken as 'high school Alice' would end up being, so I never said anything. I made a point of shifting my homework to be Aboriginal-focused even if it didn't fit the criteria, and even if my teachers would raise their eyebrows. I remember having to do a project on bushrangers for about the third year in a row and I made sure this time to find an Aboriginal bushranger instead of yet another bearded white man. I did. And I got five gold stars. But I still didn't feel satisfied.

Then I remember in Grade 5 we were given dot paintings to colour in, and I felt a sense of pride – but no grounds on which to claim my pride. I knew I identified with this thing that I loved, but without the knowledge of how to. Or something.

S: I remember I did that assignment that everyone did at our primary school, where you had to choose from a list of 'noteworthy Australians' and research them and make a poster featuring our chosen ones. It was nice they included Evonne Goolagong Cawley and Oodgeroo Noonuccal. I remember when the Olympics were on we all stayed up late to watch Cathy win.

There was one specific time in Year 8 English where we visited Brambuk as a class. You know they have all the photos of the missions in the Wimmera, including Ebenezer. Whenever I see those photos I just feel like there is this part of my identity filled in. Day to day it seems like something is missing, because we didn't have Dad around, and when there's a connection to him, it makes me feel like a full person.

A: There were a lot of things within our school, or just that small-town community environment, that I just wish would have been different. But probably still aren't. There was a yearly scholarship for Indigenous students at our school, and my class coordinator would always try to get me to enter. One year I didn't and at the end-of-year presentations they read out my entry from the previous year and gave it to me anyway. I was so angry and some people in my year made me feel shit for accepting it because I 'wasn't really Aboriginal'. There was another time the health teacher addressed me in front of the entire class about personal experiences with alcoholism, since I was Aboriginal. I told her she was a bitch and I got suspended.

I spent a lot of high school, and my time living in Horsham, feeling angry and frustrated and denied. I never once felt ashamed of who I was. I felt displaced. White people didn't accept me as black, and I felt like only my family knew me as black. Sorry to spew all of my pent-up high school frustrations into one long-winded reply. But there's one more thing I remember.

My Year 12 Studio Arts teacher was one of the only ones I liked at my school. She actually talked to us as people. We were studying Tracey Moffatt and she was reading aloud from a pretty outdated-looking textbook. Out loud rang the words 'half-caste'. I remember my stomach dropping and that weird knot in your throat that forms but you can't swallow. I expected to look up from my book to a sea of eyes staring at me in the classroom, but everyone was carrying on, unfazed. I went home and cried.

S: I'm so sorry you had that experience, my darling. There is a lot of power in those words 'half-caste' and 'quadroon'. Those are terms that were used so carelessly but defined identities and the existence of our dad, uncles, aunties, grandmother.

A lot of the time I have feelings about how my appearance, for some people, excludes me from my Aboriginal identity. It's a battle that I have internally all the time. It's social conditioning. I will never get the inclusion and membership to community simply from my looks. A lot of it is a white thing, sure, but that's also the culture we were brought up in and that takes a lot of mental and emotional undoing.

A: Slightly off topic, really, but I just remembered that an Aboriginal woman used to hang around the Preston supermarket when I lived there, and she would ask people for money, but she used to call me 'sis', so I would give her coins even though I could not afford to, because it made me happy to be recognised for who I am, but also because I wanted to help her. Then I told my friends and they were like, 'she probably just says that to everyone so they give her money'. So the next time I saw her I asked her who her mob was and she asked me back.

S: Yeah. I know identity is nothing to do with skin colour and it goes much, much deeper than that. But it's so hard when that's how mainstream Australia thinks about 'what an Aboriginal person looks like'.

A: Do you remember anything about how Dad felt about it? All Mum's ever said is that he didn't like to announce it and that 'he wanted to be given things because he deserved them not because he was Aboriginal'.

S: I know pretty much what you do about how Dad felt. Would have to check with Mum, but I think she said once that his teacher up in Swan Hill used to point him out in class as 'the Aboriginal kid'. It could have been more racist than that, but I'm not sure if that's what I was told or if that's what my childhood memory has created. I reckon I've heard Mum say that he would phrase his identity so he said that it was his mum who was Aboriginal. That stuff about him not embracing being Aboriginal seems like a self-preservation thing. Maybe internalised racism, but I'm hesitant to associate that idea when it can't be confirmed.

But, you know, I have realised a lot of that stuff is that we just didn't have the right community around us. I dunno. Of course we had our cousins and aunties, but they were only around occasionally. Plus at school there was stigma and a lack of understanding about how we specifically relate to that aspect of who we are. And if we didn't fit the idea of what they thought being Aboriginal was, then we must be lying. That's something I still carry around with me now, which seems ridiculous.

I'm struggling to find the voice to write about this because I feel like I don't have any agency or my words don't have any value. Like who cares what a fair-skinned Aboriginal girl's experience was?

A: I dunno, I guess the thing distinctive to our story is that the direct connection to our culture was missing for most of your and our sister Laura's life, and for all of mine: our dad. It's a powerful thing, and when you say that when you feel close to him you feel like a whole person, it's so true. Same with our heritage. I feel like a whole person knowing I have our ancestors helping us. Seeing a pelican fly above me and feeling so safe. We're lucky.

I agree with the struggling to find your voice for this piece. I never really feel fully qualified to say anything either. But then I get upset that I feel that way mostly because I only feel that way because of other people and not because of how I really feel myself, if that makes sense. I know who I am until somebody questions it, and then I have to start all over again. It's exhausting.

I know so many people who share those exact same feelings, and that's exactly why I think we should be doing this interview. Not necessarily to be read by anyone or selected or whatever – but because conversations are everything. And if it's only had between us then it's still not wasted. I'm really glad to be writing this with you.

S: YES! I kind of had this breakthrough at a dinner with friends the other night. I had this feeling of hovering outside myself as I 'came out' as Aboriginal to everyone at the table. Every time I speak about it my heart races, face flushes – just waiting for surprise or someone to say 'you are a liar' or some other response. This particular night I could see my desire for there to be something – either within me or in others – that changes when I explain my story.

A: I was talking to my housemate about it last night: she's Aboriginal and she's also blonde-haired and blue-eyed. She has a story of her own. Similar to ours, but hers. That makes me think just how many stories there would be across the country. And it makes me feel less alone and less insignificant.

S: For so long even talking like that, acknowledging who I am, felt like the biggest challenge for me. I know rationally that the trauma of losing our dad and our immediate connection to culture is part of the struggle for us understanding our identity. But, though it's powerful and meaningful, identity itself isn't the whole job. The real work happens with this writing. Marching. Talking. Being seen. Language. Cultural relearning. Yarning.

A: Regardless of exteriors, we both have some of the oldest-surviving blood running through our veins – and when I remind myself of that, I don't really care about that old white man on the plane to Alice Springs who told me I 'couldn't be *properly* Aboriginal', or any of my classmates who would reply to me with, 'Yeah, but you're different to them.' If I remind myself about that continuous bloodline – and if I'm surrounded by people who remind me of that – nothing else matters.

S: Hey, I actually think this is a really strong arc but that could be because I'm tired as.

A: Well, I'm reading it back and I got really emotional. Maybe I'm just really tired too. I feel like this is a conversation that could go on forever. This is literally a conversation that will go on forever.

Finding ways home

Evelyn Araluen

I wasn't a nice kid. I'll be the first to admit that. I was loud and smart-arse, scrappy and scabby, and I didn't sleep. I had eyebrows as thick as your thumb and in the front of my mouth were two rotten front teeth, so I smiled like a carnivorous marsupial. Once I ran my sister over with a bike because I was playing cross-eyed. I mostly ate noodles or crab sticks, and I lived on the dreaded silver detention seats. I was never *officially* expelled, but true god we all knew it was good that I left when I did.

I am twenty-four now, remembering a smaller and sassier me. I was born at the base of the Blue Mountains, the valley of Dharug country, by the Nepean River and Mulgoa Road Maccas. The third child of six, so quintessentially middle-child I had to share even that position with my little sister. Before the dark and stormy night when I came into the world, my father saw waterlilies.

Our Aunty Gloria gave him my name, Araluen. She's from Yorta Yorta country, Cummeragunja Reserve. They left before the walk-off in 1939, and because her father was a preacher she got to go to school. In fact, she went to every mission school in New South Wales. She has the softest voice and tells stories the sweetest you'll ever hear. But we're not from Cummeragunja. We're not from Dharug, either. We've been here a long time, but not for eternal time. Not for time immemorial. Growing up I didn't know what it meant to have ancestral country; Dad never spoke about anything in possessives, much less place. I knew that Aboriginal meant we were here before the tall ships came. Bits of us. But bits of us came on those tall ships too. I was a teenager when big sis finally told me 'The Story'. Our great-grandparents. Evelyn. Eva. Harry. Douglas. Harry. Baryulgil. Bundjalung. Then other side, maybe Wiradjuri? And what about Moonahcullah? Unslipping silence and denial through the generations. 'It's not simple,' she told me, black-gold-red-painted gumnuts rattling from her rear-view mirror. 'We're never going to be one of those families that knows everything.'

I don't like not knowing everything. I discovered I was smart in Year 3 when I won a class award. I hadn't thought that smart was something I could be. I thought smart was just for the popular girls, like pretty blue eyes and a dainty little nose. I knew I was good at reading and stories, but thought I was better at running and shot-put and getting into trouble at school. My writing got me into a 'gifted and talented' program in the next town over, but I think that place only ever taught me that I'm not very good at making friends. Recess in the library, first as lonely and then as Monitor of the Year. Lunch with the 'special needs' class. It was probably hard for them to make friends with the pimpled, big-nosed kid who thought white kids couldn't see owls and who once accidentally told the rest of her class trip that she was checking the bushes for *yuri* men. They don't see *yuri* men, but I found out they do see owls.

My siblings and I were taught two worlds pressing in on each other. We were taught immemorial time. We were taught to look for little bodies in bushes and for dog spirits by water. The desalination plant means we can't swim in the Nepean anymore, or the Grose or the Hawkesbury. Those are the rivers that wrap around Gundangarra–Boorooberongal–Dharug–Eora, flowing down from Darkinjung, where Mum's side lives. I was probably a bit of a shit on those long drives through the sandstone walls of the Pacific Highway every time we went up to stay, always fighting and asking when we're gonna get to the farm. The farm is at first the hot thick smell of week-old bread and everything after is green, green swampy grass. Billabong and the threat of bunyips. Nan and Pop bred cattle. Or they just had cattle hanging around. They also had ancient ironbarks and a brown dam, and descending crow caws, and cans of expired soft drink in the outside fridge. Our cousins, blond and indifferent. Most don't identify.

I don't think anyone in my family has ever had a lot of money and I don't think any of us would know what to do with it if we did. When Dad's mum passed away we could afford to move to a nicer part of town, to get our own rooms. Dad's mum had lemonade in big bottles in the kitchen fridge that we filled up to the top of the old Nutella glasses, and always a jar of sugared jubes. She loved us, so she pretended she could see the fairy lights that followed us around. I remember the storm that came to take her spirit away. I remember a lot of things like that.

In high school, Aboriginal didn't mean time immemorial as much as it meant the boys calling me *shit-skin* and *Abo*. Aboriginal meant I was always angry in History class, and fridge magnets and beaded bracelets at NAIDOC, and the digging stick in the study and *nangarra* above our door. It meant saying hello wherever we went. It meant that sometimes we saw things round the house and sometimes we smoked the house, that we could never kill a black snake. It meant *Respect Responsibility Reciprocity* and don't you forget it, *full-name*. It meant everyone always seemed to know my parents, knew what they did around the community. It meant that not everyone always liked my parents.

And now here I am at twenty-four, moving between Dharug and Eora for uni, for work, for friends and politics and poems, still finding ways home. Growing up, nothing seemed wrong about the kind of Aboriginal I am. Fair and a bit outcast, away from country but still in country, still caring for country, still listening to ancestors. Doing our best. Now I'm not so sure that's enough. Now I worry I am getting too big and loud, taking up too much space. I worry people want my words because of their neatness – because, in the end, I did well at school. I worry I will never have enough to give to my nieces and nephews. But Mum and Dad taught us how to manage that, how to be humble and respectful. I will always want more, but I am grateful for the culture I have. I am grateful for what has been shared with us by other families, from other nations. I am grateful for how I have been welcomed and protected across so much country.

It took me a long time to learn what I was missing. Difference never bothered me – it was absence that clawed anxious into my life as I grew older, got bigger. My teenage anxiety was the colour of earth, of big sis's skin that I so longed for. I spend a lot of time dreaming of the big black family photo, for dozens of cousins and oodles of aunties. All those brown faces like mine. Sometimes that desire blinded me to what we do have. Aunty Gloria and her kids and their kids, Uncle Greg, Uncle Wes, Aunty Charlotte: some gone now, but all remembered. Everything they have taught us. Our stories. Our spirit. Our ceremony. Big sis and I learning language. Soon we're going up north, to find the way we came to be here.

We've never been alone, and we have each other. Not everyone gets everything, and we are so lucky for so much. I'm learning my place, my responsibilities. I will always be learning who I am. We are Warragul Kia Araluen Eurobin Gwirra Guriyal. We are black snake, and our parents' best. We are the dream of our ancestors.

It's not over

Bebe Backhouse

I'm the youngest of six children – three from my father's previous relationship, and three from his marriage with my mother. My father is white and my mother is Aboriginal. However, nothing is ever as simple as that. You see, in addition to the journey that I took as a young Indigenous person, my mother was also on a journey when she was younger; we've ended up in different temporary locations, but the lessons learnt and experiences endured took similar shapes and forms.

I grew up in a small country town in the Kimberley region of Western Australia, a town surrounded by magnificent mountain ranges and ancient gorges, yet overshadowed by its larger, tropical beehive neighbour. It was a town with a population of about 6000 – the majority of that population consisting of the Aboriginal community.

My mother grew up in a like situation to mine – a white dad and an Aboriginal mum, living in a remote location. When my mum was four years old, her own mother left her family for another man. So, in turn, my mum and her siblings remained with her dad and thus began the next chapter of her journey: a broken relationship with her mum, and a diminished knowledge of, and connection to, her culture.

But that's her story to tell, not mine. However, it's important for me to acknowledge my mum's history in reference to my own, as I owe so much of my own existence, both physical and spiritual, to her.

So fast-forward ten years from there in my mother's life, my maternal grandfather had passed away, my mum had made contact with her mother again, and she'd met my dad and had my two siblings and me.

I grew up in quite a fortunate and privileged home, never being short of the newest and best materials, objects and opportunities, but most importantly never being short of food, clothing or love. At school, I had many friends who were of different cultural backgrounds, but I couldn't help feeling somewhat excluded from my Aboriginal friends, as my skin was white and theirs was black; and in hindsight, twenty years later, it was this very thought that saw me exposed to the many complexities and stereotypes of Aboriginal people. I was an Aboriginal boy, so why did I feel doubt about something that was inarguably true? Why did I feel insufficient? Why was I comparing myself to my own people, just because I didn't look like them? When I needed to go on a school excursion, receive a health injection or compete in a sports carnival, my parents needed to fill out a short form. One of the questions that was frequently asked on this form was: *Are you Aboriginal or Torres Strait Islander? Yes / No*

YES! I AM ABORIGINAL!

Acknowledging my cultural identity was such a thrill for me; there was nothing I was more proud of. For me, the ticking of this box was more than a statistical record. It was an admission, a declaration, and an affirmation that I belonged to an incredibly vibrant, surviving culture that, really, I knew nothing about.

Several communities that still practised traditional Aboriginal customs surrounded the town I grew up in. Several of my friends were getting ready to head out bush for something they called 'lore'.

'Bebe, where are you going for lore?' they asked.

'Um, I'm not sure, my mum hasn't told me,' I responded.

Now, just what they were talking about I had no idea, but I didn't want them to know that; after all, I was Aboriginal and had to know these things.

It was always a strange thing for my siblings and me. As our mum was raised by a white father, there was no cultural knowledge for her – or us – to inherit. Despite being raised by her birth father in a home filled with complete and utter love, unconditional security and protection, the one thing he couldn't give my mum was the knowledge of who she was as an Aboriginal woman. This was not his fault. I'm sure there was a part of him that wanted her to get to know the other side of her identity. Even if this were the case, he wasn't able to give her an opportunity for this, as he passed when my mum was just fourteen, which pushed her unexpectedly into the unfamiliar world of her Aboriginal heritage. So, she grew up knowing the only lifestyle she was exposed to.

So going back to that day after school, as dinner was being prepared, I asked, 'Mum, where am I going for lore?'

She looked at me with quite a shocked and confused look. 'Who told you that you're going to lore?'

'My friends at school are going, so aren't I?'

'Don't be silly', was her response and that was the end of the conversation.

I still had no idea what lore was, but I felt a little relieved – yet also disappointed – to not be doing it. Why wasn't I going? Would the lore people not let me do it because I had white skin? Had my mum banned all cultural activities?

The following day at school, I didn't let the other boys know that I wasn't going away to lore and, one by one, they vanished from the classroom and the playground, and I didn't know it at the time, but they would come back one step closer to being men than I.

When I was nine years old, I began learning the piano. 'Mum, some of my friends at school are learning the piano, but I want to learn the violin. Can I?' I asked after school one day.

The only music teacher in town was a little old lady, a nun, who had strong connections to the Aboriginal residents of the town.

'We'll go and speak to Sister tomorrow,' she said.

So, off we went to see the Sister at her studio, which was an old converted chapel with green stained-glass windows.

'Show me your hands,' she said, looking down at me through her thick steel-rimmed glasses.

Nervously, I showed them to her. She only glanced for about three seconds before telling me, 'I won't teach you the violin. Your hands were created for the piano, so I will teach you that.'

And so, for the next ten years, I would be her student, ultimately becoming her only pupil – until she returned to a convent in Perth, where she would live out the last of her days. I never expected to follow a musical path in life but, for quite a few years, it was the force behind my drive. It also proved to be a very interesting factor in the development of my true identity, encouraging me to come into my own. As if I didn't have enough segregating me from other children, other boys my age, I now had the stigma of being a pianist to work with. I always knew I was gay, but being young and growing up in a town where labels were the social norm, I wasn't anywhere near ready to willingly apply another badge to my shirt.

Despite the taunts and teasing I received, I couldn't help but feel a strong sense of pride in the steps I was taking. It wasn't until later that I understood just how much the Sister had taught me – not just about music, but about life. She taught me commitment and dedication; she taught me to chase after what I wanted in life; she made me realise that I had the potential to become anything I wanted. It didn't matter that I lived in a small remote town.

The last time I ever saw her, I could barely step out of the car in the parking lot. I'd been her student, she'd been my teacher, nothing more. Right? Wrong. She was my guardian, she was my guide, she was my friend. Before I met her, I was just a young Aboriginal boy meandering through the streets of a small outback town. Yet there I was, sitting in the car outside the convent, unable to move. I wasn't ready for what was to follow. Yet, as she had taught me when performing, I took three deep breaths and began walking forward.

When I first saw her lying in her bed, she seemed so distant, so far removed from the world we were in. She could barely speak, so I spoke for the both of us. I told her of the students I was teaching just as she'd taught me, of the performances I had given across the country, of how she'd given me the tools to unlock one of the most valuable gifts. I thanked her, gave her a hug and left. Within days, she was gone.

It may seem strange, writing of this particular topic with such emotion. And you may not see any point to it, thinking I'm rambling on, but I can tell you now: growing up as an Aboriginal pianist was an experience of a lifetime. You see: I travelled, I saw, I grew; the first man I ever loved fell in love with me as I played. I took those stereotypes that were thrown against me, and I ran with them. I became more than what was expected of me. I was dedicated to becoming someone, for my teacher, for my family, for my people, for myself.

It was during my early teenage years that I began to forge a relationship with my maternal grandmother, who had been somewhat estranged from the family. It was through my conversations with her that I came to gain an understanding of my Aboriginality and form a connection. I quickly learnt that I came from the Bardi tribe from the coastal region of the Kimberley, and the Alngith tribe from far north Queensland; I learnt that my totem is the pearl shell; that our family are the traditional owners of the land that I holidayed on as a kid. This, and so much more, through conversations with my nan. Who would've thought?

As I grew older, I continued to learn about my culture, my heritage, my history and my identity. Fair-skinned Aboriginal people are questioned about – and doubted in regard to – their 'authenticity', with comments such as, 'But you don't look Aboriginal?' As something I've faced my whole life, I questioned myself constantly. There have been people in my life who have judged me because of where I have come from. I've endured racist slurs and homophobic taunts, but I've also been judged on the successes I've encountered for myself. For me, growing up Aboriginal in Australia was an adventurous journey, one that I'm still yet to complete.

My story

Alicia Bates

Born in 1989 in Warrnambool, Victoria, on Peek Whurrong–Gunditjmara country, I was my parents' first child and lucky enough to be the first grandchild born on both sides of the family. This meant that I had many significant and close relationships with my extended family, being spoilt by my great-grandmother Ma (Dad's nanna), Nanna (Mum's mum), and my uncles and aunties. During the first five years of my life, my parents bought their first home together in Portland, where my dad was a shift worker at the smelter.

Growing up I was always told I was Aboriginal – or Koori, as I prefer; I was always proud of this fact, my country and my people. However, growing up without my father made it difficult to better connect with my culture and people. Often our Koori groups both inside and out of school contained a lot of activities originating from white European culture – or team sports, which I loathed. Having a lighter skin tone, I have been told by others, both Koori and non-Indigenous, that I am 'too white to be Aboriginal' and that I have 'more white blood than black blood'. Last I checked, my blood was red just like everybody else's, and I'm not sure when exactly or how these people measured how much 'black' was in my blood. Furthermore, I have learnt through speaking with many respected elders in our community that our people should not be judged for – or by – the colour of our skin.

When I reflect on what being Aboriginal means for me personally, I know this means: being strong and proud, having a strong connection to my home country and its culture and history, caring for others, my family and community, and having respect for my elders. #DefineAboriginal

Ages 5 to 12

These years were a difficult and challenging time: my parents separated and divorced not long after my youngest brother was born. (I have two younger brothers, and a younger sister from one of Dad's later relationships.) Dad had cheated on Mum and he spiralled into a life of alcohol and drugs. Mum tried to ensure he would see us on weekends, and although I remember some fun times with my dad, he was often unreliable and didn't show up. Mum struggled trying to raise us three children alone, and she couldn't keep up with the mortgage payments; it was a very difficult time for us all. We were living in a rough area, so Mum found herself making friends with a lot of the wrong sort of people (namely, alcoholics). She tried her best to look after us three children, making sure we were always fed and well clothed; my brothers were a handful and very hyperactive at the time. My youngest brother would be diagnosed in primary school with ADHD, and later with autism.

I spent a lot of time outdoors and at friends' places; I was very much a tomboy and most of my neighbourhood friends were boys. School was also a problem for me, as I was being constantly bullied by a group of boys in my class and felt as if I had no friends at school; my best friend had also recently moved away after her parents had divorced.

At the end of 1997, when I was eight years old, Mum declared herself bankrupt and we were virtually homeless, having to move across to Warrnambool and move in with Nanna. I remember this as a very happy time (for me personally) – I couldn't wait to get away from the bullies at school and start fresh at a new school. I enjoyed living with Nanna, but having two mothers in one home also sometimes made things hard; Mum and Nanna would often argue. I loved my new school, and felt very popular having made so many new friends. Moving to Warrnambool also made our extended family closer, and I spent a lot of time mothering and helping to look after my younger cousins and brothers.

At the end of 1998 (when I was nine years old and soon to commence Year 5) Mum was fortunate enough to be offered a three-bedroom home through Aboriginal Housing Victoria after being on the priority housing list for twelve months. I remembered being excited to be moving into a new home and being able to pick out my own bedroom. I wasn't too thrilled about having to change schools and leaving all my new friends behind, and it took me a long time to settle into my new school. I always had a love–hate relationship with school; I loved the routine and enjoyed learning but often struggled with the social aspect, again experiencing bullying during my last two years of primary school.

When I was in my last year of primary school, the events of the past few years became too much for Mum and she suffered a psychotic episode. This was a scary time for both my brothers and me as we did not really know what was happening. Mum had to be hospitalised for a long period of time and we were lucky enough to have Nanna – our guardian angel – move in and look after us.

Growing up I was very close to both Nanna (Mum's mum) and Ma, my great-grandmother (Dad's nanna). I stayed with Ma every second weekend: we would watch TV and scary movies together and she would tell me stories about growing up in a large family of thirteen. Ma was a strong and proud Gunditjmara–Kirrae Whurrong elder, who cared for many. She had raised my father and uncle after finding them in a boys' home (aged eight and nine years old, respectively) after they were left there by their mother and applying to become their legal guardian. She also cared for her sister's children and grandchildren, and raised her own four children alone after leaving an abusive marriage. My relationships with Nanna, Mum and Ma have been the most significant to me and they are major influences in my life, all having spent most of their lives caring for others and overcoming challenging and difficult circumstances with such great strength and determination.

Ages 13 to 18
I loved (most of) high school and made some great friends, some of whom I am still close friends with today. It was good to find friends

who were misfits like me; unlike the other girls, we liked fantasy, studying and animals more than we cared about boys, hair and make-up.

Throughout my teenage years Mum had other mental breakdowns and was diagnosed with bipolar; this lead to my passion for psychology as I wanted to learn more about mental illness, the brain, and people in general. During these years my brothers and I became part of a support group for children and adolescents who had family members with a mental illness. This allowed us to participate in many fun activities that we would not have otherwise been able to participate in. This also provided us with a support network of other young carers and trusted social workers who we could speak to.

Adulthood

When I completed my VCE at seventeen, I applied for a library traineeship at my high school, still not 100 per cent sure what I wanted to do next. I was successful and spent a gap year working in the library at the school before beginning my bachelor's degree in psychology at Deakin University the following year. I originally began the course with the goal of becoming a child psychologist, as I had always wanted to work with children. I achieved high marks throughout my course and, as a result, I was invited to complete an honours year.

Unfortunately, on the commencement of my honours year my youngest brother, who was sixteen years of age, had a major psychotic episode (needing to be taken to Melbourne). I decided to defer my course to help my mum and my family at this difficult time. My brother has since been diagnosed with schizoaffective disorder; both he and Mum are now doing well at managing their illnesses.

The following year I completed my honours in psychology, then a Diploma of Secondary Teaching in Bendigo, where I stayed with my aunty, uncle and cousins. After spending five years at university I still wasn't sure what I wanted to do, and still hadn't quite figured out where my passion lay. I found it difficult getting work in secondary teaching, and after eight weeks' work at a local secondary college as a student counsellor, I realised I couldn't see myself working with teenagers for an extended period of time, so I applied for a Master of Early Childhood Teaching.

I completed this course in October 2015, achieving marks within the top ten per cent of my university year, and have since been working as a teacher in the local council's kindergartens and childcare centres. I absolutely love this job and feel that it's where my passion lies and is still within my original career goal of wanting to work with children.

As mentioned, I have experienced many losses (family home, father, friendships) and traumas in my life, all of which have contributed to making me a stronger and better person. Most recent was the loss of my beloved Nanna, who passed away from cancer. I miss her every day; I treasure all of my memories and know that she was, and would still be, proud of me and all of my achievements.

Currently, while working part-time, I am a volunteer director on the Gunditjmara co-op board of directors, and also a foster carer for both Aboriginal and non-Indigenous children. I am very passionate when it comes to helping others and try to give back to my community in any way that I can. I wrote this piece hoping to aid in dispelling and eradicating some of the negative stereotypes surrounding Aboriginal people. I hope that one day we will never hear racist ignorant comments, such as 'Aboriginals don't work or want jobs' or 'They are getting a free ride, they have it easy, they get all these government handouts' or 'Aboriginals don't take care of their own or their community'. These are just some of the untrue, ignorant and unfair attitudes that I have faced all through my life and that are still with us now. Today and every day I stand with both my Aboriginal and non-Aboriginal brothers and sisters in hope that we can one day reach peaceful reconciliation.

Dear Australia

Don Bemrose

Dear Australia,
I am a descendant of the Gunggari people of the Maranoa district near Mitchell, Queensland. I am a member of a rich living culture. I grew up with a loving, generous extended family on the Sunshine Coast in Queensland and I have much to be thankful for.

I love this country and all its people for shaping the man I am today and allowing me to be me. I educate, I inspire and I entertain, but I have flaws and I have done wrong and wronged you, Australia, so I must tell of how sorry I am and ask you to please forgive me.

I'm sorry
I'm sorry I identify as Gungarri and Aboriginal. I know you would prefer I added 'part', 'quarter' or some other quantifier to signify that I am less than full; to reinforce my lesser status, and as a reminder that my people are to be bred out.

I'm sorry I am neither white, nor black enough for you to easily label or identify me as 'other'. I understand how hard it can be for you to be openly funny or casually racist when people like me are around.

I'm sorry I'm not a 'real Aboriginal' living in a remote part of Australia, surviving off the land. Sorry that I can't be herded up like cattle or sheep when a mining company decides that destroying this country is more important than sustaining it.

I am sorry I can't dot paint, play football or run really fast.

I am sorry I have only been able to become a leading opera artist, sharing the stage with some of Australia's finest classical musicians in operatic works by Mozart and Puccini, and in new Australian works, such as *Pecan Summer* by Deborah Cheetham and *Cloudstreet* by Palmer, Edwards and Sexton.

And while I may consider myself an artist, I am sorry I can't shake a leg or wear a lap-lap every time you need someone for a significant 'Australian' event. I am sorry I can't 'Welcome you to Country' because we are not one mob. There is no one Aboriginal people, and my mob, the Gungarri, we are not from here.

I am sorry I completed Year 12, graduated from the University of Melbourne's Victorian College of Arts with a Bachelor of Music Performance (Opera), and I am really sorry I went on to graduate from Charles Darwin University with a Graduate Diploma of Teaching and Learning. To have me, a blackfulla, educating the young minds of white Australian children at one of the Australian Capital Territory's best schools must be hard for you to fathom.

Finally, I am sorry I have said sorry more than once. Once really should be enough to heal all past and current atrocities I have committed against you. No explanation required. You have taught me that on many occasions.

Please forgive me

Please forgive me for being unsuccessful with my suicide attempt at the age of twenty-three. I know, one less loud-mouth, thinks-he-is-educated *Abo* would have been a great addition to your incredible world-leading youth suicide statistics.

Please forgive me for identifying as gay, because I know you hate double and triple minorities, which are such a threat to your monocultural, patriarchal, 1950s utopia.

Please forgive me for not being lazy: I know how you prefer your natives to want nothing but a free handout, but somehow I have become a 'want-for-nothing' Aboriginal who lives the best life I can.

Please forgive me for being a success! I have a loving, supportive and large extended family who have been present at every success I have had in my life and career. Please forgive them for teaching me values such as kindness, forgiveness and love. I know you would have preferred I had an angry chip on my shoulder so I could be poked and prodded to burn flags, on cue.

Please forgive me for having full-time employment and for owning my own car and not relying on that 'special treatment' all Aboriginals get. I know you create all those entry-level, short-term, identified positions to tick boxes in your reconciliation action plan, but I really am too old and too experienced to be chasing an entry-level role. I applied for and won a role against all other candidates in an open field that wasn't only for ATSI people, and it is permanent and ongoing, so unfortunately I will get to spend my cash how I wish – no cashless card for me.

Please forgive me for not putting that native title claim on your backyard ... yet! I am still researching what legal proof my family will need to secure a nice spot in Point Piper or Kirribilli – I'm a bit partial to a nice water view. And while I am talking property, please forgive me for owning my own home with my wonderful partner, which we saved for and purchased with our own money. Please forgive me for not taking all the reparations money I am owed as a First Australian.

Please forgive me for reminding my seventh-grade history teacher – and nearly every Aussie since – that Captain Cook did not discover Australia in 1788. I must also seek your forgiveness for continuing to educate staff, students and government employees of these same facts through running cultural-competency training courses.

Thank you

Thank you for never allowing me to be *only* Australian. Since that first time in the local playground when a 'true Aussie' child asked me '*what* are you?', I have always had to think quickly and justify the colour of my skin to meet the standard of answer 'proper' Aussies want and that fits with their worldview. For many, a reply of 'I am Aboriginal' was not acceptable, and I thank you for teaching me that I am not Australian but proudly Aboriginal. A human.

Thank you for teaching me I am a third-class citizen in my own country by suspending the *Racial Discrimination Act* to invade the

Northern Territory under the guise of protecting children from abuse. That was to get access to land and natural resources, wasn't it?

Thank you for keeping me humble, when I achieved a childhood dream and sang the Australian national anthem at the State of Origin rugby series in 2008, by sending me abusive emails and phone messages telling me that I had betrayed my culture and community.

Thank you for teaching minorities to hate other minorities.

It was a great early life lesson to not be able to get a date because no gay 'Aussie' male wants to date an *Abo*. It forced me to learn to love myself.

Thank you for giving me the nickname of 'Bondi floater' in primary school, which meant I was a piece of shit from a sewerage line that was damaged after a storm in the 1980s and washed up onto the shoreline. Gives a whole new meaning to BFF!

Thank you for incarcerating my family for multiple minor misdemeanours because they grew up in – and were fleeing – trauma-filled homes. It really is so much easier to deal with them when they can be neither seen nor heard by wider society and are off the gentrified streets.

Thank you for acknowledging every 26 January with such grace and humility. Thank you for your encouragement – and advice to me – to let the past be in the past, to simply 'get over it', on the day my people's land was invaded and dispossessed. And thank you for teaching me to ignore all of the massacres and racist policies that helped the British build this Commonwealth nation of Australia from the ground up.

Australia: I love you

I love your incredible coastline and beaches. I love the feel of your hot sand under my feet, the sound of waves crashing, and the coolness of diving through that first wave as it breaks overhead. I love the Surf Life Saving community that nurtured my leadership skills through my teenage years and early twenties when I was struggling to find my path.

I love the build-up of an afternoon storm and the epic lightning shows that erupt overhead. I love that I can still find places to be safely alone and, on a clear summer's night, can watch the billions of stars in the Milky Way or gather with millions watching fireworks over Sydney Harbour.

I love visiting our rivers and estuaries, searching for that perfect swimming hole or fishing spot. I love sitting by a fire telling yarns and laughing late into the night. I love our humour when the chips are down and that resilience to just get on with it. I love that we can take the piss with our closest mates and stand by one another in our darkest hour. I love watching sporting heroes giving their all, win, lose or draw.

I love the sweet call of magpies and kookaburras in the morning or evening and how loud a flock of lorikeets are when feeding. I love being able to ride my bicycle across the bush capital with ease and have picnics surrounded by our native wildlife.

I love that I have been lucky enough to travel to every Australian city and work with some of the best, most forward-thinking individuals, and coach many to extraordinary feats. I love the friendships that have been culturally safe and supported me to reach my childhood goals and taught me that our differences make us stronger not weaker.

Most of all I love that I am a mediochre (middle-colour) Aboriginal man who grew up in this sunburnt country of Australia.

Sincerely, your Gungarri brother,

Don Bemrose

P.S. I truly love every square inch of Australia. I look forward to when we realise that this country is our giver of life and will survive long after we have passed on. Maybe, then, we will each choose a life similar to that of our ancestors: one of leaving soft footprints and a light touch on this landscape, and with a kindness for each other.

My father has a story

Tony Birch

In the black-and-white photograph, he is thirteen years old, posing tough with other Aboriginal boys of Fitzroy. He is wearing a pair of denim bib-and-brace overalls and a checked shirt. My father is slightly built, has a shock of dark hair and smile full of cheek. The first time I see the photo, behind a glass frame, I immediately think of Huck Finn, and imagine his childhood as one of freedom and adventure. Imagination is all I have when reconstructing my father's early life, as he gives so little away. There are no photographs of his mother, Diddie, or his grandmother, Ninnie, the women who raised him in the narrow Fitzroy terrace they lived in after the First World War until the death of my grandmother in 1951.

His is a family of secrets. One of my great-uncles adopts the nickname 'Ranji' as a means of explaining his dark complexion. Others seem to disappear altogether. Another great uncle, Les Moodie, a lightweight boxer, often fights in Sydney, where the purse is better. Each time he enters the ring before a bout he is announced as 'the coffee-coloured coon from Melbourne'. I don't know how Les coped with the racism, but he did go back into the ring time and time again, and did well for himself. In his old age Les sits in the front window of his narrow house on Hoddle Street, Collingwood, where he waves to kids walking by. They are told by their fathers and grandfathers that Les is a Maori boxer who came to Australia to spar with the legendary Jack Johnson, the first black heavyweight champion of the world. Johnson won the world title in Sydney in 1908, and subsequently toured the country with the support of gambling czar John Wren. Les did have the good fortune of touring with him.

My father's father, my grandfather, lives with the family for only a brief period. Soon after my father's birth, he leaves for New South Wales with his mother, a woman with whom he has an unusually close relationship. He quickly marries – illegally – in Sydney, where he becomes a notorious criminal. He is shot in two separate incidents. One afternoon, following an argument with his wife, he throws her from a bus. At the trial, his mother is the star witness for the defence, as she is at many of his subsequent criminal trials. She defends her son as 'a wonderful loving boy', with tearful emotion. Nonetheless, her melodramatic performance is not enough to save him from a conviction. Some years later my grandfather returns to Melbourne, a lot heavier and wearing an expensive suit. He drifts in and out of our lives, an impermanent and occasionally menacing presence.

As an adult, my father has little contact with most members of his family, who leave Fitzroy in the early 1950s. They move to the suburbs and again reinvent themselves. My father has a habit of disappearing from the house for days on end. He sometimes takes me with him. We stay at a big, raucous house in Carlton, rented by the Onus family, a large Aboriginal mob with political and social connections across south-eastern Australia. My father feels at home there. I love being there with him, even though I feel disloyal to my mother. Many of the visitors to the Onus house play a guitar, just the one, shared around. Or they play the spoons, and even a tea chest that one old man continually drums away at. And everyone in the house can sing, men and women. My father dances around the kitchen with a woman he will disappear off with. I am left by myself with the army of kids sleeping at the house. We terrorise the stray cats in the laneways and head up to Lygon Street and watch the Italians promenading through Little Italy. When my father finally decides to return home to my mother, we walk the cold streets from Carlton to Fitzroy. He tells me we have 'a little secret' between us that must be kept from my mother. I know the secret has something to do with women, but little more than that.

Waiting for my father

feeling the heavy air
of six o'clock closing
we wait for the silence
of the jukebox

his gold tooth shines
rock'n'rolling yet
another woman across
the scuffs and scratches
of the dance floor
she spins, all beauty
flashes of colour
end on end
beehive to high heel
into him
the taps shut down
he takes her hips
and winks his children away
with fish and chips for six

As much as he likes to sing and dance, my father is an angry and violent man. He has a particular talent for smashing furniture, and can reduce a lounge chair to splintered timber within seconds. A handy boxer himself, he uses his family as a punching bag. He is always apologetic afterwards, and reminds me that our beatings are yet another family secret. My mother is not so good at keeping secrets, but when she announces to his friends that my father is a 'wife-basher' they either laugh her away with feigned disbelief or turn away from her, masking their own shame with silence. There is nothing special about my father, of course. I come to understand this each time I strip off at the local pool for swimming training, where I look down at my own bruises and then sneakily at the battered bodies of my classmates. None of us speak a word about the evidence we carry on our bodies or the stories we hold in common.

Scenes of domestic life

a Saturday night middleweight
armed with a mule kick right cross
his memories of glory
and a gathering of empties
sit restlessly in the neutral corner

a hiss of tyre rubber
spews an arc of murky
on an empty pub corner
where the children wandering
the shimmering streets search
the depths of wet bitumen
for understanding

they leave behind their portraits
in a rainbow and oiled reflection
and drift home bruised feet
dodging footpath cracks
a dance of superstition

in a Sunday morning kitchen
she sits at the family table
a fractured party face
sponging weeping wounds
my mother patiently mends
a broken vase, a wedding gift
from her mother

My father is only thirty-five when his world falls apart. He is again
absent from the house, although on this occasion he is not away
singing and dancing with other women. My mother sits her five
children around the laminex tabletop in our small kitchen. She
tells us that my father has had a 'breakdown' and that he will be
spending time in hospital. The next time I see my father he is in a
psychiatric institution. I hardly recognise him. His face has gone

missing, replaced by a blank stare. He cannot lift his feet and shuffles about endlessly smoking cigarettes. When we leave the hospital, I look back at the barred windows and listen to the snap of the door lock. I ride the bus home, having never felt safer during my life than I do after each visit to him. Although they are informed about his illness, no one in my father's family visit him, with the exception of his older sister.

The years of medication, electric shock treatment and institutionalisation change my father dramatically, almost killing him. But eventually he is saved. The Aboriginal community of Fitzroy gather around and care for him: men and women who had known him when he was a kid, during the years before any of them were ravaged by the forces of racism and exclusion. He moves to the countryside and begins working with young blackfellas in schools. The experience is life-changing, for both my father and his family. I discover, a little to my own surprise, that I love him. He becomes open about his own failures. He is also apologetic, and this time he means it.

One day I am sitting with him and ask him about his childhood. Curious, I eventually ask him if he witnessed the bulldozing of his Fitzroy home, which was knocked over as part of a slum-clearance program in the early 1960s that would change the landscape and culture of inner Melbourne. I don't expect him to remember much, if anything at all. He goes quiet, coughs nervously and then tells me a story that is both wonderful and terribly sad.

I grew up in a house with six beautiful women. My mum, my Nanna, two sisters and two aunties. The house was crowded but really comfortable. I shared a bed with my mum until she got sick. I was about to turn fifteen and I was working at a shoe factory in Collingwood when I found out that she was dying of cancer. I came home from work one afternoon and a doctor was at the house. He told me that my mum had died. She was laid out on our bed and I ran into the room, jumped on the bed, wrapped my arms around her and wouldn't let go. I didn't want her to leave me. That night we sat around the kitchen table drinking tea out of the same pot in which she'd made hundreds, no, thousands of cups of tea. The house I grew up in, it was a house of love. But once she was gone I felt nothing but fear.

Soon after my grandmother's death my father found himself alone. And abandoned. He lost his way for many decades, but remarkably he survived. He also found the pathway to recovering his identity, the sense of self he carried as a boy but was separated from. Without the love and support of Aboriginal people, a good outcome would never have been possible, not for my father, his children or his grandchildren. We have no 'tribe' or 'totems' in our family. We know why this is so and we know it without shame. We also know who we are and where we are going.

Away

the warmed hollow
of your childhood bed
the place where you
once laid and rested
is away

your young breath singing
rising through morning air
to fill the rooms of houses
and the life you had –
away

fingerprints marking time
on a kitchen table
a bicycle wheel turning
its windmill in the yard
playful hands swept through
locks of hair to untangle –
away

and along the road
running away from us
where secrets are told
with darkest whispers
I see your gentle feet

leaving their dance
in a red dirt track –
away

Murri + Migloo = Meeks Mob

Norleen Brinkworth

I was born in 1947 at Yarrabah mission, an Aboriginal reserve run by the Anglican Church of England near Cairns, north Queensland. This mission was where my grandparents, both paternal and maternal, grew up from around the turn of the twentieth century.

Taken from other places in Queensland, they became part of what has become known as the 'Stolen Generations' or 'stolen children'. The government policy at the time was to assimilate them away from their mothers, family and familiar environment, placing them in an institution that was highly controlled by total strangers to these children. Sadly, many of these young children would suffer from the repercussions of this ordeal both then and there, and also later in life.

Unfortunately, none of my grandparents or my parents lived long enough to hear the words of the then prime minister, Kevin Rudd, in parliament on 13 February 2008 when he said: 'We reflect ... on the mistreatment of those who were Stolen Generations – this blemished chapter in our nation's history.' I think closure of some sort would have been provided to them if they had.

I have spent much time researching my family history. Records show that my paternal grandparents, Ronald and Ada Meeks née Jeffery, were taken to Yarrabah mission as very young children and placed in the children's dormitory. Ronald was taken from his mother in the northern Queensland town of Cooktown when he was three years old. Ada, along with her two brothers, was taken from their mother in the western Queensland town of Winton. Both Ronald's and Ada's lighter skin clearly indicates that they were fathered by European men, and this resulted in these children being removed in accordance with the government's policy for the 'Stolen Generations' and were known and referred to by the derogatory term of 'half-caste'.

Vital information about Ronald's removal from Cooktown was obtained from a descendant of a former prominent landowner in Cooktown, who allocated a part of his property to be used as the 'blacks camp', a safe haven for Indigenous residents in the region. Only full-blood Aborigines were accepted here, as the landowner was firmly against miscegenation. Sadly, therefore, my grandfather was taken away from there and his familiar surroundings, his home and, most of all, his primary caregiver, his mother, who never saw him again.

My research into Yarrabah mission history shows Ronald's age as three on his baptism record, and names his mother as 'Dora'. His father is simply shown as 'Unknown European'. In the dormitory, these children were segregated by their sex until they reached an eligible age to work and were old enough to be married and live elsewhere in the mission. This was the start of the Ronald Meeks mob.

The records reveal my paternal grandparents, Ronald and Ada Meeks, and their family were exempted from Yarrabah mission in 1936 and became residents in Cairns. My father, William, returned to Yarrabah mission some years later with my mother after meeting her in Cairns, where she regularly visited her sick mother in the Cairns Base Hospital.

After the death of my maternal grandmother, my parents, William Meeks and Audrey Sands, were married, which meant she was no longer subjected to the daily Anglican religious doctrine she claimed was imposed 'morning, noon and night' in the female dormitory where she lived. Her freedom from the dormitory led to a new life as a married woman, and so began the William Meeks mob in Yarrabah mission.

I lived at the mission for the first ten years of my life with my parents and my five siblings plus my maternal grandfather. Having lots of cousins and aunties and uncles in the small mission community with the surname Sands, I was always surrounded by – and had constant contact with – relatives, but none with my surname.

I remember as a first-grade pupil travelling by boat with my family to Cairns to meet some of my father's family in Anzac Park, a popular meet-and-greet place used regularly by Indigenous people as they sat talking under the tamarind trees that bore tasty fruit that the children searched for. When we met the Meeks family it became obvious that there weren't that many of us, as Ronald Meeks did not have any siblings.

During this period, travelling from Yarrabah mission to Cairns, a distance of approximately forty kilometres via sea, could only be done aboard the mission motor launch, as the huge mountain ranges between these two places had no roads, only walking tracks that were used mainly by fishing enthusiasts.

For me, the greatest joy travelling on this boat occurred when my family were given a day 'leave pass' to attend the annual Cairns Show in the month of July. This annual and much-anticipated outing – that every child on the mission wished for – could only happen if our parents obtained a pass from Mr Wilcox, the mission superintendent at the time. This required the whole family waiting their turn outside the mission's office to request a leave of absence. I believe us children were on our best behaviour when waiting for this pass, as I have vague memories of my mother threatening to take us back home if we didn't sit still, be quiet and be patient. The day pass, if granted, recorded names of all family members visiting Cairns and the date of their absence from the mission, as it was necessary for Cairns police officers ('bullymen' as these law enforcers were commonly referred to by the mission people) to sight this pass in order for Yarrabah mission residents to visit the town.

My first four years of education were spent at the mission school, which didn't have a dedicated dress code, and we all walked barefoot to school daily. There was little memorable about those schooldays, apart from sports day, when the foot race was my main interest that I focused and thrived on. It was my running ability that helped me cope in the next school I attended, Parramatta State School in Cairns, because my brother Joseph and I were always selected for running events in various sporting teams.

In 1957 several residents in Yarrabah mission went on strike and spoke out about various issues, including the restrictions placed upon them in terms of their movement away from the reserve, the lack of food and health care, and work safety issues. Needless to say, some of these protesters were expelled and officially exempted by the Anglican Church, which meant that these residents and their immediate families were banished permanently.

In 1958 my family was also exempted from Yarrabah mission and we moved to Cairns. I never knew the full reason for our exemption, but I suspect my father was critical of the administration, as they took no action to improve living conditions for the remaining residents despite the strike action.

Leaving Yarrabah mission permanently for Cairns as a ten-year-old child wasn't as traumatic for me as it was for my mother, as she was leaving her large extended family knowing that she wouldn't be allowed back to attend any family functions or even if a loved one died.

It was around this age that I became curious about my surname, having been called 'Meeks fruit' by other children, which annoyed me because all I knew was that was something used in making cakes; I guess that bullying only further fuelled my curiosity to find out why we were the only Meeks family living on the mission. Furthermore, I wanted to know why we – me, my father and my siblings – had lighter-coloured skin than my other relatives in Yarrabah mission.

Meanwhile, I continued my education at Parramatta State School, where wearing shoes and school uniform daily was the least of my worries. What did stress me out in the very first two days in class was not knowing what the elderly, cranky spinster teacher meant when she reminded the children to do their 'homework' as they left the classroom. For me, 'homework' was helping my mother with household duties, such as carrying my crying baby sister on my hip or washing up.

In class the next day, the teacher asked if I had done my homework. I said yes, but when asked to produce evidence of homework in class I was totally confused. I felt embarrassed and ashamed to stand in front of the class and discuss my 'homework'. Needless to say, when I started talking about my household duties, the class started laughing and sniggering, and I soon realised I was in trouble.

'Homework' was never part of the school system at Yarrabah mission when I was a pupil there, hence my confusion with this word. Books, pencils, slates and other tools used in the classroom were supplied and never taken to school by children, nor were these items taken home or taken out of the building. Hence no homework. On reflection, education on this Aboriginal reserve at that time was basic compared to schools with pupils not under the *Government Protection Act*.

Another ordeal I encountered as a new pupil at Parramatta State School was making eye contact when spoken to. The cranky teacher became annoyed and angry when she stood in front of me and reprimanded me because I wasn't making eye contact with her. Obeying her 'Look at me!' command and seeing an adult's eyes was frightening and meant I was disrespecting an elder. Growing up in Yarrabah mission, it was a cultural custom not to look an adult in the eyes when speaking or being spoken to – a silent sign of respect with eyes averted. I soon adapted to looking most people in the eye when spoken to, but my mother's slap across my face when I was talking to her made me realise this cultural tradition still stood at home.

Apart from the misunderstanding over 'homework' and learning to make eye contact with most people, I survived the education system and returned to it years later, once I was a mother of two boys, since I wanted to be a role model to them and teach them the value of education. This action resulted in my completion of tertiary education with a teaching qualification.

My curiosity about our lighter skin colour never subsided. I remember as a teenager asking my father this very question about our appearance. I was shocked and saddened by his detailed explanation, but I never questioned him about how he knew such information.

Sadly, I never got to tell my father the correct answer to that question of mine, because he died without knowing about the wonders of DNA testing, which is now freely available to the public. In 2012 I turned to DNA testing for the answer, because although the intense research I'd done on former residents of

Cooktown – and the information my husband obtained from the internet – was exciting and convincing to me, it was up to this point unproven. Hence, I needed DNA testing so I could confirm that my hypothesis was 100 per cent correct.

However, before DNA testing could be done, more time and effort was spent looking on the internet to try to locate a living family member of the man I suspected was my great-grandfather. Reading the electoral rolls and then the Brisbane *White Pages* finally led to my making a telephone call to a likely male descendant, Alan Meek, who readily agreed to participate in the DNA testing. Consequently, the DNA testing of Ronald Meeks' grandson, Joseph (my eldest brother), and the Brisbane man proved that Ronald Meeks was the progeny of a liaison between Dora and an English naturalist who was living in Cooktown – and this resulted in my grandfather becoming part of the Stolen Generations at the very early age of three. The DNA results also refuted my father's answer to my question 'Why do we have lighter colour skin?' His long-held belief that his grandmother was raped by a cattle-station owner has now been proven wrong.

I'm very grateful that my great-grandmother Dora had the courage in 1898 to give her son the surname that he and his descendants (mob) are still known by. Without this surname, there would have been no clue linking him to the naturalist; my grandfather's surname has the letter 's' added on the end and that is the only difference from the surname of the English naturalist. There is no evidence that my great-grandmother Dora used or was known by that surname while she was pregnant. In fact, I have found a marriage certificate signed in Cooktown for the naturalist and another woman and dated 1898, the year my paternal grandfather was born in Cooktown.

While researching this naturalist, I saw a photograph of him on the internet, which helped to confirm my suspicion that there is a definite connection between the naturalist and my grandfather. In my opinion, the similarities of their facial features cannot be disputed.

My paternal grandfather spent seventy-four years as a victim of the Stolen Generations – that '*blemished chapter* in our nation's history'. He left this earth on 6 May 1975 as a loving, kind, caring, generous, compassionate man despite the traumatic upheaval forced upon him as a three-year-old toddler, the consequences of which he endured until he found love years later with another Stolen Generations victim at Yarrabah mission. Ronald Meeks and Ada Jeffrey were married on 6 November 1918 and thus began the only Meeks clan at Yarrabah mission.

Easter, 1969

Katie Bryan

The day before my fourth birthday my mother made a magnificent cake. She had found the design in one of her magazines – the witch's cottage from *Hansel and Gretel*. I watched, entranced, as she carved the vanilla pound cake into sections. A fat square for the base, and two triangles wedged above it for the roof. The layers were glued together with thick butter icing; not ideal for engineering, as by the time my party came around one-half of the roof was listing badly in the Brisbane humidity. The entire production was on the verge of collapse, and a hasty fix with toothpicks would be needed to prevent it from toppling, minutes before our guests arrived. Family and friends might be impaled by the lurking infrastructure, but the star feature of her party table had been saved.

But that was later. For now, a brown paper grocery bag of sweets sat just out of my reach on the kitchen bench, ready to decorate the cake after the fiddly procedure of icing it. My mother had three bottles of food dye to tint the butter cream – red, green and yellow. I longed to add the drops, but being heavy-handed and partial to primary colours, the end result would gleam like the Rastafarian flag. And in this instance, my mother stood firm.

'No, Kate. If you add too much colour, people won't like it.'

The same rule, it transpired, applied to her guest list. So when I said to her, 'Can we invite Dad's cousins? The nice ones, from the beach?' she hedged, and we began to argue.

My birthday follows Easter and, a few months earlier, my family had motored out to the bayside suburb of Scarborough for some respite from the late summer heat. My mother packed our rusting metal esky with a picnic. Ham sandwiches, cake, biscuits, oranges, a flask of fruit-cup cordial. It was an hour's drive, but it was at least five degrees cooler on the bay than in our home in the western suburbs.

Dad parked his prized green FB Holden Special on the sandy verge, and my mother spread our navy tartan picnic blanket on the grass overlooking the sepia arc of Queen's Beach. My sisters, moody teens, grumbled that they'd rather be at Surfers Paradise. Scarborough has always been a safe haven for children who are too small to be confident in the open waves, but in those days there were no shops, no cafes, no pirate park and no junk food. In short, there was nothing to tempt a restless teen. Just the beach, the pub, and a fish and chip shop, and perhaps a Mr Whippy van, if you got lucky. So while the prospect of a trip to Scarborough was enough to fill a child under five with delight, it was guaranteed to produce a state of resentful ennui in her siblings over twelve.

What Scarborough did have was Norfolk pines that offered shade, which Main Beach did not, and this was the clincher. My sisters had smooth olive skin a few shades lighter than Dad's; they could stay out all day in the sun and would simply tan to gold. My skin was like my mother's: fair, flecked with freckles and moles. Too much time in the sun would turn us both lobster red, and any exposed flesh would burn and peel cruelly in the following days. My father hated when I burnt, and so my sisters' hopes for a more glamorous destination were dashed. It was simply one of those times when having a baby sister was a drag. They resigned themselves to a day of sullen moping, far from boys, shops and psychedelic 1960s fashions, relegated to building sandcastles in 'the swamp' for the chubby-legged source of their tribulation, and muttering scornfully that Scarborough was 'square' and 'uncool'. The best they could hope for was that their friends would never hear of it.

It was here, beneath the pines, that I first realised my father had secrets. My mother, alarmed that my face was now redder than my bonnet, had reeled me in off the beach and had set me to playing in the shade. Following my own interpretation of what constituted 'shade', I scuttled off to join some children who were sliding down the steep grassy embankment on flattened cardboard boxes. These had been cadged from the pub. Kids these days may have Xboxes; but back then we had Four-X boxes. And they were ripping good fun. But the hill was steep and my legs were short, and my sisters grew weary of pig-a-backing me up the incline. So when I spied a family group rounding the headland, and their father called out a fond greeting to mine, I trudged back to our picnic to see what it was about.

A man with smooth dark skin and a look of my father stared down at me. For a moment it seemed to me that he was suffused with light. As if the spirit that lit his amber-hazel eyes was at once a beacon, a magnet and the warmth of a homecoming camp fire. Years later I would describe it to an elder. He would rock back in his chair and stare at me intently before he spoke: 'Ah. That's kin-ship recognition. That's how you know your mob.'

The scowl on my mother's face told me that she could see no elfland glow. She looked out at the world through eyes that saw calloused hands and bare feet and muddy streaks on lithe brown limbs, and frayed clothes that had weathered years of hard toil and had been ruthlessly boiled clean in an old copper. Her eyes were at first disapproving, and then suspicious.

But the man paid no mind to her; he was looking at me.

'Is this your little one, Tom? Jeez, look at those eyes. She'll be a heartbreaker when she grows up. Doesn't she look like Ruby!'

'She looks like her mother,' my father growled, a warning look in his eyes.

'Who's Ruby?' I had never heard the name before.

'Ruby? Why, Ruby's your grandmother. Your dad's mum.'

I had never met my paternal grandmother. She was a patient, loving voice that chuckled at my stories on the far end of our phone line.

'Oh, you mean Marnie. But she lives in Perth. How do you know her?'

'Well, me and your dad grew up together. We're cousins.'

'But Dad is an only child. And so's Marnie. We don't have any cousins.'

'Well, maybe so, but there's all kinds of cousins. My mother and your dad's grandmother were sisters. So me and your grandma Ruby are first cousins. And that means me and your dad are first cousins once removed. So I'm your cousin too. And this lot.'

He gestured at his children, and launched into a long and involved explanation of our degrees of separation. It was too much; I was still struggling to comprehend how my grandmother could have a cousin who was younger than my father. The man looked at me kindly and ruffled my bonnet.

'Never mind, love. You'll understand when you're older. Hey! Is that Kaye? And Dodi? My god, you've grown. You'll remember my girls, surely.'

From the uncertain look in my sisters' eyes, I wasn't sure that they did. But girls their own age were an improvement on my company, so they nodded and went along with it. There was a tall boy with the man too. Perhaps four or five years older than me. The boy was staring at me, gobsmacked, and understandably so. We looked alike enough that a stranger passing by might have taken us for brother and sister.

My newfound cousin rested his hand on his son's shoulder, looking at him with affection and pride.

'This is my youngest, Dan. Listen, love, your dad and I are just off to the pub for a drink. We served in the war together, you know. And it's been a while. We've got a lot to catch up on. Dan, you take your little cousin back to her friends to play, and mind you look out for her.'

Ever my father's shadow, and confident there'd be pink lemonade to be had from it, I elected to follow him and this intriguing new development in extended family into the pub across the road. In the 1960s, you didn't have a lot of choice when it came to fizzy drinks in a bar. Pink lemonade was exotic; it was produced from combining plain lemonade with a sweet red syrup and, if a long trip with a garrulous child was in the offing, a good strong nip of cherry brandy. And possibly it was this that prompted my father to drop his guard. He forgot the age-old wisdom that little pitchers have big ears, regardless how charged up they may be on Dutch liquor.

My father cut to the chase. 'Olly, you can't go telling people we're Aboriginal. Especially not my wife. It isn't safe.'

'But there's nothing wrong with it!'

'That's not what they think. My wife's father – he's a doctor. He thinks that anyone with Aboriginal blood has something wrong with them. He thinks Aboriginal people are primitive. Another species. He wouldn't want to think his daughter married one. He'd think there'd be something wrong with our kids.'

'But that's rubbish!'

'It doesn't matter. It's what they think, and if something goes wrong, they'll take your kids away. It happened to me, with Kaye and Dodi, when their mother died. I couldn't look after them, and I had to put them in a home for a while. One of those church orphanages. Somehow they found out, and they turned on me. I nearly lost them forever. I was lucky that I found Katie's mother. I wouldn't have those girls now, if I hadn't married Barb.'

A long and involved discussion ensued that went right over my head. I think it shifted between politics and eugenics. What was clear to me was the fear the two men felt. I saw it in their eyes. That, and something that might have been disappointment, and a sense of hurt and betrayal. They had given up the best years of their lives to fight Nazis and they hadn't reckoned on coming home and marrying into families that espoused similar views.

'You can never tell anyone. Not even your kids … they can let things slip. And definitely not your wife. If things go wrong …'

I felt my father's fear, and I climbed up on his lap to cuddle into him. 'I love you, Daddy. I don't want the bad people to take me away.'

He held me close. 'I'll never let that happen, Katie darling. Whatever I have to do, I'll do it. I'll never let them take you away.'

Dad's cousin was pensive. 'It's alright for you: you're blond, you're blue-eyed, you're a generation further away from it than me. How the hell am I meant to explain this?' He made a sweeping gesture that drew in the totality of all that he was.

Dad shrugged. 'Tell them you're black Irish. Or Spanish. Anything. They're idiots. So long as you stick to your story and cover your tracks, they'll never know.'

'What's a Black Irish, Daddy?'

'The real thing. Unlike your mother's father: he's Orange Irish.'

'What's that?'

'English. And someone who pretends to be something they're not. Ha! Perhaps I've got more in common with your grandfather than I thought.'

Peals of laughter rang out. The bar was full of gnarled wiry men with rich tans and broad noses and ears, and deep heavy lines around their eyes and their brows. They smelt of sweat and strong tobacco and almost all of them wore dark navy singlets – a shift must have just finished, down at the docks. My father and his cousin grinned. They were safe here – they were amongst their own. Looking more at ease, they ordered another round.

My father spoke the language of the docks, but my mother never knew it. Like other Aboriginal children in the 1920s, he was obliged to leave school at the age of twelve and went out to work as a labourer, loading fish. He had been raised by his mother and his grandmother with the support of his great-aunts and -uncles in a multicultural area of north Perth. Weekends of his youth were spent camping with his mates at the beach. They volunteered as lifesavers at their local surf club. When the war came and the army recruited SLSC boys for their courage and their discipline, his opportunity to rise up in the world came along.

The ADF did IQ tests and my father scored in the top five per cent. Acknowledging his genius for mathematics, they sent him off for training with the RAAF. He became a navigator with Bomber Command and spent five years in the UK, flying missions over France and Germany. His experiences would haunt him till the end of his days but, by the same token, the war provided an opportunity for upward social mobility that would not have been possible otherwise.

My father was charismatic and mercurial, a born entertainer. In another life he would have been a natural on the stage. He was a quick study and a talented mimic, and by the time the war was over he had used his ear for music to develop a resonant, cultured speaking voice. It was enough to fool my mother into thinking the dashing RAAF officer with his two pretty little motherless girls was a part of her world. They had married in 1961, and they had a good life together until I came along. My sisters had drawn my parents together; I drew them into the cultural chasm that would tear us all apart.

Back in the pub, those two cousins had the double bond of kinship and their war service, and they did indeed have a lot to catch up on. They lingered over their beer long enough for my mother to be annoyed. She'd been left to make small talk with our cousin's wife and when we returned it was plain from the look on both their faces that the discourse had agreed with neither of them.

The shadows had grown long and it was time to pack up. My mother shook the crumbs off our picnic blanket and folded it away. Our cousins waved and walked off, picking their way over the rocky foreshore like long-legged seabirds. Cousin Olly called back over his shoulder that we should stop in for a cuppa on our way home.

I was looking forward to this stopover, so when we drove past the turnoff and headed for the toll bridge, I threw a monster tantrum, jumping up and down on the back seat of the station wagon. There were no such things as seatbelts back then; children were restrained by their mothers reaching over into the back seat and administering a stinging slap to the back of your thighs. The last thing I remember from that trip is my sisters drawing away from me to stare out the windows, after giving me 'the look'. As in: *one day you'll learn not to argue with her, you can't win, you know*. They grimaced at me as I screamed and drummed my feet on the bench seat until, finally, the cherry brandy kicked in and, to everyone's relief, I dozed off.

My father began to sneak out to the bayside to see his cousin. They'd meet up in the Seabrae Hotel at Redcliffe or the bar near the Sandgate War Memorial while my mother was working, my sisters were at school and I was riding shotgun in my father's taxi. My father was a different man when he was with Cousin Olly. He seemed comfortable inside his own skin. For a while he would shed his cloak of artifice and guarded vigilance. It made him short-tempered and ill at ease when he took it up again as we returned home. The easy banter and laughter that flowed between the cousins was in stark contrast to the grim wall of silence that grew between my parents, brick by brick, with each deception, every lie.

I loved these sleepy afternoon sessions in the bars, and not for worlds would I have ratted them out. But four-year-olds are not reliable secret-keepers, and it was only a matter of time until I slipped up. The timing was unfortunate. One of my mother's friends, Hilary, had invited us to a garden party, and while my father and my sisters had found pressing reasons to be elsewhere, I was looking forward to it almost as much as my mother. All her old private-school chums would be there, along with her colleagues from university. Forays into her old life must have been bittersweet. Motherhood had brought home the reality that in marrying my father, she had taken a step down in the world, and it was beginning to dawn on her that she lived with a complex man who she barely knew. Moreover, I had the unhappy knack of embarrassing her in front of her important friends, so she extracted a promise from me that I would be on my very best behaviour.

The motivation to follow through on my oath was high. I liked Hilary; she was what my mother called 'a good stick'. She lived in a grand colonial plantation house set on acreage out past Moggill. Every room was a treasure trove of books and fine art and antiques. The twin living rooms had pressed metal ceilings and a chandelier and an ornate tiled fireplace. The verandah was encircled by iron-lace fretwork, and from there landscaped gardens sloped down towards the tennis court and the narrow brown bend of the river. Peacocks trailed languorously over manicured lawns by a shimmering fountain and – glory of glories – there were ponies in the paddock adjacent. It was the life my mother must have imagined for herself, and the life that her own mother had been born to. It was undoubtedly the life that her parents had anticipated she would attain by an advantageous marriage. Their collective disappointment in my father was always palpable.

The day of Hilary's party arrived. Matching linen frocks in a delicate pastel pink hung on a hook in my parents' bedroom, safely out of my reach while my mother busied herself with her toilette. She had left me to play with my scrapbook and colouring pencils, having confiscated my felt-tip pens due to my past indiscretions. She would not have me appear (again) before her friends in a frieze of rainbow-coloured stripes and dots that invariably seeped into my skin while I was preoccupied with my artwork.

I sat at my play table in my vest and knickers, my hair pinned up in rollers, and pondered what to draw. Resenting the loss of my treasured felt-tips – and certain that my subject would sympathise with my plight, I selected the most colourful character I knew. I began with a large ship, crossing a staccato line of waves. Aged fifteen, so he told me, Cousin Olly had run away from an unhappy home life and had gone off to sea. The anchor tattooed on his arm symbolised his service in the navy and the swallows that flew around it tallied the number of times he had crossed the globe. Given my mother's moods of late, running away seemed an enviable life goal, and I gave myself over to memorialising it in art. My mission achieved, I tilted my head to survey my handiwork, trying to recall how many swallows Cousin Olly had.

At least two, or was it three? Mine thus far numbered fifteen.

Perhaps I'd rather overdone it with the swallows.

My mother agreed. Rounding the doorway in her starched linen frock and pearls, she spied the ballpoint pen reserved for her shopping list in my hand and she shrieked, aghast. In my quest to be like Cousin Olly, I had inked a fair likeness of his anchor onto the length of my forearm, and in anticipation of how far and how often I planned to run away, an entire flock of swallows soared in flight from wrist to shoulder.

My mother was livid. Naval tattoos, it seemed, and the accompanying language that I turned on her when she tried in vain to scour mine off, were not a part of the image she had hoped to present to her society friends. Tattoos, I was given to understand, were the insignia of the working class; not only were they vulgar, they were *common*.

An unpleasant scene erupted later that evening, when she held up my wrist to display the lingering ink to my father. It was undeniable evidence of our guilt and, disturbed that Cousin Olly was getting under my skin, she decreed that all contact with him must stop. He was unsuitable company for a child. Henceforth, the men of her family would guide the development of my character. They were of unimpeachable moral virtue and could be trusted to check my natural inclination towards deviance. It was the end of our happy visits to the peninsula and, to ensure it, my mother enrolled me in crèche. If my father kept the visits up, I didn't know.

So there was no hope that my mother would relent and allow Dad's cousins to attend my birthday. Her parents would be there, and to have them under the same roof with Cousin Olly would be untenable. My maternal grandmother and her sisters still spoke with unyielding English accents, despite it being over a century since their family had arrived with the first fleets of free settlers. They upheld a rigid devotion to God and Empire and a social system based on wealth, class, caste and colour. Cousin Olly had the same rough voice and silty skin tone as the gardener who tended my grandfather's roses and the domestic who came each morning to clean my grandmother's house. He was beneath them. If they'd joined us, my mother would never have heard the end of it. Only the 'right sort of people' could come to my birthday, and every other one to follow. My mother would see to that.

So much still pending

Deborah Cheetham

It's not a question you hear very often: 'When did you grow up?'
But it is one I have asked myself many times. Yes, you read it right
the first time and, no, I didn't mean 'when', I meant *when*.

I'm certainly a child of the 1970s – one look at my ABBA collection and that is plain enough to see. But that's not *when* I grew
up. At least not when I grew up *Aboriginal*. No, that happened
much later. If I am really honest with you, I'm probably still getting there.

If you were here with me now I would probably sing you a song
about it. That wouldn't necessarily establish my authenticity in your
mind. I just like to sing. I always have. Not many opera singers in
our community. I'm happy to say there are a few more now than
there used to be, and I am proud to have had a little bit to do with
that. But I digress – you'll get used to it. In the end the upper word
limit for this account of my life will corral my wandering thoughts
into a story that I hope will shed light on how it is I managed to
grow up at all, and if it makes sense to you – well, even better.

My earliest memory is of me leaning up against my mother in
church. It is the evening service and so I am probably dressed in
my pyjamas. Fortunately I'm only three years old, so I'm young
enough to get away with such an outrageous fashion statement.
My mother is singing a hymn and, if I close my eyes, I can still hear
her voice:

Jesus is calling the wanderers yet, why do they roam?
Love only waits to forgive and forget.
Home weary wanderers, home.

I always wanted to be a singer. I gave my very first audition when I was just seven years old. It was 1971, and I was in the first class at Mortdale Public School, in the southern suburbs of Sydney. 1971 was the year Greenpeace was founded, women in Switzerland won the right to vote, and late-night shopping was introduced in Australia. It was also the year Mortdale Public School decided to record an album – well, more like a 7-inch single to be perfectly honest.

The song to be featured was 'Little Sir Echo'. You know the one ...

Little Sir Echo, how do you do?
Hello! (Hello!) Hello! (Hello!) etc.

The infants department had been rehearsing this song for what seemed like weeks. I had the words off by heart long before anyone else in my class, and I was quietly confident of making it into the choir.

Finally the audition day arrived, when only the very best would be selected for the recording session. In typical infants department fashion, we were lined up in the playground and instructed to sing 'Little Sir Echo' over and over while the choir mistress – a rather imperious and formidable Mrs Brown – made her way up and down the lines, tapping those who were successful on the shoulder.

Those who did not make the cut were not offered a lucrative recording contract like some of the *Australian Idol* runners-up. *No.* Those who were rejected were sent to the sewing mistress for lessons in elementary needle threading. I knew I just had to make it into that choir!

As Mrs Brown approached our line I began to sing louder and louder. I'd also noticed during my time at school that those who managed to sit or stand the straightest were often chosen for the prized activities, like cleaning the blackboard or collating the worksheets – and so I had worked this strategy into my audition in order to give myself an edge. Closer and closer Mrs Brown came until she was almost in front of me, tapping my friend Diane Moore on the shoulder. I took this as a very good sign: as Diane hardly even knew the words, so surely I would have no trouble getting in.

The moment had arrived.

> *Little Sir Echo, you're very shy.*
> *Hello! (Hello!) Hello! (Hello!)*

To my amazement and horror Mrs Brown passed me by. I felt no tap on the shoulder. Surely this was some terrible mistake! Before I knew what was happening I found myself being marched towards the sewing rooms. This was a disaster! Something had to be done. Seeing no alternative, I decided that I would be so naughty for the sewing mistress that she would be forced to send me to the deputy for disciplinary action – the deputy being none other than Mrs Brown!

My tactics worked, up to a point: I still didn't get to sing 'Little Sir Echo', although I was permitted to join in on the B-side of the recording, which just happened to be 'Advance Australia Fair'. I've had quite a few chances to sing that song since my Mortdale Public schooldays and I'd love to catch up with Mrs Brown sometime and let her know.

The last time I sang the anthem was in 2009. It was at the memorial service after the terrible bushfires that swept through Victorian communities, indiscriminately claiming vegetation, property and lives. I decided to use a fantastic orchestral arrangement that I had sung a few years earlier, which included the of clap sticks and yidaki (didgeridoo) in a powerful combination. I was accompanied by the Melbourne Symphony Orchestra and the Melbourne Philharmonic Choir: the performance was everything it needed to be for that solemn occasion. Many emails and letters of thanks for the performance arrived in the days, weeks and months following. I was proud to have made a contribution. I still am.

But then a comment appeared in a newspaper that shook me. Journalist Andrew Bolt called into question the need or relevance for clap sticks and didgeridoo and, for that matter, an Aboriginal singer. What did the horror and devastation of the worst bushfires in over half a century have to do with Aboriginal people? And there it was. My coming of age had arrived. Insensitive and ignorant to the fact that Aboriginal lives were counted amongst those lost on that day, Bolt proclaimed that the anthem had nothing to do with my Aboriginal self and, although it pains me to credit such a person with a role in my personal growth, he was right. I finally realised that this song had nothing to do with me.

More than that, it has nothing to do with anything. I used to justify the lyrics by saying that Australia was a young nation and the many injustices and errors of judgement around the treatment of Aboriginal Australians were a product of youth and inexperience. Like many Australians, I had blindly accepted this premise. Even setting aside 70,000 years of Indigenous cultures for a moment, it has been more than a century since Federation and we're over two hundred years into colonisation, so, at the very least, you would have to say the anthem's words lack a certain level of accuracy. As Australians, can we aspire to be *young* for the rest of our lives? If we are ever to mature, we simply cannot cling to this desperate premise.

This was a hugely significant moment in my journey of growing up Aboriginal. Finally I recognised that no amount of justification could make those words right. That as a descendant of the longest-continuing culture in the world, our national anthem has no business to tell us that we are *young*. Equally, I would have to say that until the day my partner Toni and I can celebrate our relationship (twelve years and counting) with an overpriced, over-catered affair for two hundred of our nearest and dearest, I'm not that thrilled with the word *free* either. So what was to be done?

Within a year the solution presented itself. Later in 2009 I was approached by music legend Judith Durham and Mutti Mutti singer-songwriter Kutcha Edwards, with words they had written for a new national anthem. A song with the inclusive kind of language that could change the way we think about Australia forever. Honouring the Dreaming, our sacred land, and the many and diverse cultures that combine to make Australia what it is today, with a call to live in peace and harmony. It was a brilliant anthem, and participating in the launch of those new lyrics was yet another rite of passage.

The chance to test out these new lyrics came in 2015. Sadly, this was a year when Adam Goodes, one of the great champions of AFL, had been subjected to the kind of racism that would crush a lesser being. I received a call from the event company responsible for staging the AFL grand final preshow, which of course includes a performance of the national anthem. The AFL wanted to show support for Aboriginal Australians and somehow make it up to Adam, and I guess they thought asking an Aboriginal singer to perform the anthem would make a positive statement. I agreed to sing the anthem on the condition that I would be permitted to replace the words *for we are young and free* with *peace and harmony*.

Australians all let us rejoice in peace and harmony

Friends were urging me to just do it. Just insert the new words. I could have, but that would have created a different conversation to the one we are having today, and no doubt provided the likes of Andrew Bolt with several column inches of vitriol. In the end the AFL said no to my request and they found another singer – who inadvertently got the current lyrics muddled anyway. But through the process of saying no to one of the biggest gigs in the Australian calendar I had come of age and gained a level of maturity in my understanding of what it truly means to be an Aboriginal Australian.

My ancestors come from the rich green land of the Yorta Yorta nation, which embraces both sides of the Murray River. We call this river Dhungala, and the Dhungala has been home to the Yorta Yorta people for more than sixty thousand years. My grandfather James came to Yorta Yorta country from Wallaga Lake in the early 1930s and married a local girl. Her name was Frances McGee, although she was fondly known as Sissy. Together they had seven children, the youngest of whom was my mother Monica, while Colin, Betty, Freddie, Ernest, Madeline and the eldest, Jimmy, were my uncles and aunties. I am one of nine children myself.

It would be fabulous to tell you some hilarious story about growing up with so many brothers and sisters, uncles and aunties and countless cousins, but I can't. You see, I didn't grow up with them. For the first thirty years of my life I didn't know anything about them. At just three weeks of age, I was taken from Monica.

I am a member of the Stolen Generations. So, you see, the voice that I can recall from my childhood wasn't that of Monica, but of my adopted mother, Marjory, singing in church. Still, all my life, the voices of my ancestors have been calling to me from the banks of the Dhungala, even if for more than thirty years I couldn't hear them. When I finally heard the calling, my response was the opera *Pecan Summer*.

Pecan Summer tells the story of the walk-off from Cummeragunja mission station in 1939. This was a moment in history when the women and the men of the Yorta Yorta nation took their destiny into their own hands and walked off the mission in protest at the appalling conditions that had been imposed on them by seventy years of intense colonisation. I chose this story for its obvious dramatic content: the exodus of the Yorta Yorta people from their homeland, and their inevitable and unending search for belonging are themes of an epic scale perfectly suited to and deserving of an opera.

Less than a month into researching the history of the walk-off I made an astonishing discovery. The Aboriginal grandparents I had never known – James and Cissy Little – were actually part of the story I was telling. They had carried their firstborn son, Jimmy, off the mission, crossing the Dhungala from New South Wales into Victoria. Suddenly I had a family that stretched beyond the limitations of my knowledge. And people were telling me how much I reminded them of my grandmother Cissy and how she had been a singer with a beautiful voice known to one and all. Suddenly I had a past that linked up with my present and my future and I just happened to be writing an opera about it.

Sadly Monica and Cissy did not live to see *Pecan Summer* come to life in 2010, but their stories are threaded through each page of the libretto and their voices can be heard in every note of the score. Writing, composing, directing and performing in *Pecan Summer* has provided me with an opportunity to connect with my community, family and history, and has finally given me the chance to grow up Aboriginal. Even more than that, it has set me on the path to helping Australia take that same journey. Just as I have gone from not-knowing to knowing, from youth to maturity, I think it is fair to say that, in Australia, we could all benefit from growing up a little more Aboriginal.

Aboriginal, Indigenous, Koori, Yorta Yorta, Australian, adopted, stolen, lesbian, soprano, daughter, mother, sister, partner, wife (still pending marriage equality). These are all facets of my identity and my experience of growing up Aboriginal, and I carry each of these identities in equal measure. I'm happy to say that I am still learning. There is no other way I can or would rather be, and accepting this has made all the difference.

'This is Nat, she's Abo'

Natalie Cromb

Coonabarabran, 1995

Staring out the window as the flat plains turned to rolling hills, I knew it wouldn't be long before we were pulling up in the driveway of our holiday sanctuary. The plains turned to scrub, and the dirt turned red and sandy; the hills were inviting, and the air crisp and cleansing so that your body relaxes and you can breathe better. I didn't know it then, but I know it now: that's what it feels like when you're on country after an absence.

This was my childhood: school holidays spent on country with the biggest mob of family. I was part of a family of five, with an older brother and younger sister, but in the holidays we grew and multiplied with grandparents, aunts, uncles and cousins.

As the youngest, my sister was always in the middle seat and would ask about twenty times, 'Is this the big hill?' Each time my brother would shoot her down, and I would pretend not to be as hopeful as she was.

Seeing the final big hill before we hit town was a thrill and from there it was mere minutes before we were turning into Jubilee Street, where we would take off our seatbelts and launch out of the car before Mum and Dad had a chance to turn it off properly. The screech of the screen door had us flying up the steps to Nan's and Pop's waiting arms and laughs.

As Mum and Dad lugged in our bags filled with clothes, we were already in the house with Nan and Pop, deciding where we were putting our mattresses and planning what games we would play, when we would see our cousins, when we were going down to the weir. Meanwhile, Nan and Pop were already clanging crockery and setting out plates for us to have a feed.

Because we lived two hours away in a bigger town where work opportunities were better and schools even more so, they'd want to know all about school and we would pull out our pictures and they would take pride of place on the fridge, and show any awards or certificates and be told how clever we were.

We were 'home' with our people and this was our refuge from the rest of the world. The rest of the world stopped when we were on country for the holidays and staying at Nan and Pop's. We would wake up early and be given Weetbix and Milo and then hook it for the day with our cousins to the oval to play footy or basketball, to the weir to try to catch yabbies, to the park to feed the ducks and play on the equipment. We would return home for food, and for money for the shop where we always got our mixed lollies.

If Pop had a charge, by the time we got home he would be yarning up about the old days. At the time we would giggle and think how funny he is – but looking back now, this is how I got to know my history and culture, and also that the world was not going to be easy.

Pop would yarn about rations and the labouring jobs that all our people had to do; he talked about the visits to Sydney he had with cousins and his time inside. Pop told me about bush tucker and cooking and five-corner fruit.

On Sundays the house was a revolving door of visitors as all the old ones – aunts, uncles, cousins – would roll in for Sunday lunch and Pop would serve the biggest feast and everyone would rave about the food.

That's how Nan and Pop showed love the best – with food. Whether it was Pop's rabbit stew, curried yabbies, scones, damper or sweets. Everybody who needed a feed, no matter how close or distant, was welcome at Nan and Pop's for Sunday lunch, where the elders would sit at the dining table, the other adults would be throughout the lounge room, and us kids would be all over the backyard eating and playing games.

The aunts would row over who'd won at bingo, and the uncles would be looking at the form guide for a bet, and the kids would go down on their bikes and put on the bets because we would be given change to grab mixed lollies at the top shop on our way home.

All the floors were covered in foam mattresses with little bodies every night, as all the cousins slept over and talked long into the night while the adults would sit up drinking tea and coffee and telling us, 'Go to sleep!' We'd laugh and dare each other to jump out the window and do a 'knock and run'.

We were told stories of Mother Tongue Bung to get us to behave and would try to big-note ourselves when we went out the mission and dare each other to go closer towards the big hill where she lived.

Sunup to sundown we were on the go doing things with our cousins, but on the last day of the break, we would all wake up with long faces and a sense of foreboding. Not because we didn't want to be with Mum and Dad or get back to school, but because our little refuge and the free feeling it created was going to be left behind until the next school holidays.

When you're a kid, a ten-week term waiting to get back on country with your mob is forever. And the two-hour car ride home felt even worse. There was no excitement, just resignation.

Tamworth, 1998

> *All the Aboriginal students, please go to the quadrangle immediately.*

Cringe.

High school.

Difference brought shame, and in country New South Wales nothing brought more shame than being Aboriginal. There weren't many other nationalities, so the main 'difference' was black and white. The difference was announced by being called out of class over a loudspeaker for meetings concerning just the Aboriginal kids. It might have been to discuss camps or reconciliation events or cultural activities. It didn't really matter why, but it felt like being singled out (there weren't many of us Kooris compared to the vast majority of white kids).

I knew all the black kids at school – some of them were cousins or cousins of cousins. We would go away on camps together, and we all got on and laughed and had the best time when it was just us. When we were mixed with the white kids, our difference stood out and we were quieter, but I do remember how it felt to look into the eyes of the other Koori kids as they passed by in the course of our day. I felt in that moment as if I wasn't alone.

When that loudspeaker would go off calling us to the quad, I would sometimes just go and ignore the snickering; other times I would cringe and pretend I hadn't heard it until one kid would invariably pipe up, 'Natalie, you're Aboriginal. Time to go do Aboriginal things before your people think you went *walkabout*.' In those moments I wanted to be swallowed up by the ground. I would go bright red and leave the classroom angry, with a huge chip on my shoulder about being black.

That chip I carried – that ranged from shamed to angry – always fell away when I was on country in the school holidays. I would forget all of the teasing and taunting from some of the shite kids and just laugh and roam and play with my cousins.

Two worlds, 2003

Growing up Aboriginal in country New South Wales throughout the 1980s, 1990s and early 2000s always left me feeling confused and unsure of where I stood in the world.

I was lucky to grow up with a massive extended family and have my connection to country and culture through this family and our school holidays at my Nan and Pop's. From Pop's stories, I learnt black politics young, so I knew I had to move on from the country and go get 'book smart', as my old Pop would say. He'd tell me, 'You got so many brains, baby girl. You gotta get out of here and get down that big smoke and use 'em.'

I didn't really want to leave, though, not my family or my country, but in my final year of high school, I knew I had to. By then I'd dealt with thirteen years of schooling in a country town where my Aboriginality was pointed out and ridiculed by numerous peers, but for the most part my close friends never engaged in the jeering that made me feel ashamed.

Until an eighteenth birthday party in 2003, when a friend of mine introduced me to someone at the party.

'This is Nat, she's *Abo*.'

Now I had been called *Abo* before, along with many other names all intended to upset and embarrass me. Being ridiculed for my Aboriginality was not new; I had copped it to the point that I had almost tuned it out, but this introduction has stuck with me since that evening in 2003.

I remember the shock at a 'friend' calling me that term and using it to introduce me, but also the look of horror on the face of the person I was being introduced to, and my friend's follow-up 'but she's cool', as if their qualifying statement removed the clear abhorrence of my being Aboriginal from the equation.

So at eighteen, having just finished high school, I moved from country New South Wales to Sydney all by myself. I didn't know anyone in Sydney. You see, us 'bush blacks', as we called ourselves, rarely mixed with 'city folk', but the minute I moved here I immediately connected with other Aboriginal students going to university and we formed a tight-knit mob who looked out for one another, and over a decade later I now consider them my brothers and sisters.

Resolve

Growing up Aboriginal in Australia is both beautiful and painful and tests you. The holidays spent with cousins I now rarely see were the best moments of my childhood. We were 'thick as thieves' and I'm sure many in the town who subscribed to the stereotypes thought we were *just that*, but the freedom of walking around town and finding things to do – fishing, yabbying, playing sports and going bush – was simply the most exquisite act of connecting not only to mob but to country. All the shame fell away when I spent time with my people on country. After all, we are Gamilaraay – and together we are home.

Thanks for the childhood travels

Karen Davis

Dear Mum and Dad,

Thank you for taking the time and making the effort to encourage what I consider to be the single most influential factor in my formative years: a sense of adventure. Although we weren't rich, through careful household and financial management, you managed to take us on adventures that I – we – still value today.

Travelling with kids in the 1970s was immensely different to today's standards. No tablets or DVD players to keep the kids occupied. No seatbelt laws limiting the number of people who could be carried in a car. Despite the lack of technology and safety laws, we arrived at our destinations in one piece, while having fun along the way (not to mention the occasional scrap!).

Growing up in north Queensland, you took us to places of great family significance – Mossman Gorge and the Atherton Tablelands – and interesting places in between, such as the Curtain Fig Tree, Gentle Annie Lookout, Kuranda, Mount Hypipamee Crater and the Babinda Boulders. Do you remember the time we stumbled across the little house shaped like a UFO in a paddock near Yungaburra? These locations and experiences piqued our interest in seeking out new adventures, near and afar.

To pass time while travelling between locations, you bought us little songbooks that included the lyrics to the hit songs of the day. I recall countless trips to Cairns as we belted out the words to

'Fernando' at the top of our lungs. How you managed to concentrate on the driving, Dad, I can't imagine. But we had fun, and we took delight in the musical magic we created, even if it was only in our imaginations. As the oldest, Rona provided humorous relief on each trip with her insightful observations and her ability to take on various characters. This kept us amused for many journeys. And, indeed, many years thereafter.

Dad, your job as a Queensland Rail station manager gave us ample opportunities to travel by train up and down the east coast of Australia many times while growing up. We knew the *Sunlander* route well – extended stops at Townsville and Rockhampton; struggling to maintain our balance as we crossed between carriages; the excitement of climbing the bunks in the sleeper carriages each night. I remember travelling on the *Sunlander* one New Year's Eve and hearing the carriages erupt with cheering, clapping and laughter as the New Year ticked over.

Mum, your pre-dinner announcement of 'Dinner is now being served in the dining room' functioned as a comic nod to the *Sunlander* dinner ritual for many subsequent family dinners throughout the years, and is a now a classic family one-liner!

In 1977, you decided to take us on a road trip to Darwin. The year before our trip, you'd taken a blue Holden station wagon for a test drive. I recall the wild delight in our eyes as Kirstine and I discovered the rear window could be 'wound' down with the simple touch of a button. Wow, the marvels of technology! 'Buy it! Buy it!' we urged. You bought it.

We camped our way to Darwin via Townsville, Hughenden, Julia Creek, Mount Isa, Tennant Creek and Katherine, up to the Top End. I'm so happy you fitted the car with an air conditioner and an eight-track cartridge player, making the trip cooler and more entertaining, with the music of Elvis, Charlie Pride and Johnny Cash emanating from the speakers. The dry dustiness of the outback made the swim at the lush oasis of Mataranka memorable as the warm, crystal-clear waters of the natural springs washed off the stickiness of the Northern Territory heat. Along the way we collected stickers at each town we visited and proudly displayed them as badges of honour on the rear side window and bumper bar of our station wagon.

Three years later, in 1980, you took us on a summer road trip to Melbourne, via the inland route on the way there and along the coastal highway on our return trip. To keep the costs down, we pitched our tent at the end of each day in small communities we'd had no idea existed before then, but still remember today. I laugh when I recall one of our breakfast stops by the side of the road near Moree. The flies were atrocious, and Ron and I wrapped towels around our heads like the desert nomads we pretended we were, removing the towelling just long enough to allow us to eat while keeping the flies out.

It wasn't just daylong car travel either: along the way, you took us to visit attractions as well, such as Dubbo Zoo, the Parkes radio telescope observatory (where we listened to the stars and got the t-shirt to prove it), the Bacchus Marsh lion park, the Byron Bay lighthouse and the Big Banana, Orange and Pineapple, to name a few. I loved the trip we took to Thredbo. It was midsummer but we were so excited that we were finally going to experience snow – albeit icy snow – on the mountain. The small snowballs we threw at each other felt more like ice cubes than soft snowballs!

On our approach to the New South Wales–Victoria state border, a series of large road signs warned motorists against taking fruit into Victoria. So you made sure we pulled over on the side of the road well before the border to eat all the fruit we were carrying. 'There's no sense in wasting good food,' you said. You still laugh today at how you discovered a whole bag of uneaten fruit under the front seat after we arrived in Melbourne.

I remember that on our return trip our car broke down near Maffra, which delayed our travel by a few days while it was fixed. During this unplanned stay we met a few of the locals and at one invitation to dinner tasted rabbit for the very first time.

Our stopovers in Sydney were exciting, especially when you walked us across the Sydney Harbour Bridge. The goings-on on the harbour below held our attention and distracted us during the arduous 1.5-kilometre trek across the bridge, which seemed more like five kilometres. You were somewhat amused at the relief on our faces as four little Murris, exhausted and spent, collapsed on the cool soft grass at Milsons Point. As tired as we were, we joked and laughed while regaining our 'next wind' for the return journey.

Upon reflection, I cannot recall experiencing any overt racism during our travels. Perhaps I was too young. Rona tells of the time we were travelling through outback Queensland when a car of young, white males sped up behind us and yelling the directions for the nearby mission. Our belief is you likely protected us from experiencing the harsh realities of life faced by many Murris in those days. At a time not long after the abolishment of 'The Act', you would have wanted us to grow up with a belief that we had the right, as Australians, to travel freely across Australia.

Mum and Dad, I guess what I'm trying to say with this letter is this: Your desire to take us kids to different places, introduce us to a diverse range of people, and allow us to experience a variety of foods has created the adults we are today. For this start in life, thank you.

Love,

Karen

Growing up beige

Ian Dudley

Do I know much about growing up Aboriginal? Nah, I don't. See, I didn't grow up black; I grew up beige. Latte. Occasionally caramel after a long, late summer, with the first school term of the year and Easter holidays spent shirtless and shoeless roaming the streets and shorelines of home after the true baking heat of a South Australian summer had passed.

Heritage was something mentioned obliquely. 'Look at your father. Don't tell me there's not a touch of the tar brush in his family somewhere,' Mum said regularly. Like many of her era and upbringing, she was a master of saying borderline racist things while at the same time considering herself as avowedly progressive in all matters.

Not that Dad cared too much. Both his dad and a sister had tried digging up the family tree and found more questions than answers. Supposedly dead first wives for whom there was no real record of existence. Birth certificates not issued at all or, stranger still, with dates that didn't quite match the lives they documented. Apparent relatives living on the same Adelaide street who only spoke to each other at Christmas, and even then only grudgingly. 'We're dark because we're Spanish' repeated down the line, despite the fact the carriers of the Spanish line were demonstrably not the dark ones in the few old photos that were still around.

It was a mystery for my young mind, but looking back with the benefit of education our family story has all the hallmarks of the Stolen Generations, though in our case even that is supposition. Someone, somewhere, could have been given up willingly, adopted legitimately. Or maybe, rootless and disconnected already, she saw the writing on the wall and grabbed the 'dog tags' when the chance was there, betting everything on the 'them' at a time when the 'us' seemed to offer no future. Ultimately it could be as simple as saying that we are what the assimilation policy was supposed to achieve.

Whatever actually happened, it seems that for at least the three generations before mine my family weren't properly black then either. But there were traces. *Love of the bush and the ocean, respect for all things, treat people well, know the land you are on.* Optimism. But also pessimism. *Trust religion barely, and the government not at all. Trust the police even less. Laughter is the best medicine, but don't ever let them laugh at you. Failure isn't worth the risk of trying. Shame. Sometimes getting drunk is the only solution.* With hindsight and an unflinching eye, these are the lessons that we all seem to have learnt in our hearts somehow.

And also the connection to other outsiders. There were always a handful of kids throughout my primary school years – both Nungas and those who were 'other' in some other way – who were my friends for a few days or weeks until they invariably moved on from our small town with its small minds and limited opportunities. I was incredulous that so many classmates seemed to place so much judgement on skin colour or eye shape. Wondered aloud why it even mattered. Making myself a target for all the cocky farm boys but knowing intrinsically, vocally, that the jokes and taunts of the schoolyard were blatantly wrong as well as mostly unfunny.

At twelve, we took a road trip up the desert. Dad had been working in a community around that time, and our old Econovan's tape compartment held dubbed copies of Coloured Stone, Warumpi Band, Yothu Yindi. The words, sounds and snippets of meaning bursting from the speakers – that my expanding mind suddenly 'got' – all merged with the landscapes we wandered through and the people we met to create lasting impressions. Of country. Of history. Of self. At Uluru we unanimously decided as a family that we were walking around, rather than up. I can't remember if there were even signs asking visitors not to make the climb back then, but the blokes Dad knew had told him about it. Other tourists looked at us like we had rocks in our heads, but it made perfect sense to us. *Respect.*

A year later, and I was at boarding school. A regional city. Catholic. Despite the town having plenty of blackfellas, there was only one other black kid in the whole school at the time. She was in my year, stylish and sassy, and I gravitated to her inevitably. Infatuated doesn't adequately cover it. Certainly I was as deeply in love with her as any thirteen-year-old can be, but in hindsight I think it was her connection to culture just as much as her own being that I was mesmerised by. She had language, knowledge, colour, stories. For two years, before family pulled her across the continent I pretty much worshipped the ground she walked on, wide-eyed and loyal as any puppy, without ever having the courage to do anything about it. Too shame for sure.

As time went by, music again helped my black sense of self grow. Not exclusively Aboriginal this time, but global. Public Enemy and De La Soul. Rage Against the Machine. Red Hot Chili Peppers' songs from before they were famous, touching on life from a First Nations American perspective. Mostly white punk bands from working-class backgrounds who understood that some forms of the struggle transcend – or at least aren't exclusive to – any one colour or culture. Also the Bob Marley records I found in my parents' collection. So this was consciousness. Holy shit!

A few other formative processes occurred in those mid-teenage years. I started being useful enough to help the old man out around the farm. From rabbit control to harvesting to revegetation, he was always busy. Usually barefoot, to feel the warmth of the dirt beneath us. *Love of land. Learning to give back if we were also going to take.* And I finally got brave enough to follow him out the back on days when the surf was pumping, or to dive down deep looking for abalone, crays and the big turban snails we always called *warreners* (a Tasmanian Palawa word apparently, to add another layer to the mystery of our heritage). Not exclusively black pursuits obviously, but still more fodder for a growing sense of connection to the physical world around me. Also, through surfing and football I started to meet a few other crew from up and down the coast who were in the same boat. Mixed heritage. Varying degrees of connection. Not black enough to be black, always too black to be white. Some of them are still my mates today. Some didn't make it this far.

For a while a few school peers tried to rag me with 'throwback' and 'coony', but it never seemed to stick. Probably because by then I was starting to see it as a badge of honour rather than a source of shame. *Chip me if ya want, but unless you're serious I'm gunna ignore you.* The abuse I got was more along the lines of 'Why don't you put a land claim in for the detention room? Tell them it's a sacred site or some shit so we don't have to go.' Pretty harmless, really.

As life rolled on to university, some patterns stayed the same. Gravitate to dark skin, but don't try to be something you're not in case you look like a fraud. Pick a career that'll give something back somewhere. Don't be selfish. But also don't reach for something too far out of your comfort zone. Failure would be worse than predictability. Hiking barefoot through the nature trail when city life got too much. Taking subjects in the First Nations Centre. Blown away that you could learn this stuff and get graded on it. Still growing. Listening to strong, smart Nunga men and women. Including people paler than me. One old white bloke delivering speeches in fluent Kaurna. Turned out he's an elder. Mind blown again. Imagine still having that?

Other patterns too, of course. Walking back with a Tiwi brother from the Bottle-O one night. Multiple carloads hurling abuse. Caught in the wind, less than half heard but still fully understood. 'Don't worry about it, bruzz. Fuck 'em,' he said. Imagine being dark enough to cop that shit all the time. White people couldn't handle it, that's for sure. Breathtakingly weird conversations with supposedly educated people. Certain, for example, that before 1788 we cannibalised babies and also routinely died en masse on hot summer days. No air-con, you see. And the amount of racist graffiti on the toilet doors in that place of higher learning? *Too puzzling!*

But life always rolls on. Even now, pushing middle age, I am still growing up beige. Still searching for culture using the means I have available. Bush tucker is my current passion, though the knowledge I've collected has come more from hours stuck in books than countless generations of ancestors. Likewise, I have learnt more about culture, language, law and just what community means from half-a-dozen years as an Aboriginal Education Teacher than from any family history we've unearthed. Students from across the spectrum of modern Aboriginality, big-hearted and cheeky. Smart, compassionate and thoughtful, regardless of what their report cards said. Who have grown into deadly young adults out shaping their world to suit their purposes. They have been my teachers, at least as much as the other way round. *Respect.*

And now it's come full circle and I'm back in my hometown, for a while at least. At school here there are a few Nunga kids, and I'm trying to grow the culture. Connecting with parents, organising guests and experts. Getting them out of the classroom and into the bush. Not just for them, though, but for all the kids. Our country needs it. The land and the people. After 230 years of this nation trying to make the black people white, I think it's dawning on us that, just maybe, if we made the white people a little bit blacker instead the place would be in better shape.

And I'm also teaching my own kids. Their mum is white so, as tanned as they get without trying, my tribe of little girls will, like me, never grow up black. No matter how many pigface fruit they eat in summer or quandongs they pick in winter, they still won't know all the trials and triumphs of being Aboriginal. But despite that, will they be increasingly proud to grow up beige, latte and caramel as their own lives and learning journeys unfold? I hope so. Because then I'll know all the things I've learnt have been worth it.

Yúya Karrabúrra

Alice Eather

I'm standing by this fire
The embers smoking
The ashes glowing
The coals weighing us down
The youth are buried in the rubble
My eyes are burning
And through my nostrils
The smoke is stirring
I breathe it in

Yúya Karrabúrra

I wear a ship on my wrist
That shows my blood comes from convicts
On the second fleet
My father's forefathers came
Whipped beaten and bound in chains
The dark tone in my skin
The brown in my eyes
Sunset to sunrise
My Wúrnal mother's side
My kíkka who grew up in a dugout canoe
In her womb is where my consciousness grew

Yúya Karrabúrra

I walk between these two worlds
A split life
Split skin
Split tongue
Split kin
Everyday these worlds collide
And I'm living and breathing
This story of black and white

Sitting in the middle of this collision
My mission is to bring
Two divided worlds to sit beside this fire
And listen
Through this skin I know where I belong
It is both my centre
And my division

Yúya Karrabúrra

My ancestors dance in the stars
And their tongues are in the flames
And they tell me
You have to keep the fire alive
Between the black and the white
There's a story waiting to be spoken

In every life
There's a spirit waiting to be woken
Now I'm looking at you
With stars in my eyes
And my tongue is burning flames
And I say

Yúya Karrabúrra

The sacred songs are still being sung
But the words are slowly fading
The distant cries I'm hearing
Are the mothers burying their babies
The elders are standing strong
But the ground beneath them is breaking

Yúya Karrabúrra

Now I welcome you to sit beside my fire
I'm allowing you to digest my confusion
I will not point my finger and blame
Cause when we start blaming each other
We make no room for changing each other

We've got to keep this fire burning
With ash on our feet and coal in our hands
Teach Barra-ródjibba
All them young ones how to live side by side
Cause tomorrow when the sun rises
And our fires have gone quiet
They will be the ones to reignite it

Yúya Karrabúrra

These flames
Us
Will be their guidance

*

This poem is about identity, and it was a really hard thing to write in the beginning because identity is such a big issue. It's a large thing to cover. The poem is about the struggle of being in between black and white.

I knew that before I started to write about myself, I had to write about Mum and Dad, because that's everything in my life: my whole upbringing – the two different worlds I grew up in, the city and the bush. They are such polar opposites, from convict history to remote Aboriginal Arnhem Land, from one place that was settled at point of contact to one that has only been settled since the 1950s.

I think my whole life has been quite blessed to have elements of both sides, but it's always been tough trying to figure out what part I take on which side. It's always been hard balancing both worlds. It was tough growing up because I did have identity issues, and I went through a lot of depression not knowing where I fully belonged.

My bábba, Michael Eather, met my kíkka, Helen Djimbarrawala Williams, in the 1980s by following his sister who was a linguist in the Maningrida community of the Northern Territory. My father is from Tasmania. His ancestors came on the *Neptune* in the Second Fleet in 1790. Apparently that was the roughest ship. My mother is a Kunibíjdi woman who was born on a little island, Mardbalk (Goulburn Island), in Arnhem Land. My ancestors on my mother's side have lived in Arnhem Land from sunrise to sunset. Kíkka is a traditional owner and spokesperson for our community. She grew up around the saltwater, travelling in a dugout canoe between the islands and the mainland.

There weren't many whitefellas around Maningrida at the time, so for my dad to be up here having brown children with an Aboriginal woman rocked the boat on both sides of the family. There were elders here in Maningrida saying, 'Why are you with a white man?' and his family down in Brisbane saying, 'Who's this woman from Arnhem Land?' Dad crossed a lot of boundaries, but that's what made us – my two sisters, Noni and Grace, and me – who we are today. I'm actually glad he crossed those boundaries, because it allows us to be able to cross those boundaries too, in a really good way.

I was born in Brisbane, my older sister, Noni, was born in Darwin, and my younger sister, Grace, was born in Derby. Kíkka never stayed in one place. That was a big part of our lives, always travelling between different homes. After Mum had me in Brisbane, we were back and forth all the time. We have four older siblings on our mother's side, and two younger sisters on our father's side. When I was a bubba, some of my older siblings and family on my mum's side came down to Brisbane to get away from petrol sniffing. I was born in 1988, and they came and helped look after me, to get out of the community. We lived with Dad there and we went all the way through school, but in between all of that we were driving back and forth. Dad had a big Toyota and he'd chuck us in and drive up to Arnhem Land. Then when we were old enough, we'd fly. We ended up in a lot of places as kids.

My bábba kept us connected to a really strong culture in Brisbane, through his gallery and his art. He allowed us to be ourselves and not feel pressure to be in any other place than where *we* were. He gave us space and choice, education and a good home. Everything we needed. He challenged us and our thinking and surrounded us with people who did likewise. A lot of our education came from school, but it was also from the people in our lives – artists, poets, writers, travellers and singers. I think that culture in Brisbane, and a very loving family – the Eather family – were the important things about growing up with him.

Kíkka never let our skin colour identify us; it was more our connection with her and having our Ndjébbana language and a really strong family. That's what we identified with rather than the colour of our skin. She reminded us every day that we had land, and culture, and story: 'You're my children, this is your land, this is your place, this is your belonging.'

I think that's why the half-caste skin-colour issues never bothered us. It would come up in conversations or funny little stories or jokes, especially with people who had similar upbringings or split families, but I always felt lucky to have really strong parents who encouraged us to feel as if that never had to be an issue.

Mum always kept our language alive while we were in Brisbane. She used to send us books in Ndjébbana. We always sang songs, busked and read stories in our Ndjébbana language, so when we came home everything was still familiar. Ndjébbana was never a foreign tongue to listen to or talk in.

The term half-caste has travelled everywhere with us, from the Northern Territory to Queensland. It always sparked a lot of conversations about the history of Australia and the Stolen Generations. It wasn't just a simple term that could be thrown around. Knowing that we could go back home to Maningrida and be with our family and still have brown skin put things into perspective for us. I was struck by the contrast with the many people who had brown skin like us but had everything taken away from them.

We always had to be very careful in the way we talked about things like that: having empathy and listening to other experiences of Aboriginality. There were Koori, Murri and Nangar mob we met who had a very painful history. There were people who had lost a lot of things who found it really hard to hear our story. We had connection back home and a language that was still alive that we could speak openly and freely at home.

That's another struggle. There were people who identified as Aboriginal but 'looked' less Aboriginal. One girl at school got bullied by other Murri kids who would call her a coconut, and sometimes I would think, 'Thank god I have dark skin.' But then I would come back up to Maningrida and it was a different story again. Being too white or being too black, and seeing other kids deal with those issues – that was hard.

When Bábba would walk around the city with us, a proud man with blue eyes and curly blond hair and his three brown girls holding hands, people would look at us. They could never work us out as a family. Dad would say later that he hoped people didn't think this was a Stolen Generations scenario. Sometimes we would ask why people were staring at us, and he would just say, 'It's because you three are all so beautiful, that's why.' He'd never mention colour. But I remember thinking people would never understand our story, how mixed and beautiful our family is, and that we were so happy that that's just the way it was. I think the fact that we understood our family, we knew where we came from and who we were made it so hard for other people to understand.

The most important thing I've learnt from Bábba and Kíkka – and especially for Australia, it's almost the definition of reconciliation – is that things don't need to be that bad and we can all actually live together. We're lucky enough to have a really multicultural family. Our Christmas tables are so long – we have our Aboriginal side, our French–English side, our Scottish family, our Serbian family, all coming together. It's really special.

I graduated in 2005 from high school and did a bit of study but I didn't know what I wanted to do and I didn't like the way people operated in the city. Everything felt a little bit trivial and shallow.

I felt as if I didn't really belong there, which led to my depression. I was going around in circles and I was admitted to clinic four times and, every time I thought I was getting better, I ended up back in the psych wards on a lot of anti-psychotics and antidepressants. Bábba was a rock; he got me through all that, and there's no way you can get through a depression like that without so much support. It was really huge because I was dreaming a lot and there was so much calling me to come back home to Kíkka and to Maningrida.

I remember we got money together and I flew back to Maningrida. Coming back here was a big thing because it was a place of belonging. It's where I knew my language belonged, and my mum belonged. I wanted to come home to country.

Once I was back in the community, however, I realised it was very different from how I'd experienced it growing up. Back then we would go straight to the beach looking for crabs and oysters, and Kíkka would throw our shoes away. It was so fun having all our family in one place, in one little house. We would fall asleep hearing stories every night by the fire, under the stars. It was so comforting.

A lot of my friends I grew up with had had babies. There were so many different stories. The stories you don't tell kids. The stories you hear when you're an adult. That really shook me up. All I did was write. I wrote everything I saw and that was my way of processing my experiences and the challenges I'd grown up with; all the writing was part of the processing and healing, because I was acknowledging what was happening and not ignoring it.

That's when I started seeing the health issues, hearing the welfare stories, and I started questioning everything. Why are all of our families in this state? What has happened? What happened to the old people who I remembered as a child in Maningrida? I started noticing that our people were dying at a really young age. Overcrowded housing was making our people sick. Kids were growing up without parents because of suicide, incarceration and alcohol abuse. That was really hard.

Why was my brother in jail? Why was all of our family split up? Why are there so many funerals? But the biggest thing I remember about that time is that I used to try and make a fire every night at Mum's house, and every day I would try and find a boat to go out to the island – to Kíkkas's country, Kabálko Island. Wúrnal country. There were dodgy things that happened, spark plugs breaking and boats half sinking in croc-infested waters. But that never made me want to give up just being on country. That's where I found peace.

Kabálko Island is not far from our house in Maningrida, in the mouth of the Liverpool River. It's where a lot of our family found peace. It's where, back in the day, they would leave petrol sniffers. It was a healing place, and it still is.

When I moved back to Maningrida, Mum said, 'You're not going to be half-caste anymore, you're going to be *over*cast!' I love the fact that Mum said overcast from being exposed to the Arnhem sun. My adopted brothers say that any time you think about being half-caste you start feeling like an outcast because you're not white or black enough. That's why my poem is so important. It's letting people know that my mum is black, my dad is white, and I'm here; there's nothing else. It is what it is.

In Maningrida I started working as an assistant teacher at the school, where I was eventually given the opportunity to study to become a teacher through the Remote Indigenous Teacher Education program at Charles Darwin University. I realised this was my way forward. I graduated as a teacher in 2013. Now being in the classroom is a big part of my life. I can teach in both English and Ndjébbana. I feel as if I'm in the perfect position, but it's still really hard.

I was trying to get out all of my anger in my poem. I was also try-ing so hard not to be negative, because there's too much negativity said and written about Aboriginal people in communities. You either go down that road or say something that can make people stronger. Not just 'people are dying' – everyone knows that, and everyone wants a solution. I didn't want it to become so negative that no one would actually want to hear it because it would have been so depress-ing. This is the time when I began to realise that bringing people together was more powerful than pushing people away.

When I perform this poem, it is spoken really slowly. Every word needs to be heard, every syllable. Colleena, my eldest sister, said that the poem reminded her of ceremony, where fire is the main thing that keeps everyone together and alive on country. Fire can represent so many things.

Every day here in Maningrida, people are processing pain. It's an everyday battle to sustain our Aboriginality and balance Western culture. Our people don't get enough recognition for how strong they are and how they have fought so hard to keep living with so many pressures. Change is happening so fast. The change is very inviting, and can be exciting, but it's also very scary and it can be hard to be a part of. That's when people get frustrated and start blaming each other. It's a lot to take in.

Growing up between two worlds, it's *still* a lot to take in. The pace of change is so fast and we are just expected to keep up. You see it out here firsthand, in the schools, in the government services, the programs being run. The community has already changed rapidly since it was established as a trading post in the 1950s. Nothing is ever going to stay the same, but it's about listening to each other and moving forward. Not letting everything happen mindlessly, but being part of conscious change.

When there's a suicide: whose fault was it? Why has that person taken their own life? You hear about it in the papers. There is something fundamentally wrong if there are young kids taking their own lives, and these are not one-off stories: these are stories everywhere. That's a sign of distress in a community. It makes me think back to my own depression and the number of times I tried to commit suicide. I am so thankful every day that that didn't happen. Because I can actually help. I can sit with kids and family members and say, 'I can feel your pain.'

I really do feel that pain.

The poem is about who I am and about teaching our children. There is always more than what you first see. Bábba calls it looking at the world with x-ray vision. I have always listened to Bábba's voice of reason and Kíkka's voice of cultural integrity. Their voices guide me in everything I do.

When we were growing up Bábba talked a lot about 'keeping both campfires burning'. This was always a struggle, but I've kept those fires alive and now I've found my medicine: teaching our children.

Out of all of this, this whole story, I believe we have to take responsibility for ourselves and what we do in our lives, and pass that on. Ma. Rdórdbalk.

Ndjébbana language words:

Yúya Karrabúra – fire is burning
bábba – father
kíkka – mother
barra-ródjibba – children
Kunibídji – Ndjébbana-speaking people from the Maningrida region
Wúrnal – my clan name from my mother's side
rdórdbalk – good
ma – ok

White bread dreaming

Shannon Foster

One of my earliest memories is of eating white bread sandwiches with my dad. Not Vegemite or peanut butter or devon and tomato sauce sandwiches like the other Australian kids in our working-class suburb of south-western Sydney. No, we ate oyster sandwiches with vinegar and pepper and salt. Sydney rock oysters out of a jar smashed onto bread slathered in margarine. Dad would say that we are salt-water people; we love the sea and would eat anything that came out of it. We are D'harawal Guriwal – whale people – and I wondered, who was everyone else? Were they D'harawal too?

I don't ever remember being told I was Aboriginal. I just was. There was no one defining moment; it was just one of the pieces of grass that intertwined with the others to create the dilly bag that held all that was me. I had no idea what it meant to be Aboriginal because I had no idea what it meant not to be Aboriginal. It is only now with the vision of adulthood that I can trace back the grassy strands of knowledge to their origins in the foundations of that dilly bag.

My D'harawal dad is an excellent storyteller. He speaks with warmth, meaning, expression, gravity and humour. I had no idea as a child that my father's storytelling was an ancestral ability born of thousands of years of knowledge sharing. I never gave it a second thought as I lay in the bedroom I shared with my sister in the little fibro home we lived in on the outskirts of Bankstown, which, at the time, was a very Anglo-Saxon area. I say that because now Bankstown is the quintessential, multicultural melange, rich in diversity and 'inclusivity' – who is including who, though, is never clear.

Dad would tell us stories of our family, of an aunty so black that she died in the bath trying to scrub the black off her skin. She scrubbed herself so much she scrubbed herself into oblivion. Or the uncle who never clipped his toenails until one day he fell over and his long toenails stabbed him in the chest and he died. His feet were now memorialised in a museum, and Dad promised to take us one day and show them to us. Looking back, I can see the messages under these children's stories of the fantastic and the surreal; at the time, I had no understanding of the layers of knowledge that could be revealed when you peeled back the veil of naivety.

By far the stories I loved the most were the clever ones where Dad would tell us how to fix things, how things worked and where to find things. My earliest memory of a clever story was on a warm Sydney winter's day. We were having our annual sports carnival in the back paddock of our primary school, and Dad came along to watch and cheer. As we sat on the itchy buffalo grass waiting for our races, Dad showed us how to find little sweet berries in the grass that you could eat. I thought all dads did this. I thought all dads knew how to find food in the back streets of suburban Sydney. It would take many years of walking and talking with aunties and uncles through the remnants of Sydney's saltwater, freshwater and bitter-water country to understand the full depth of what my father was teaching me – that the land can and will provide everything you need, without exception; and that is when I first became aware of the idea that Aboriginal people live in complete harmony with the land and never take more than they need.

This is what I grew up to believe it meant to be Aboriginal: to be Aboriginal meant that you were smart, intelligent, inventive and resilient – just like my dad. I had no idea that I should be ashamed of being Aboriginal and hide it like the family I read about in Sally Morgan's book *My Place*. Where I lived you didn't have to be ashamed – you just had to be silent. Just never mention it. There was no way Aboriginal people lived in this blond-haired, blue-eyed suburb of Sydney; Aboriginal people lived in the Central Desert. You were told, 'You don't count –you're not a *real*

Aborigine.' It felt real to me. It never felt more real than when my father would come home from his factory job and I would hear him telling my mother the things that the men there would call him. 'Dirty black bastard' was the least of it. I thought they were commenting on the black dust from the welding machines that shimmered on his skin when he came home from work. But he seemed so cranky and sad about what they said. I didn't understand why. Just have a shower and it will wash away?

My sister is my most constant memory from when I was growing up. She is only fifteen months older than me, and we were inseparable. If she got into to trouble for something, I wanted to get into trouble too and I would stick my hand out alongside hers for punishment. As we grew up and my sister was taunted and called horrible names because she was Aboriginal, I wanted to be called horrible names too – I was Aboriginal too! But I was excluded from the overtly racial slurs because I had lighter skin so they would say I 'wasn't really an Abo'. Strangely my sister was and so was my brother, and they heard it all, just like Dad. I wanted to be included with them. They were my favourite people in the world, but the world was telling me I wasn't like them. I was different.

None of the teachers at school ever talked about Aboriginal people. 'They' were never mentioned. Australian history started in 1788, and in the background of the photocopy of a First Fleet ship that I had to colour in was a tall thin man with a long stick and a scrap of cloth over his privates. I had no idea what he was doing there and I guess neither did the teacher, because she didn't seem to notice him.

So the world around me was silent, which started to make me louder and louder and my father prouder. At every opportunity I would talk about being Aboriginal. I would write about being Aboriginal. I would paint and draw and sculpt about being Aboriginal. I would see people twitch uncomfortably and some-times even let their ignorant thoughts out: 'But you don't look it?' 'From how far back?' 'Do you get lots of handouts?'

I started to notice that it was not considered good to be Aboriginal, but I just didn't understand. During high school I began to learn the stories of what happened to Aboriginal people around Australia. I started to hear the stories my father told me differently and to understand what my father's stories of his childhood as a 'half-caste' were all about. I realised that I was considered a 'quarter-caste' and could be easily assimilated into white society and not have to mention being Aboriginal. Apparently I had a 'choice'. I had a choice to deny how I really felt based on how I looked. I had a choice not to be my father's daughter. I had a choice to ignore what he had taught me. It didn't feel like a choice to me. This was me. No changing it. No choosing it. It just was. With every question and cruel remark a piece of frayed grass would come loose from the dilly bag, but there was no way I would let a hole develop. I tightened the strands and twisted them hard against the constant picking.

And so, with complete surrender, I delved into learning everything I could know about my 'Aboriginal-ness'. I traced back my father's stories and found more strands of grass for the dilly bag. My father's story is a long one. Dad was born in a mission at La Perouse, Sydney, to Fred Foster, a D'harawal snake man and performer, and Jesse Russell, a white woman. The first few years of my father's life were spent living in a tent with his older brother and sister on the La Perouse mission during the mid 1940s, but it wasn't long before the authorities started coming through to take half-caste kids from their families and send them to orphanages to be assimilated into white society. Dad's family moved around to avoid the authorities and ended up in the Hearne Bay reserve. Soon after, the family was offered a housing commission house in nearby Narwee and that is where my father spent the rest of his childhood, in a violent, alcoholic home amongst the middle-class white kids, being taunted mercilessly until Year 7, when he left school for good and began working in factories.

My dad told us many stories about him and his brother and how they survived their horrific childhood. My uncle would say that he would never get married and have kids because he would be just like their old man and make his family's life a living hell. My father promised to be the opposite – he was true to his word and is still a wonderful father who lives for his family. My uncle, though, did not have the same fate. He was a loner who turned to alcohol and, after a night of drinking, was picked up by the police and taken to a cell and bashed. He spent the days following feeling gradually worse and worse with a bad headache and dizziness. My cousin took him to a doctor and the doctor brushed him off and told him to go home and sleep off the grog, even though he hadn't had a drink for days. He went home and fell asleep but never woke up. He died in his sleep from a blood clot on the brain brought about by a blow to the head. He was forty-four – that's my age now.

It was around the time of my uncle's death that my father decided to go to TAFE to do an art certificate. He struggled with literacy and especially essay writing, so my sister and I would teach him what we were learning at our good school, which my parents struggled to pay for. Dad graduated from TAFE with a portfolio of impressive work and a growing feeling of confidence and self-worth. On the back of his new qualifications, Dad landed a good job with the government, helping people to find jobs after being on disability benefits. This was around the late 1980s and early 1990s, just as white Australian society was beginning to change and the government was becoming aware of Aboriginal people and our unique needs. My father took on a role as an Aboriginal Liaison Officer, helping Aboriginal people throughout Sydney to negotiate the government systems and bureaucracy, while also helping the government and their associated business clients understand the individual ways and needs of Aboriginal people.

He is a great man, my dad, and he is loved by so many. He has inspired people everywhere with his life story of a little black boy rising up from the depths of poverty and abuse to help and inspire untold numbers of people around the world. Just before his retirement, his career culminated in an address to the United Nations on behalf of the Indigenous people of Australia – an accomplishment that I am sure was driven by the spirits of our ancestors and that of my great-grandfather, who was a devoted soapbox activist in the Domain.

It is hard to believe that my father came from his father, Fred Foster, but Fred did not have an easy life either. As an adult, I can clearly see the same cleverness and courage that I see in my father in the stories about Fred, who was undoubtedly a brilliant and creative man. A snake man from La Perouse, he fearlessly stuck his hands down snake holes in the waterways that weave around Sydney to catch snakes for his shows. He kept king brown snakes and red-bellied blacks at home. My father was raised with Eugene the red-bellied black snake, an affectionate family pet that would curl up with my dad in front of the fire. Dad had no idea he was deadly – he loved Eugene but he definitely didn't like the brown snakes; a baby brown had snapped at him once, luckily only on the fingernail, but that was enough for my dad to stay clear of them slithering around the house. Fred was quite the entertainer and would paint himself up and do corroborees, put on shows and boomerang displays with his father, Tom Foster.

My great-grandparents, Tom and Eliza Foster, lived at the turn of the twentieth century and were a major part of one of the world's very first civil rights marches. Tom and Eliza were brave, committed and courageous and they led the charge with Aboriginal activists Jack Patten, William Cooper and Doug Nicholls in the 1938 Day of Mourning march in Sydney, petitioning the government for equal rights for Aboriginal people. This was thirty years before Rosa Parks, Martin Luther King Jr and Nelson Mandela hit the headlines, and second only to Ghandi's Salt March. They were involved in world-first events in history. My family. My little Aboriginal family from white-bread suburban Sydney.

And this is who I come from. This is who I am. To deny being Aboriginal is to deny their courage and resilience and the way they paved for me and all who come after us. They were soldiers on the frontline of a war that is still being waged. To succumb to the naysayers and deny this is to surrender – to wave a white flag and admit defeat. Assimilation complete.

I have now grown up to be a storyteller like my dad, if only half as good. I make sure our stories and knowledges do not sleep anymore. That they are not silent or silenced. That they live on for the next generation who will grow up Aboriginal, because to grow up Aboriginal is to be just one of a large community; not just a living community, but generations of family who you have a responsibility to – ensuring that our songlines continue and that there is a culture and 'Aboriginal-ness' to own in the future.

So, is my story of being Aboriginal any less of a story for being set in modern-day Sydney and against a backdrop of fair skin and green eyes? My story is born of 'Aboriginal-ness';

discrimination and persistence; injustice and innovation; sadness and success; dispossession and belonging. To not honour this is to deny the torrent of saltwater that runs through my veins, propelling me forward with the singing of a thousand voices in my ears and the sands of all time under my feet, for I am Aboriginal – and Aboriginal is me.

There are no halves

Jason Goninan

I am a Gunditjmara man from my mother's side. I am Irish from my father's side. I was born in Sydney at a time when my biological parents (my 'bios') were living there, however, the rest of my family were born and have lived and been raised in and around Melbourne and throughout Victoria, including Lake Condah, where a mission was located.

How do I identify? As Aboriginal, first and foremost, although this was not an easy path to take. My parents, who I love and call 'Mum' and 'Dad', fostered me when I was six months old. That was a silver lining to someone else's cloud. They couldn't have children of their own and were given the opportunity to do so, but obviously this came at the expense of others' hardship.

My biological mother was a survivor of the Stolen Generations. To this day I still don't know the intricate details of her life. I know that she and her brothers were removed from the Lake Condah mission, and were separated and placed in various state-run homes. There was abuse and sadness and all the harshness that is synonymous with accounts of the Stolen Generations.

Sadly, as with many other survivor stories, the trauma resulted in substance abuse, crime and bad relationships. Luckily a decision was then made that it was best for the innocent to be given a better chance in life, and I was placed in a state-run home for children.

My mum and dad first met me while I was awaiting placement in a children's home operated by the Child Welfare Board. As Mum tells it, the moment she saw me, she knew. She knew that I was her child. It always heartens me to witness the emotion and love she displays each and every time she tells that story. She and her best friend went and bought a crib and filled it with all things 'baby' that a new parent could need and went on trying to figure out parenthood, as most parents do.

My folks are not Aboriginal, and the Department of Community Services encouraged them to be open and honest with me about how I came to be in their lives and about my Aboriginality. They did this from day one, and I can't ever remember a time when I didn't know who I was or the reasons behind me being part of their family. I have met other people where this wasn't the case, where a bombshell was dropped or a 'discussion' was had and lives were drastically changed forever.

My mum experienced a similar family circumstance of being fostered to a different family, not her biological parents, as a young girl. My dad was born in Australia and has a very strong sense of his family history, which traces back to Cornwall, England. He tells the same stories of family and kinship that Aboriginal people do when meeting each other or having a yarn. So in some ways it was fortuitous that I was connected with these two amazing people with experiences that could inform my upbringing.

Although they had no personal involvement with Aboriginal communities prior to having me in their lives, they were always supportive of my decision to connect with my own culture. Mind you, this didn't come until later in life for me. I still vividly remember the day when in Year 3, after I had recently changed schools, I told a 'friend' that I was Aboriginal. I didn't think anything of it, until that 'friend' told his older brother and his mates. That's when the taunts and slurs began, the random pushing and shoulder barges in the hallway, and it was reinforced to me over time that it was not okay to be Aboriginal.

Without any guidance or peer support, I became ashamed of my identity, embarrassed to be part of the oldest living culture in the world, and made to feel like my identity was something to be kept secret. Over the years, I would meet amazing people who changed my thinking and taught me to be proud of who I was, to never be ashamed or let others make me feel that way. While at the Koori Centre at the University of Sydney, one aunty asked where I was from, to which I replied, 'I'm half-Aboriginal', which is what I'd always been made to think. She corrected me, 'No, bub, you *are* Aboriginal ... there are no halves.' Those few simple words changed something in me forever. Something which I bring my own children up believing. They have an Aboriginal father and a mother with a Filipino background so they *are* Aboriginal *and* they *are* Filipino. They should be proud of that because they are lucky to have such strong cultural backgrounds and that is something to cherish and encourage – not to be stamped out – especially in people so little.

I took a trip to the Northern Territory in 2006 to take part in some conservation work around Uluru. It was life-changing. It was not my country, but there was something about working on such sacred ground, meeting local community members and elders, working on country and being proud to see Aboriginal culture thriving. It ignited a spark inside me, and I knew it was time to reconnect with my biological family.

I contacted the organisation Link Up and asked them for assistance in locating my bio-mother (Dee*). I started meeting regularly with a case worker, Sandra, to discuss the steps in the process, what the outcomes might be and what to expect. It felt weird having such a big decision taken out of my hands, but Sandra and the Koori grapevine worked wonders and, before long, I received news that Dee had been contacted. Coincidentally, she had been looking for me at the same time.

My mum, Sandra and I travelled down to Melbourne to meet the family. We walked into the Koorie Heritage Trust and immediately the women working at the front desk greeted us and commented that I looked exactly like Uncle Mark. Who is Uncle Mark, I thought? Having grown up as an only child in an extremely small family and not having anyone in my family look like me, it was mind-blowing to think that not only did I have an uncle but that this man actually bore such a resemblance to me that strangers were commenting on the likeness!

At that first meeting, I met Dee and my two youngest half-brothers. I formed a bond with them straight away and felt an affinity that only people who experience strong relationships with their siblings would recognise. We laughed, told stories about our own lives and found common ground even though we were complete strangers to one another.

Dee sat me down, explained the reasons why she had to make the decision to try to find a better life for me and told me about the family history. She had even gone to the lengths of bringing a printed family tree with her and talked through the various relationships, including the other siblings, aunts, uncles, aunties and cousins that I would soon meet. Sandra later explained to me that it was a way of imparting knowledge, of a mother teaching her child about the kinship system. It dawned on me that it was something so simple yet such a strong part of Aboriginal culture and that, in that moment, thousands of years of cultural knowledge and practice had continued.

The rest of those initial days were spent meeting other family members and, by the end of the trip, I was mentally, physically and emotionally drained. I had such mixed emotions. I was happy to have finally met them and completely overwhelmed that I was part of such a large family. I was conflicted that while I had enjoyed such a privileged life, my biological family had in so many ways been living a completely reverse reality. How was this fair? Why did this happen to me? What would've happened if I'd stayed with them? These were questions to which I had no answers, and that I still ask myself today.

Growing up, I always knew that I'd been extremely fortunate to be in the situation I was: a good family, good schooling, friends, life opportunities. In some ways though, I knew the opposite was also true: that having no connection to kin, culture and language was a detriment not only to my sense of self but also to the survival of the culture.

In 2008 I married the love of my life. She had been by my side through the whole crazy ride while I had reconnected with my family and had provided her unconditional love and support through every moment, even though she confessed to not understanding what it was I was going through. In fact, I knew she was the 'one' right from the very start of our relationship. After our first date, during the 'get to know you' stage, she asked me to tell her something about myself. On a whim, I thought I would tell her about my family background and the journey that I had just begun (at this point, I was in the process of organising the trip to Melbourne). It was a gamble because my past experience meant I never knew how people would react to being told I was Aboriginal, but I trusted her. She was amazed. She asked questions, showed genuine interest and gave me her support – I knew right away that she was special.

Knowing that we wanted to start a family, my wife and I decided to take an extended honeymoon and went travelling around the world for the next few months after the wedding. It was towards the end of our trip that I received a call from my sister telling me that our mother had passed away from a stroke. I was speechless and suddenly felt alone again. The person who had brought me into this world – and my connection to family and culture – was gone. I felt a lot of feelings similar to those I had the day I first met her. Pain, confusion, sadness. I didn't understand how this could have happened, particularly at a time when things were only meant to be positive and there was so much more we were meant to experience together.

We ended our trip so we could attend the funeral in Melbourne. We spent a few days helping to arrange the funeral, meeting with family members and supporting each other through this process. Amongst all the craziness, I was asked to deliver a speech at the funeral. I didn't know whether I even had the right to do this but I accepted the offer. I was asked by one of my uncles if I'd ever been to an Aboriginal funeral before. He asked in a way that was not condescending but showed that he understood I'd been raised under different conditions. He told me there'd be a lot of people. And that some of the cousins and uncles who were in jail would be there for the service, so there would be police too. He wasn't wrong about any of it.

The day itself was a blur, but I do remember walking up to the front of the church and seeing hundreds of people staring back at me, waiting to hear something that would take away their pain. I don't know whether I gave them what I wanted but I felt such pride to see and hear how many lives Dee had affected. She was a role model not only for the Aboriginal community but also the broader community. A champion of people's rights, and a voice for some of society's most vulnerable.

Some years earlier, Dee had fought hard, along with many other community members, to gain native title rights and she rang me proudly the day the High Court's decision was made. I shared in her excitement but I felt hollow at the same time. I hadn't known that kind of struggle. I was naive and didn't understand what it was to have to fight for something that had been ripped from you. I didn't appreciate what Aboriginal land rights were: a belonging and connection to the land. Not ownership of something, but custodianship to care for and nurture it.

I made a promise to Dee on the day of the funeral that I would always be strong, as she had been through so much of her life. I wanted her to look down and be proud of me, to know that everything she had both accomplished and endured would not be in vain.

Flash forward to today. I work for the government in supporting Aboriginal communities. There are some necessary evils in the world and I believe this is one of them. I once worked as an Aboriginal Education Assistant in a low socio-economic area. I thought I could change every student and make the world a better place overnight. It was a hard lesson for me to discover that there are many forces far greater than my own goodwill that many Aboriginal people face every day of their lives. Over time, I've also learnt that sometimes the best way to change things is from within.

I always felt I was too white for the blackfullas and too black for the white folk. But maybe that's helped. My experiences have allowed me to bridge divides and understand both sides and where they come from. I'm not suggesting other people aren't able to do this or that I'm better than others, but that my particular circumstances are unique. For so long I viewed them as a detriment rather than as something to be embraced, even if I didn't have the luxury of having my Aboriginal culture, family or friends around me.

But what is identity? For so long I thought it meant you had to look a certain way, talk a certain way and act a certain way. As I grow older, and through my interactions with other Aboriginal people from all walks of life, I realise that nothing could be further from the truth. I also believe this is something non-Aboriginal people need to understand. That just as with any other community, Aboriginal people can't be pigeonholed into stereotypes for convenience. We don't just play sport, and we don't all look the same. We also don't practise culture in the same ways, but we do all share an understanding of what it is to be Aboriginal through unique lived experiences. That is going to look different for every single person.

I am proud to be able to tell people that I have two families. It isn't conventional, but that's the beauty of it. It doesn't fit the stereotypes that I grew up with and was conditioned to believe were 'normal'. And that isn't my *fault*, which it has taken me a long time to accept, because I was made to feel ashamed and guilty about it.

I keep in contact with my bio-family. My daughter shares a birthday with my bio-niece, which I think is a wonderful connection between the two families. I look forward to seeing which path my journey will take. In my own opinion, there is no one way to be Aboriginal. There is no rulebook. We each have our own lives to live. How we do that is up to us and we can only make the most of the opportunities that are afforded to us and not let others define or judge who we are.

Name changed for privacy.

The sporting life

Adam Goodes

I grew up in a lot of different places. My family moved around a fair bit when I was a kid, moving closer and then further away from the extended family. Being the eldest was tough growing up. I was supposed to know better, and I was always punished for the mistakes my brothers made. It was nice to be the man of the house but it came with high expectations.

I spent a lot of my childhood in Horsham, Victoria, and I remember always being in the backyard playing cricket, volleyball and tennis with my two younger brothers, Jake and Brett. It was great fun having younger brothers: we spent so much of our time outside, playing games, riding our bikes, swimming in the river. The camaraderie we had with each other was great. Of course, we didn't have computer games back them. Sometimes we just had a tennis ball and a bit of stick, and maybe a cricket bat if we were lucky, but we were always able to entertain ourselves for hours on end.

After school – and on the weekends – it was all about sports. If it got too hot, we might climb a tree or build a cubby house. If we were lucky we'd go to the river and grab onto the swing rope, swinging right over the river and dropping into the water. We had the river and we had dams, and we also had the local pool in Mildura. The best part of the pool was jumping off the towers, which were five and ten metres high.

One time I was called to the principal's office. I think he wanted me to tell on whoever put a hole in the wall. I knew who did it, but I didn't want my friend to get in trouble. I'd been friends with these guys for a couple of years since I moved high schools. I knew that we were probably all in the wrong because we'd been wrestling each other in the hallway. We were just being a little bit – okay, we were being very – silly. Then one boy got thrown into the wall, and that's how the hole happened.

We didn't agree to stay quiet, but you just knew that the other guys wouldn't say it was you, and you wouldn't say it was them. For me it was about being loyal, but also about being honest. I don't think I was being dishonest to the principal by not telling him who was there. I really didn't want to get my friends into trouble. But at the same time, I wanted the friend who caused the hole to put his hand up and take responsibility. I thought by being quiet I was giving him the opportunity to stand up, because I'd learnt that when you do something wrong it's good to take responsibility for your actions.

I didn't really get into that much mischief at school, but I did make some mistakes. I remember once I went on a field trip to the zoo and the teacher specifically told us not to make eye contact with the gorilla. But ... well, me and a friend thought it would be a good idea to do the exact opposite of what we were told, so we climbed up on the ledge, looked into the enclosure and made eye contact with the gorilla.

When you stare at a gorilla, it actually means you are challenging them. Of course, I didn't know that at the time – I was just doing it because they told us not to – but I later learnt that's the way gorillas communicate with each other. And so, on that day, the gorilla started beating his chest, running around and throwing bamboo at us. We just laughed because we got a reaction. We thought it was funny. But then the teacher saw what we were doing and we got in trouble. It wasn't until I found out more about gorillas that I realised it was actually very bad behaviour on our part.

I always liked school because I enjoyed making friends. I enjoyed talking to people and getting to know them, and watching people, but it was hard because we changed schools a fair bit. I reckon I went to five different primary schools and two high schools.

In primary school I had two teachers when I was in Grades 4 and 5. They shared the responsibility for us in those years, and they were our sports teachers as well. The best thing was whenever we finished our work quickly we were allowed to go outside and play sports and games, so it was a real big motivator for us to do our work, and do it well. It was the way the teachers rewarded us. I remember those being really fun times. I think a lot of kids, including myself, just wanted to be outside playing. I think most kids today still genuinely want to run around outside and burn energy.

When I was a kid, I wanted to be Michael Jordan, the basketball player. I had posters of him all over one wall. I liked how he did a slam-dunk, and I wanted to be just like him. I played soccer until I was thirteen or fourteen years old, when we moved from Adelaide to a place called Merbein, in country Victoria. When we got there, there were no junior soccer teams, only a senior soccer team. We watched them play a game and it was very aggressive and there was a lot of bad language being used on the field. I was a young kid and my mum didn't want me to get involved in that.

It so happened that there was a game of AFL being played on another oval nearby, and I walked over and asked what it was about. It was the under-14s, and it was perfect. If I'd stuck with soccer, though, I reckon I could have been Australia's Lionel Messi! The best thing about playing junior sport is that you get to give everything a try – different sports and different positions. If I was good in one sport, then why not try another sport? I liked challenging myself and learning something new – that was always how I felt about it.

I was about eighteen when I decided I wanted to play AFL seriously. In AFL I played back, forward, ruck, rover and wingman. There aren't many positions I didn't play with the Sydney Swans, but I really loved playing in the midfield because I wanted to be near the action. I liked being in a position where you had the most influence on the team winning or losing. I didn't like sitting on the bench much, but the good thing about today's game is you're only on the bench for a minute or two before you're back on the field. These days you're not on the bench for the wrong reason – it's more about rotating the players to get a rest.

I was sent off once. I elbowed somebody in the back when they weren't looking. It wasn't an accident – I deliberately struck him on the back. I was reported by the umpires and missed a game because of my actions. There was no excuse for what I did, and I got a one-week suspension. I deserved the week out and I learnt my lesson.

I remember kicking my first goal. It was my first-ever game for the Sydney Swans, back in 1999. I was nineteen. It was round one, and we were playing against Port Adelaide at the Sydney Cricket Ground. It felt great. It was a set shot, so I marked the ball and went back to do my run-up. I knew my mum and my two brothers were in the crowd watching. It was a really enjoyable moment and I remember thinking I was glad I could share it with them. I remember kicking my last goal too. It was against North Melbourne at ANZ Stadium in the 2015 Semi-Final. I kicked two goals that day and I kicked the last goal of the game, but we lost by twenty-six points.

I believe in having a dream and setting goals to achieve it. If you really want to be the best at anything, then you have to have the knowledge to do that. So you need role models, you need to be a good listener, to learn from your elders (people who have done it before). You have to have a great work ethic and, most importantly, you need to have fun and love what you are doing.

A Tasmanian Toomelah tiger

Jodi Haines

'You're not a real Aborigine.' 'You don't look Aboriginal.' 'How much Aboriginal is in you?' These are the consistent comments I have listened to throughout my childhood. The judgement and questioning of my identity became engrained into my young psyche and created loads of confusion about who I was growing up. I knew I was Aboriginal, but ignorant people and institutions around me continually questioned me.

My father is a Gamilaroi man from the New South Wales–Queensland border community of Toomelah, a mission that was set up by the New South Wales government. He was a boxer and was invited by the local copper from Goondiwindi to follow him to Hobart. Dad arrived in Hobart and boarded with the people who would become my grandparents, my mum's mother and stepfather. Nan and Pop were musicians in a band, and I remember as a child the big amplifiers that occupied the lounge room and hallway, ready to be taken to their next gig. This is where Dad met Mum. She was a shy fifteen-year-old who obviously became smitten by this handsome, dark Aboriginal man with all the charm in the world. She was young and naive; they eventually married and had three girls – I'm the middle child.

My mum has Irish ancestry but, due to her mother being adopted, their family tree is a bit limited. Mum was passionate and committed to ensuring we knew we were Aboriginal. She defended us many times growing up from racist attacks in our neighbourhood. I remember that one day she was hanging out of the lounge window with a wooden spoon in her hand yelling to the boys in our street to stop being racist or else (or words to those effect)! Mum says she doesn't remember this, but I do; I was both embarrassed and proud of her staunchness.

The first four years of my life were spent with Mum, Dad and my two sisters. Dad was a champion boxer, and a good musician, storyteller and cultural man, but he wasn't home much, always busy making new friends with the local Aboriginal community. Some of our elders in Tasmania have some good stories to tell about their time with Dad. Mum pretty quickly became a single mum. We had lots of visitors and support from family and community, especially Nan (Mum's mum). We also had another Aboriginal family whose matriarch originally came from Cherbourg. She became our second nan and would often visit to check that we were doing okay. My nan became nan to their children too. I have strong memories of Dad coming and going, pushing us on the swing, having conversations around the kitchen table, and then he was gone for good. I was around four years old. Mum said my older sister would stand at the lounge window waiting for him to come home.

Another strong memory I have of Dad before he left was when he took me to a park to teach me how to throw a boomerang. I remember running with glee trying to chase it. Dad made and designed this boomerang and gave it to us girls; he engraved a picture and our names on it, and it takes pride of place in my bedroom today.

Dad eventually left Tasmania and returned home to his beloved Toomelah and family. We moved to another humble housing commission area and eventually Mum met a new partner, who became our stepfather. As I continued to grow up I became very aware that my sisters and I were different from the other kids and I kept being reminded of these differences by regular neighbourhood calls of *nigger* and *boong*. Where was Mum and her wooden spoon when I needed her! People were often too scared to come out of their houses to tell me their ignorant version of Australia's history in person. I never really understood their meanness and certainly didn't want to be like them. We also had a dead kangaroo carcass dumped on our doorstep one night when the American slave movie *Roots* was on. Despite these negative experiences, I was proud to be Aboriginal, albeit a little confused about why it offended so many people.

I remember one day receiving a photo from Dad of him on a crane, showing off his job. I remember feeling proud of him but wondering where he was. I especially needed him when I was nine and took my boomerang to school for 'show and tell'. At recess I went outside and threw the boomerang with an Italian school friend – I didn't know Italians threw boomerangs too! I took it to the toilets to wash off the dirt, and some older girls in the toilet grabbed it off me and said that it wasn't mine because I wasn't Aboriginal. I remember feeling deflated and lost for words. Where was Dad to prove my right to hold this boomerang?

I was extremely shy and retreated into the worlds of sport, art, *Young Talent Time* and *Countdown*. I loved AFL and fell in love with North Melbourne because of the Krakouer brothers, who were brilliant. I would wear my football jumper every day and night, and play kick-to-kick across the road in the bush council area by myself or with my stepbrother. I was obsessed and pretended to be the Krakouer brothers. I was a classic tomboy and being called a boy made me quite happy – they seemed to have more fun than girls anyway.

When I was twelve Mum got word that 'old Ma Haines' (Dad's mum) was dying of cancer and wanted to meet us three girls before she passed away. The local church and the local Tasmanian Aboriginal community supported us to go to Toomelah for the first time ever. I remember Mum and we three skinny-legged Aboriginal girls flying to Sydney and then getting on a small plane to Moree, where we were met by a special uncle who looked after us. I remember the heat hit me like a suffocating hot velvet blanket. I pretended not to let it bother me, always trying to be strong.

We then travelled north by car until we pulled over to the side of the road and were greeted by an Aboriginal man who put his head inside the window. Mum said to him, 'Well, aren't you going to say hi to your children?' It was Dad! I don't know what I felt at that moment, but we all shyly said hello. We eventually made it to Toomelah mission and were greeted by smiling aunties and uncles and little blond-haired cousins all staring at us. We were presented with beach towels and food. Everyone was too shy to speak, but they smiled a lot and made us feel welcomed. I kept that beach towel for thirty years.

It was obvious our grandmother was very special to everyone. I remember seeing her for the very first time as she lay in bed unwell. It didn't stop her from growling at us kids when we made too much noise playing outside her window. It was great to play with our cousins and, although I didn't realise this at the time, not be questioned as to who we were.

We spent ten days getting to know our family, visiting and saying hello to everybody and everyone. Gee, I had a lot of 'lations! Dad was very proud to show us off. He organised a concert and fundraiser in the local hall for our return home. He wore a red satin shirt and gave me some coins from the fundraiser. Probably about two dollars' worth, but it was the thought that counted. I remember feeling sorry for him; I sensed he wanted to give more, but it goes alongside my boomerang and the crane photo as my prized gifts from him.

We would swim in the local muddy river to cool down from the heavy heat, and other kids showed off their skills by swinging from high trees into the river. One of my oldest cousins gave me a necklace in the water. It was the Aboriginal flag and he explained what it meant – my first political lesson. I wore that necklace for twenty years, but eventually lost it; I have a tattoo of the flag on my shoulder instead. I always remind him of this thoughtful gift when I go home to Toomelah – it's our special connection.

After that intense first visit we returned back home to our normal routine. My older sister found it hard to transition back into school, as this trip had obviously awoken something in her. She started to engrave land rights flags into the desks, question authority and assert her individuality. My younger sister was also set on a political path and questioned the claims that there were no Aboriginal people left in Tasmania. Both of my sisters continue to excel in their chosen fields today, giving voice to Aboriginal issues in their areas of expertise.

I continued to be a shy kid but gained confidence through art and sport. (My music development came later in my mid-twenties.)

I had plenty of Aboriginal sporting role models to identify with who, I suppose, replaced that early absence of my father. Now that I had visited my family, I knew where to return to once I left school. I have visited many times since, trying to keep my connections strong. I've gone to many funerals and sung original songs as a way of showing my love and support. My song 'Toomelah Woman' is written about old Ma Haines and my first visit there as a twelve-year-old, as described in this story. Finally knowing my extended family always sat deep in my heart, mind and soul, and would often give me the strength to be confident in who I was and to answer the continual dumb questions about my identity.

My dad and most of my immediate uncles and aunties have passed over to the Dreamtime now. I have younger brothers and sisters from my dad's second family, and all of my first cousins have children and their children have children so we come from a big mob. I love them all and am proud of my Gomeroi people. I'm grateful to my mum for showing me how to be strong and compassionate, and to my Tassie nan and aunties who looked after me too. I'm proud of the Tasmanian Aboriginal community for their resilience, and continue to enjoy working beside them today.

I remember

John Hartley

I am Ku Ku Yalanji Bama. My name is Karranjal John Hartley, and I was born in Kogarah, New South Wales, in 1956. My ancestral homeland is in far north Queensland.

I wrote this spoken-word piece for a men's talking circle when I was in my mid-thirties, some twenty-five years ago. It covers some of my earliest memories over a period of some thirty years, from when I was four years of age and living in returned soldiers barracks at what was then called Herne Bay and is now known as Narwee.

*

I remember rows of paint-peeled tinderbox homes, paper-thin walls, wooden floors and a kerosene fridge. Long wooden tables that stretched forever with church-like chairs, black and stained, where I sat straining to reach my dinner.

I remember communal washrooms, wire fences, electrical transformers and old dirt roads, and two Dutch friends. I remember open fields, two swings and a roundabout, a snow-white horse roped in a grass-filled paddock, and how I rode that horse without climbing on its back.

I remember farewells, the moving, and a freshly laid cement path leading all the way to a newly built war-service home. Mum, Dad, Granny and Granddad, my brothers and sisters, photos on the doorstep, and the metal outline of 'a Mexican seated beneath a palm tree in perpetual siesta' living lazily on our front-door screen.

I remember the black-tarred roads in our neighborhood that would feel the constant weight of my shoeless feet, and how my feet would blister on melting summer days, and how my blue twenty-four-inch Malvern Star with back brakes would leave skid marks on its surface for days.

I remember it was the road that always led me home, and it came to be the road I walked away on and left behind.

I remember being the new kid on the block, trying to fit in but just never quite.

I remember sitting in the bush on my favourite rock for hours, never tiring; the spirit of that place would send my mind walking to places far and quiet.

I remember being a welcomed guest in that eucalypt and paperbark country, except for when the sun went travelling, and shadows grew tall and hungry, and those red-eyed *Quinkins* (spirits) chased me home.

I remember Mum pointing out the tracks left by the ancestors of that country, the waterholes and sharpening stones, the many hidden shelters. I remember how we would map and name features of that country: the big rock, the big tree cave, the little saltpan and the paperbark mob.

I remember a sense of place becoming embedded in my marrow.

I remember the visitors to our home, black and white of all nationalities; the long political talks and conferences, the '67 referendum, the never-ending bottles of DA lager empty and drained, and me forever watching and wanting to catch the eye of my father.

I remember going to work with my dad and how I had to dress just like him.

I remember walking up the gangplank of the passenger ship *Oriana*, marching alongside Dad in the May Day rallies and feeling ten feet tall, but remaining unseen, hidden beneath the banners and the militant gait of working-class giants. I was safe and complete, and I didn't know a damn thing, and nothing mattered, as long as I was walking beside him.

I remember being told to be proud of who you are and where you come from.

I remember visiting my father's father and mother, the train trips and ferry rides, the steep climb to their home that would put an ache in your legs that burnt for days; the fruit salad and ice-cream and the endless supply of barley sugar. I remember their smiles of greeting and their waves at parting, their hugs, their fare-wells and so-longs.

I remember the old musty smell as I ventured through their home, and the view over the harbour through binoculars that I strained to hold, and how I loved my grandparents.

I remember lying in the big room at the end of my parents' house on a double bed that you could get lost in. I remember float-ing in the warmth between my mum and dad, curling their hair simultaneously with my left and right index fingers.

I remember Dad getting up to go to work for the midnight shift down on the wharves and never returning.

I remember the stillness of the morning I still wish had never come, and my mother taking me to the blue fold-out vinyl lounge where our visitors often slept with full bellies and warm blan-kets. She sat me down and I looked up at her, knowing and feel-ing the deep sadness but not knowing what was to come. Hugging me, she whispered brokenly: *Your father has died; he won't be com-ing back*.

I remember the light in my mother's eyes becoming dim; I became weightless, without anchor, and darkness entered my life also.

I remember becoming numb that day; I remember being told to be strong, that I was now the man of the house and I had to look after my little sister and mother.

I remember my aunty saying to let me cry; I never did – men don't cry. I remember I wasn't a man: I was eight years old.

I remember being in third grade and informing the class that my father had died. I remember them laughing. I remember sink-ing under the floorboards, dissolving, evaporating like water on hot coals.

I remember my mother struggling to make ends meet; to my shame, I only ever made it harder.

I remember my father was a wartime hero with citations from President Truman. I remember he was deported from America as politically undesirable.

I remember they said he was a working-class hero with the respect of his fellow workers and how thousands lined the streets of Sydney for his funeral. I remember watching his casket go into the fire and, just as bravely, I watched his spirit quietly leave, and something in me left also.

I remember never reaching out again. I remember not believing, and searching for him in the places we went, but never finding any trace.

I remember being an eight-year-old man of the house, who did nothing but grow angry. Anger was a feeling; anger was understood; anger was tangible; anger, I thought, got results; anger was a moat; anger was protection and brought a pulse to numbness.

I remember in third grade being told I was not Aboriginal, because I was not black. I remember being educated to feel shame just because of who I was and where I came from; I remember becoming nothing. I remember being educated into forgetting who I was and no longer feeling where I belonged; that I just didn't fit.

I remember objecting to the teachers' description of the 'Aborigine' and being told I was too 'fair of skin' to be Aboriginal and to stop being silly and to sit down; and yet, I felt the pull of the earth and the call of my ancestors, too strong to be anything else; but yet, I was told I was not who I was brought up to be – I was not, they said, 'Aborigine'.

I remember learning racism in school: that we live in a world of colour; that it was your colour that made the difference, was the determining factor on the ladder of 'success'. I remember being brought up proud of my people and my cultural heritage, yet 'educated' 'teachers' were telling me I could not be at home in my culture due to my skin colour.

I remember burying who I was. That day in the classroom, they dispossessed me of a proud and strong culture. Like an ancient gum protesting the march of 'modernity', my roots were torn up and I floated aimlessly without connection when they said I wasn't black.

I remember my mother taking us up to meet our relations in far north Queensland: Granny Caroline, Grandfather Edgar, my uncles, aunties, cousins, nieces, nephews, brothers, sisters, mothers, fathers, the ancestors of the rainforest; going for the obligatory swim in the Davis family waterhole at the Mossman Gorge.

I remember the run-down conditions of the Bama settlement and butter-box homes. The tin house where my mother grew up in silent dignity. I remember the termite-crushed floors and sugar-bag doors; a smile, a cup of tea, a feed and a warm bed, and places to heed.

I remember the prejudice and the eyes of disgust that followed you in lily-white northern towns. I remember sitting in the front row of the picture theatre in baggy canvas seats as we watched with strained necks, because that's where the blacks were allowed to sit. I remember being told I could sit anywhere. I remember I sat in that front row: I sat with my family; I sat proud in my resistance.

I remember the feeling of dismissal from blackfella and racism from whitefella, all because you don't fit a mould – I remember constructs of invasion and other colonial stings designed to hasten the death of ancient memory. I remember thinking I don't need this shit; black of mind, white of skin, where do I lay my head when others have already made my bed?

I remember the feeling of feeling nothing. I remember I made a choice. I remember I cried.

I remember 'Aboriginal' is coloured by a colonial construct. *Bama* is belonging: it is family; it is connection; it is lawful; it is colour-less.

I remember loneliness is a state of mind, and family are never far from mind. I remember the ache in my heart when I began to feel for others again, and not being fearful of the feeling. I remember tears are cleansing.

I remember each day the pain in my body. I remember we can't go back; nothing changes the past, only how I tell it. I remember tomorrow can change, but I don't remember it yet.

I remember I am not one-eighth, one-quarter, half, three-quarters, full, fair, red, yellow, copper, brown, dark or black ... I am memory. I remember I am eight pints of 'full-blood' human being.

I remember I can change … if *we* change.

I remember the tightness in my chest, the ambulance, looking up at white-panelled ceilings, the wires and the beep of bedside monitors and thinking this is it. I remember the ancestors came and said: *Boy, you have to go back to your culture.*

I remember, I am not broken or bygone. I am not the neatly framed picture nailed-tight to a well-constructed wall.

I remember Aborigine is a colonial construct.

I know very well my law and my culture.

I am Ku Ku Yalanji.

I am Bama.

I am Karranjal.

I am proud.

Born of ancient song.

My blood is in the country and the ancestors know me there.

I remember, beneath this skin

I am continuance.

I am resistance.

And … yes.

I am living memory.

Some call 'Aborigine'.

The streets of my youth

Terri Janke

I can clearly remember Jones Street in Cairns, where I grew up. The street was flat and straight, no gutters. If it rained for more than a day, the puddles would become lakes then rivers. My siblings, Toni and John Paul, and I would have fun splashing and catching tadpoles. When it didn't rain, we rode our bikes up and down Jones Street. One day I strayed away from our street alone. A kid on a dragster bike called out, 'Get out of here, blackie.' My legs pedalled fast to get back home.

It was safer in my street because everyone knew us. My young parents rented the orange Queenslander from the housing department. Our next-door neighbours, a white family, had a pianola that played music by itself. I used to like sitting on the polished wooden bench in front of it, with my bare feet on the pedal, and pretend to be a famous pianist. The German woman across the road sold dolls with crocheted skirts that could fit over toilet rolls. She would let us watch her coloured TV. My Aunty Betty and Uncle Dick Williams lived a couple of streets away with their six kids – they were like my grandparents. Then there was my mum's brother, Uncle Tony, and his family. They were always over my house for barbeques where we would eat, tell stories, play the guitar and sing. There were many happy times when we were all together at Jones Street.

As a kid, I had red scaly, itchy skin that turned purple when I scratched, then white when it flaked. I stank like rotten fish from the concoction of ointments my mum applied to my skin. I had chronic dandruff, bung eyes and a snotty nose. I went to the doctor's, but they couldn't help. I went to Uncle James, a traditional healer, who gave me natural plant remedies to bathe in and rub on my skin. These provided relief when I used them, but nothing would deal with my skin problems in the long term. My mum constantly worried about my skin.

My parents were the centre of my universe. My mum was the most beautiful woman in the world, with her long black hair that she combed with an orange brush. She wore brightly coloured headbands that matched her miniskirts. She worked at the Department of Education assisting Aboriginal and Torres Strait Islander kids who'd come from the Cape and the Torres Strait to go to school.

My dad was the activities manager for us kids. He made us a go-cart out of an old crate, which didn't really work well on such a flat street, so he used to push us around. He played golf, and I used to go with him sometimes to caddy at the North Cairns Golf Club. I liked watching him concentrate to line up the putt. He would bend his knees, tuck his head in, make his arms stiff and clip the ball into the hole. My job was to pick up the tees, which was fun until one day I got hit by a ball. My brother got the more glamorous job of lifting up the flag at the green.

Dad worked at the post office sorting mail and then, in 1972, he got a job as a law clerk at the new deputy crown solicitor's legal aid office, one of the many changes implemented in the Whitlam era. At nights, Dad studied journalism and he volunteered writing newsletters: for Apex, a local business group; and also Opal, 'One People of Australia League', which did a lot of work to advance Aboriginal people in the community.

I remember the day Dad told us that we were moving. 'I've got the chance to be paid as a journalist,' he told us. 'Your father's going to work in the government,' Mum said. 'It's colder there, and it will be better for your skin, Terri.' Dad went ahead to work in Canberra for a few months, and then we all packed up the house and left.

I don't remember how I felt about leaving Jones Street – the place that was my childhood world. I didn't really mind leaving my

Catholic primary school: I had no friends to play with, and I wasn't enjoying my lessons. I was never encouraged by my teachers and I didn't feel smart. In fact, I felt invisible.

I don't remember how my sister, Toni, felt about leaving Cairns. She had many friends and was always being invited to birthday pool parties. She was going into her final year of primary school and was probably going to be elected the captain of the red sports house.

My little brother, John Paul, was in Grade 3. He didn't talk much, but his thing was playing soccer. I don't know how he felt about school. As we went to a Catholic school, he was due to leave our primary school and go to the all boy's college up the road.

I guess we all saw the move as an adventure. We had never been on a plane before. We arrived in Canberra in March 1976. Malcolm Fraser was the new prime minister. Our new temporary home was the Aboriginal hostel in Carruthers Street, Curtin. Later we moved to a house in Pethebridge Street in Pearce, a suburb of Canberra under the shadow of Mount Taylor. We made friends with the neighbourhood kids. I rode my bike, but when I went further up the hill, there were older kids who tried to be tough and scare me.

John Paul went to Marist College, and Toni and I went to Sacred Heart Primary School. I loved that school. From the very first day all the girls were so friendly. The teachers assessed my level of education, and to my surprise Mrs Glover, my fifth-grade teacher, told me I was smart. I liked writing, and I was in the top class for maths. I liked my new friends. I was a true competitor at lunchtime handball, and my skinny black legs could run fast so I won most of my races. I remember going to see *Storm Boy*, starring David Gulpilil, at the pictures with my new friends. 'Is that your people?' my friend asked me. 'Yes,' I said, 'kind of, but I come from Cairns.'

Did the cold weather help my skin? Well, not really. I discovered I had an allergy to wool, which made my skin even worse. The itchy, weepy, scaly skin pattern continued, but I learnt to look after it better as I got older.

Canberra in the 1970s opened my eyes to the political and social world of Indigenous Australia. Mum and Dad both worked in the public service, as did many other Aboriginal and Torres Strait

Islander people who had moved from all over Australia to take up new careers. They formed a little community. I got to know many of the Aboriginal and Torres Strait Islander leaders in government at the time, or who later rose to have prominent careers in their fields. But Jones Street was never far from my mind. It was my first home, my first world, and it's still vivid in my imagination after all these years.

What it's like

Keira Jenkins

'You wouldn't know what it's like, I guess,' he said very casually down the phone to me. 'Your mob is from top camp – that's not a real mission. You probably don't know what it's like to be really Aboriginal.'

I had to hold back a tirade. I had to hold back laughter. Here was a white man who'd been married to an Aboriginal woman years ago, and he thought that made him an expert on being Aboriginal.

'Okay, thanks for your call. I've got another line ringing so I've got to go now,' I said, perhaps a little tartly, hanging up the phone before I could hear his reply.

I don't make a habit of hanging up on people – especially not at work – but you tell people who you are and they make judgements. I've had enough of that in my lifetime. Yeah, maybe I don't know what it's like to be what you think an Aboriginal should be, ignorant white man, but I certainly do have my own version of being Aboriginal.

I was six years old, sitting cross-legged on the floor in my checked dress, which was slightly too long for me, looking eagerly up at Miss Brown – at least I think that was her name – the first time I had a blow to my sense of identity. We were learning about Aboriginal people and I piped up very proudly.

'I'm Aboriginal.' I waved my hand in the air.

'No, you're not,' my friend Alison said. 'You're too white to be Aboriginal.'

I don't remember what happened after that; I just remember feeling ashamed. I think Miss Brown berated Alison for making the assumption that Aboriginal people had to be dark. I think she knew my parents actually, and knew all about my heritage, that's what happens in a small town like Moree.

Yeah, Moree, I hear you mutter under your breath. You'll know it from the artisan baths, the freedom rides maybe; maybe you'll know it from the domestic violence statistics as a 'rough town'. But, even though I spent only a small portion of my life in that western New South Wales town, I never saw it like that.

I grew up playing with the kids over the back fence, seeing how high we could swing, climbing trees, having memorial services for the ants whose nests we ran over with our bicycles.

Mum would let me ride my bike to the park; she'd have my little sisters in tow, a baby in a pram and a toddler on her hip at the time.

We might go all the way to visit 'Uncle Corey' – one of Dad's oldest friends, not an uncle (not even a blackfella) – at the corner store he worked at and have an ice-cream each.

I remember having parties with my sisters and my cousins; there'd be a jumping castle set up in the backyard, and the adults would pull out the plastic green chairs and sit around chatting, food and drinks in hand, while the barefoot kids would chase each other on the dried-out grass, trying not to get a burr to the foot. We'd take ice cubes out of the esky and suck on them to keep cool on those summer evenings. It was never a tough life for me, but I know it was for some of the other kids growing up in that town.

I didn't know that doing it tough was part of what made you Aboriginal until someone told me so. That man on the phone, he was just one of the many people in my life who tried to strip me of my culture, my pride, because I'm educated (and everyone knows blackfellas can't be educated), because I'm only a little bit brown, because I'm just as proud of my Norwegian and English heritage as I am of my Aboriginal heritage.

Mum and Dad always told me I was Aboriginal. They told me to be proud of that – and I was. It wasn't until I went to school that

I really had to consider what being Aboriginal meant. A lot of my cousins were darker than me, but I never considered that. It just was what it was. Nan and Pop and Dad and my uncle and aunty were dark. Mum was white and I knew that. I didn't think that because she was white it made me any less Aboriginal until that day at school.

We moved to the north coast when I was eight. Mum wanted to get me into the best school possible; I was excelling in my classes and I loved to read and write. I went to Wyrallah Road Public School; Mum later told me one of the local private schools informed her I'd be put in the lowest class there because of my race. My mother was dealing with discrimination for me before I even knew what it was.

I made friends quickly at school and loved my teachers, loved my classes, loved afternoon art classes and took an art-enrichment course. I remember one day coming home to tell my parents about a really cool Aboriginal dancer who'd come to school and played the didgeridoo for us and danced in all his traditional get-up. Dad told me it was my cousin. I just thought it was a great spectacle, just like all the other kids sitting in that assembly that day. When we learnt about Aboriginal Dreamtime stories or did the annual NAIDOC colouring-in competition, no one pointed out that I was (or wasn't) Aboriginal and for years I flew under the radar at school.

At home we used the Aboriginal words we knew, and I repeated them to my friends to sound cool that I knew some language, the same way I used the sign language Mum taught me. '*Budghan*,' I'd say, pointing to a cat, and my friends would laugh as they tried to copy the guttural sounds. It was a great game, and my peers were impressed I could speak even a little of another dialect. Dad would sometimes sing 'Boggabilla Road' to us, and when Pop came over he'd sing 'My Boomerang Won't Come Back' or some other little ditty that we just assumed he'd made up. I spent a lot of time in the sun, trying to get blacker. I wanted to look Aboriginal so I could claim my Aboriginality.

When I got to high school, though, that's when the real shock to my identity came. That's when people started telling me it wasn't a good thing to be Aboriginal. High school was when I started being ashamed of my heritage. I'd never had many Aboriginal friends at school; we'd been in different classes, which didn't bother me, and it's not something I ever thought about. At high school the other kids would look at me with this strange mixture of shock or disbelief, a bit of jealousy and, at worst, disgust when I was taken out of classes for an Aboriginal students' meeting or an Aboriginal students' excursion, and I hated it.

It got to the point that I'd pretend I was sick if I knew there was a meeting coming up. I was embarrassed, so from Year 7 I started missing classes because of who I was. It didn't bother me if I missed out on those 'Aboriginal things' (as my classmates used to call them) anyway. I hated going fishing and thought meeting football-ers was tedious, and sausages were about the only thing I didn't eat. But that's what those reward activities were all about, because that's what Aboriginal kids like to do, right? Sports and fishing and having a sausage sizzle. Not me. Maybe I'm the only black kid in the world who has no interest in these things. Maybe it's another warped way of society telling me I don't fit the standards set to be Aboriginal. I knew who I was, but I guess being surrounded by people who thought these things – the things I didn't particularly enjoy – were rewards for Aboriginal students made me feel less Aboriginal.

That was a common thread throughout my high school life.

I grew up middle-class, and I'm not afraid to admit that. Privileged. I've been described using that word by all kinds of peo-ple. Even my parents remind me of my privilege, but not in a nega-tive way. They tell me they have fought hard and worked hard to give me that privilege, so I can go to any school I want, can go to any university and study anything I want, can have pretty much anything I want if I work for it. Not everyone has that opportunity and I know that.

I'll always remember the ways I've been torn down, by my own people, by white people, by people I had considered friends and allies, by institutions and societies; the times I cut my thighs, my wrists, my chest just to see if I bled the same or if there was some-thing in my blood that would prove to me that I was Aboriginal; the nights I lay in bed, stressing about if I'd be taken out of class the next day. That's how the girl who's told she's not Aboriginal enough struggled.

The first time I was attacked by the hand of society it was because they wanted to make sure I could read. My parents got a note at home saying I had to take a basic reading test. They were confused; I'd just got to high school and been put in the English class with all the advanced kids. They tried to work out why I'd been selected to take the reading test – none of my friends or classmates had to do the test.

Dad went with me when I took the test, and I remember him having a heated exchange with the teacher when he realised I had to take the test because I was Aboriginal. I got defiant right about then – that's a common thread throughout my life, and probably why I've done half the things I have, because I want to defy expectation, prove wrong the people who've thought so little of me. I read what they gave me with flying colours; it was the kind of thing I was given to read in kindergarten.

I got award after award at school. It was exhausting for my soul. That sounds a bit full of myself really, but it exhausted me having to think: 'Did I deserve this, or did I just get it because I was Aboriginal?' I had a friend – at least I thought she was a friend – and she'd tell me whenever I was awarded with something, 'Oh, you just got that because you're Aboriginal.'

Mum told me she was jealous when I'd come home in tears. But you hear something enough and you start to believe it. I look at some of the awards I got back then and I think, yeah, you were a token. Then I think, no. You worked hard at school. You did well. If you are rewarded for that, you use that, you use the institutionalised racism that they throw at you, and you use it to your own advantage. You use that same racism to prove what you can do. Now that's contentious, isn't it? Ah, some will say, just another Aboriginal taking free stuff; others will say I've sold my soul to the white system. I say I've done what I need to survive in the world that has proven again and again to be hostile to me.

But don't worry if you're white. This is not an attack on you – no way. I'm proud of my heritage and that means the heritage that was passed down by my mother too. I've grown into myself a bit now, and I'm not ashamed of who I am anymore. It took until I was twenty years old. I remember the moment I realised who I was again and that I should love myself. It was Anzac Day and I was at the march in Redfern, I had a friend with me, and while I was mingling, chatting and just being part of the day, she looked very uncomfortable, pulled out a book and started to read, ignoring what was going on and the people around her.

Maybe I was wrong to be angry, but I was livid. I never would have done something like that at something important to her. That realisation, that not only was this important to me, but that I wanted it to be important to other people was the moment I was proud again.

But sadly, even if I know who I am, there's never a shortage of people who want to tear that pride down. I get asked where I'm from a lot. I look different, and I like that. I even get a bit of a laugh when people tell me to go back to where I came from; because I've got olive skin, people sometimes assume I'm Middle Eastern.

That's something I learnt from my family – to laugh it off. It makes you more resilient. What I hate is people telling me 'you're only half Aboriginal, you're not really Aboriginal' or telling me 'you're pretty for an Aboriginal' or 'you're smart for an Aboriginal'. *It's just ignorance. Don't let it bother you.* That's my mantra.

When the people you've looked up to – activists who you've modelled yourself on – say things like 'I told my kids not to bring any white sons- or daughters-in-law home' or you're told 'half-castes are genocide on our bloodline' or when a white man says 'you probably don't really know what it's like to be Aboriginal', you find yourself reeling with not knowing who you are, but you're still proud. But are you? Is it enough? Am I Aboriginal enough if I was ashamed of it for so long, if I grew up middle-class, if most of my friends are white?

Yeah, it is enough.

I have struggled my entire life with racism. I've seen my grandmother get followed around shops; I've been denied jobs and rental houses because of my heritage; I've seen my sister get school detention for 'lying' about being Aboriginal.

Who gets to decide who I am and if it's enough? Me.

I grew up in this skin – and I'm still growing up in this skin – I get to decide who I am, even if it takes my whole life to figure it out. So far it's only taken twenty-three years. So I don't care if you're 'black, white or brindle' (ah, that saying; I hear it so much): you don't get to tell me I don't know what it means to be Aboriginal.

My life's voyage

Patrick Johnson

From the first moment of taking a breath, I had the salt air in my lungs and the wind on my face and my mother's touch. My mother, Pearl Marriott, gave birth to me on a speedboat racing from Yarrabah Aboriginal mission to Cairns base hospital. My mother was Aboriginal, originally from Lockhart River (Kaantju), and my Dad is Irish from a town in Ireland called Carlow.

My mother's family were moved from Lockhart to live in the mission of Yarrabah, and my father travelled from Ireland to Australia when he was sixteen. The world is an amazing place, full of opportunities and coincidences.

Unfortunately, when I was only two, my mother died in a car crash outside Yarrabah. My father decided to do his best as a single parent and bring up his child on a boat in far north Queensland. The exciting diversity of the towns and places I visited at a young age allowed me to view life as an adventure: to see, smell, taste and notice every moment. I'm not saying there weren't tough times, such as making friends and then moving and never seeing them again, and other disappointments and heartaches arising during my early years at school and as a kid growing up, but I tried to use them all as opportunities to build my character.

I lived on a boat in far north Queensland for almost seventeen years and attended over twenty different schools along the coast. I had to be very adaptable and learn to take responsibility for my actions from a very young age, looking after dinghies, watching out for Tiger sharks or for when the anchor got stuck. I have always travelled but feel firmly rooted in the richness of our country's Aboriginal and Australian culture.

When I was growing up, my father was constantly questioned about who I was, by both non-Indigenous and Indigenous people. In Australia in the 1970s, a white father looking after his Aboriginal son was a rare sight. He tells me their concern and interest was genuine and not about racism.

In life, you will always come across people who will try to label you, stereotype you or judge you without knowing anything about you; it's not confined to any one race, region or culture. In my case I choose to live my life not influenced or affected by negative people who have different views about how I should live and behave. My personal view is that some people are genuinely missing out on being enriched by other people's true abilities, cultures and full potential. So I have always approached life and people with both eyes open, both ears listening and simple respect.

Growing up in Australia for me was never about my nationality, colour or religion – what was important was my character and how I treated others. I am who I am, and I'm proud of the richness and depth of my Aboriginal culture, and the humour and toughness I inherited from my single dad with his Irish wit and intelligence. My true connection was always to the land, the sea and the natural world around me, and that is a direct product of living on a boat for seventeen years.

In 1989 I won a scholarship to Aurora College in Moss Vale, New South Wales, an international boarding college. I was the first Australian ever to attend the college. My fellow students were all from different parts of Asia. Boarding college was a culture shock, but it strengthened my appreciation for other cultures and languages, which led me to continue to study Asian and political studies at the Australian National University. This led me to work at the Department of Foreign Affairs and Trade for almost ten years.

At the age of twenty-four, at the Australian University Games, I began my journey into the world of track and field with no training background. In my youth, I did win a few athletics carnivals in the many different schools I attended, from Magnetic Island to Cooktown to Airlie Beach, but I never dreamt of running or competing in the Olympics. I loved any type of sport, given that I lived much of my time on a boat. I didn't have any sporting heroes or a well-known public hero back then: my heroes were my dad, my mother and my grandmother. Here's an interesting fact: I do not know what my mother looks like and have never seen a picture of her; I hope I have done her proud.

Three years after the Australian University Games, I competed in my first Olympics – Sydney 2000 – in the 100 metres, 200 metres, and 4x100-metres relay. Three years later I broke the Australian and Oceania records for 100-metre sprints, becoming the first-ever person of non-African descent to break the ten-second barrier, running a time of 9.93 in Mito, Japan. Currently, I am still the Oceania and Australian 100-metre record holder. In my twelve-year sporting career in track and field I feel I've had an opportunity to show that, through sheer will, passion, discipline and determination, the impossible is possible if someone is given a chance to believe in themselves.

My passion has always been in the health, wellbeing and leadership space, partly as a result, unfortunately, of many of my family passing away through chronic health issues. Hence my transition from elite sport into community-controlled health, and I currently work as a leadership project officer in AMSANT (Aboriginal Medical Services Alliance NT). Leadership lies in our communities, families and friends, and local heroes. I strongly promote, nurture and develop our leaders, making sure that we give due respect to our past, current and future leaders. We must recognise the contribution of local heroes in Aboriginal leadership in our communities.

Our upbringings, relationships and experiences all influence us. Each of us can find our true passion. Don't fear the unknown – we are the creators of our own destiny. We can empower ourselves through education and knowledge to determine our own paths. Choose the life you want for yourself, and lead by example to empower yourself and the next generation.

Red dust kids

Scott Kennedy

Red, flat and dry. Condobolin was hard and didn't take too kindly to the weak – and no one was as tough as my pop. Even though I'd started school and was a big boy now, he could still hold me above his shiny bald head, looking up at me with his round chubby face and his wide Koori nose. I was so high – if he'd dropped me from up here I would surely die – but his big smile would ensure me I was safe in the King's hands.

We had the best lawn in the street, and a shiny new HR Holden in the front yard. Pop ruled our street, and I was his five-eight, his china plate. No one could touch me (except the wrath of my mother; not even the King could save me from that). I suppose that was why Uncle Mark and David hated me so much.

Mark was four years older than me, and David five. We were more like brothers, and with me being the youngest they would make my life hell at times. Mark was small for his age so had to fight for everything. He was the only blond in our family so I used to think he was not really one of us – like there was something broken in the link. David was the opposite: slow-witted, tall, and he didn't seem to have the fight in him that Mark and I did.

Saturday afternoons were my favourite time of the week; we would all go to the picture theatre. This one Saturday, the Pawsy kids from the end of the street walked up to our house as usual. I had a huge crush on Sandy Pawsy so I would be louder than usual, showing off, but didn't have the courage to let her know how I felt. Then, under my mother's control, we would start walking, picking up the Doogle kids on the way – then another few Pawsy kids, their cousins – then the Burns kids. By the time we got to the cinema, we were a small mob led by my crazy mother, who nobody dared to mess with. We were untouchable.

Even though Mark, David and I were at each other's throats most of the time at home, in a social environment we were as thick as thieves. We had a good reputation for being bad. Even with my little sweetheart there, you couldn't pry us apart – plus obviously the best way to impress her was to be one of the boys.

Once in the theatre, we got our choc-top ice-creams. The three of us boys had one main objective, to break away from the mob, away from my mother's rule, so we headed upstairs to the balcony seating. Leaning over the rail, eating our ice-creams, we'd watch the place fill up. Mum was down below up the front, in our view. It was perfect.

After we finished our ice-cream, with our heads hanging over the rail, Mark dared me to spit. They would dare me to do stuff like this all the time – and being the little one, taking dares was a good way to ensure my place with the big boys.

Mark said, 'Go on, Scott, spit. What are you, chicken?'

David, on the other side of me, knew I would do almost anything for a dare and said, 'Go on, we dare you.'

Mark started flapping his wings making a chicken noise, and then David started too, saying, 'He won't do it, he's got no guts.'

There was no way out of this. I saw our mob down near the front, and Mum was looking up at us keeping us in check. Then she turned back around to face the front. As scared as I was, I thought to myself, if I'm going to do it, now is the time. So, I coughed up a huge golly, tipped my head back, then we all leant forward together over the rail as I spat, launching it into the crowd below. We watched it fall as if it was in slow motion.

It hit Billie and Jack's dad on the head. He put his hand in it, then tilted back to look up at us. Mark and I leant back, but David stayed there.

I pulled David back. 'What are you doing, idiot! Now he's going to know it was us.'

Although Jack was nothing to fear, Billie's nickname was Blue. Not because he had red hair – it was blond – but because he loved to blue and, him being a year older then David, we were in trouble. The theatre lights dimmed as the movie projector light hit the red curtains, which were opening as the previews started playing.

Shitting ourselves, we sat through the entirety of the movie hoping Billie and Jack's dad, or Billie himself, wasn't going to come up behind us and give us a flogging or – even worse – tell my mother. Mum was passionate about her floggings, so if it was one of hers, we would be dragged outside, 'cause they're not the type of floggings you get in front of people.

As the movie ended we watched the theatre slowly empty, and I could see Mum and our mob starting to make a move. I finally got the courage to look over to see if Billie, Jack and their dad had left.

'They're gone. Let's sneak down the stairs and see if they're in the lobby,' I said.

We snuck down the stairs. We couldn't see them in the lobby so we started to head to the front windows, but we couldn't see them out the front of the theatre either.

'What are you up to?' My mother had come up behind us and scared us half to death.

'Nothing,' we all answered together.

'I'll bet,' she grunted with her stiff upper lip.

*

Come Monday, we had to go to school, and I was wondering if that was when our luck would run out. At the end of the school day, I could see Mark and David walking through the gate amongst the other kids, just like any other day, so I ran to catch up. We didn't say anything to each other; I guess we were all feeling relieved that we got away with the spit dare.

The next day was the same. Then, the next day after that, I started to forget all about it.

Come Thursday after school, I could see a small group of kids forming a little red dust cloud outside the gate. I was thinking, 'It's a fight', and ran up to get a closer look. By the time I got there more kids had joined the circle to see what was going on, so I had to push my way to the front.

Then, my heart dropped. It was David and Billie.

Kids were yelling, 'Fight! Fight! Fight!'

David got a punch in the face.

'Smash him, David,' Mark yelled out.

With his fists up, David looked at me – I was so scared he was going to say it was me. Then he looked back at Billie and punched him in the face. There were a few wild punches and it went to dirt. Billie ended up on top, punching David in the face, over and over again.

Mark yelled, 'Get up, David.'

After a few minutes that felt like hours, Billie stopped, stood up and spat on David and said, 'Cop that, ya *coon*.'

The crowd slowly dispersed, most following the victor. Mark helped David to his feet. I grabbed David's school bag, and just stared at him with tears welling up in my eyes. I wanted to say something but couldn't get a word out.

David smiled at me with his bloody nose and fat lip covered in red dirt. He ruffed up my hair as I bent under his shoulder to let him lean on me. Without a word, we walked along the dry, red, dirt path into the streaming sunlight.

When we got home, Pop was on the verandah watching us coming through the gate. Usually I would run to him and jump up for him to catch me, but this time he just smiled at me as Mark and I followed the battle-scarred David into the house.

December 21

Sharon Kingaby

That day, 21 December 1967, didn't start out as anything out of the ordinary, but then I was only seven years old; how would I recognise extraordinary anyway? No, it started out like every other day I had ever spent at Joyce Wilding OPAL (One People of Australia League) Home in South Brisbane, with me and my younger sisters, Coralie and Lillian, waking to the smell of hot Vita Brits from the nearby factory. Although my memories from OPAL Home aren't good ones, I still love that smell!

The building seemed purpose-built, but could have been a converted Queenslander, with a number of rooms for sleeping, and communal dining and bathroom areas. OPAL Home was set up for Aboriginal women and children, although I have a (possibly erroneous) recollection that there were men housed in the downstairs area. But, if so, we never had anything to do with them. What memories I do have about the home are snapshots. For instance, I can picture the bed and the room in which the three of us slept. The room contained our bed (we slept together) and at least one other, but possibly more. I'm pretty sure they were single beds, and I think there was a teenaged girl staying in one of the other beds.

I can picture the dining area, which seemed to seat about one hundred, but might have been fewer. I vividly recall that we would line up for our meals. I have no memory of what the meals were like, but I'm sure I would have if they had been unpalatable. I've learnt over the years that our memories can be deceptive and they're relative to our age and experiences at the time. I do remember missing our mother.

Non-Aboriginal families would sometimes come to the home to give one of the children the opportunity to go and stay with them. Sometimes it was just for a weekend, sometimes a bit longer if it was school-holiday time. I used to think the way it worked was a family would come in, tell the matron preferred age and gender, and someone would be sent to fetch children who fit those criteria. It probably was a lot more involved than that, but the only person who could have told me has now passed on. Those children selected would then gather outside the matron's office awaiting 'inspection'. The white family would then choose between us. We learnt to smile and shyly say hello if we wanted to go. And from what I remember, we usually wanted to go. It was a good way to get away from the home for a few days, and we knew, from our own experiences or those of other children, we'd probably be given new clothes and shoes and maybe even go on outings. I remember at least three instances of being chosen, once by a lady from Wynnum, once by a family who took me to Fraser Island (which I thought they owned), and the third time was the one that occurred on 21 December 1967.

All the families I ever stayed with, when out of OPAL Home, were Caucasian Australian, with varying opinions about how a small Aboriginal girl should behave, what she should do and how she should talk. Most of them let me know that I had no value, no worth beyond what I could 'do' for them: from washing dishes and sweeping floors to putting things inside of me that shouldn't be there. Oh, and that I should be grateful for their charity. Being grateful meant being quiet, following orders, not making a fuss.

That day, I was sent back to the bedroom to 'collect your things', although I don't recall *having* any things except a beautiful yellow floral ladies handkerchief. I kissed my sisters and – wow, things are coming back to me that I didn't know I remembered – Lillian cried. I told her to be good and that I'd be back soon. Then I left. It was to be forty-eight years before the three of us would be in the same room again, but that's another story.

My journey away from my family and culture and connections had begun. It began the same time as my journey towards assimilation. I didn't know what assimilation was then. I didn't know what it was for nearly another forty years. But when I learnt about it, I recognised its face immediately. It looked like me.

And I let it happen. I let it happen because I didn't know how not to assimilate. I was told the same things that other Aboriginal people speak of, both from back then and right up to today. Certain phrases were said with admiration: 'You don't look very Aboriginal.' 'You don't sound like an Aborigine.' Or the insidious, 'But you're not like other Aboriginal people, you're different.' I was an impressionable young girl, desperate to fit in, to be accepted and liked in a world that didn't look kindly on my people.

There are lots of ways of surviving; people have used them all since time began, including aggression, adapting, hiding and so many more. My way was by adapting. So I constantly adapted, shifted and changed the way I was, to become the way I was most accepted. In my case, that meant being compliant. It also meant I learnt how to play down my Aboriginality; I learnt not to announce it. I never denounced it, but I rarely put it out there before someone else did. When the (it seems) whole world thinks your people are 'worthless alcoholics and a throwback to the Stone Age', it's not the easiest thing for a small child to try to dispute. It was a survival mechanism that I'm learning to forgive myself for. I'm ashamed to say that I learnt so many 'jokes' aimed at my people and used them to prove to my entirely non-Aboriginal friends that I was 'not like those people', so they would see me in the positive light I was cultivating for myself.

I laughed with (white) co-workers about my heritage and how I was different. I struggled constantly to be thought as good as any of them; I was diligent and always went the extra mile. No one was ever going to say I was a lazy *boong*. I got married at seventeen so I could 'legitimately' start my own family. When my first child was born when I was eighteen, I made sure he was clean, fed and well-mannered, to the point of absurdity. And I made sure no one could ever say I didn't know how to look after my kid.

I had absolutely no deliberate interaction with other Aboriginal people until a friend, to whom I will always be grateful, basically bossed me into applying for a position as an Aboriginal Liaison Officer at a local primary school. She seemed to think I had the necessary skills to work at a primary school with the Aboriginal students and their families and, amongst other things, advocate on their behalf. I was terrified. Clearly the two elders who sat on my interview panel saw the same thing she did, because I got that job. I was welcomed into the role, the school and the Aboriginal community by the grace of those elders and that of the families with whom I worked.

And from then on, I learnt. I learnt what these – my – people have gone through since colonisation, from massacres to removals. I learnt what we're still going through, from institutionalised to casual racism. I learnt that our people are generous and big-hearted, proud and loud, and funny and loving. And I learnt that we still, *fifty years later*, face so many of the same things that little seven-year-old girl hid from.

Growing up, grow up, grown-ups

Ambelin Kwaymullina

My people are the Palyku and we are born of the red dirt, purple hills and blue skies of the Pilbara. But I grew up amongst the tuart trees and winding rivers of Whadjuk Noongar country in the south-west of Western Australia. The arrival of my branch of the family in Perth was the result of a journey undertaken by my great-grandmother that was not her choice. Like so many others, she was a member of the Stolen Generations, as was my grandmother after her.

People ask me sometimes if I experienced any racism when I was a kid. Questions like that always make me wonder where the other person is living. They seem to be speaking to me from some kind of magical Australia where it's possible for an Indigenous person to escape the effects of racism in a colonised land. But that's not the Australia I know. It would be surprising if it was, given that the entitlement of the colonisers to the soil was founded on the alleged superiority of Western Europe ways of life over those of Indigenous peoples. Unravelling a bias so fundamental to the formation of the Anglo-Australian nation and the institutions and laws that govern it is no easy task. No wonder, then, that Australia still has a way to go.

Yes, of course I experienced racism. It's like standing in the sea and having the waves crash over you; it's regular and relentless and you forget what it's like to be able to properly breathe. Or, at least, I forget until I walk into a safe space. Then I notice as air rushes into my lungs and goes to my head; I am dizzy and my horizons expand to infinity. I don't remember many safe spaces when I was a kid; certainly school wasn't one of them. But I find more safe spaces now.

I write for children and teenagers, and work at a university with a young student population. Most of my time is spent with people who are in their teens or early twenties, and some of it is with student advocates, Indigenous and non-Indigenous alike. They grow impatient with me as I launch into the explanations of privilege and power that I've crafted over the course of decades and spoken many times before. 'Yes, we know all that,' they say. 'What we're interested in is: what do we do next? What do we do *now*?' And so I am continually challenged to turn my mind towards solutions and to finding pathways into a world where all voices are heard equally and all voices are equally heard. And I think to myself, if these are the young then I don't want to grow up.

It is often when I find myself speaking in my 'grown-up voice' that I like myself the least. The grown-up voice is less hopeful than many of the voices of the young. The grown-up voice warns Indigenous youth of the unfairness of existence, of the need to navigate as best they can the barriers that will stop them realising their potential, barriers that have nothing to do with their merit and everything to do with their Indigeneity. And I know it's necessary to speak of the strategies they can use to try to protect themselves, because we don't live in a magical Australia where it's possible for Indigenous people to escape the effects of racism. But I wish we did. And I do see that Australia coming.

I want to be old in the way my ancestors were old, those brave, wise men and women who survived the colonial cataclysm. Their lives were ones of grinding injustice and yet they never lost their sense of hope or their sense of humour. It was they who carried the future and held it safe within themselves in the face of determined efforts to destroy all of what makes Indigenous people who they are. Like them, I look forward to an Australia in which everyone can breathe. Perhaps I will never see it in my lifetime.

But I think the coming generations will realise it in theirs.

Far enough away to be on my way back home

Jack Latimore

My father enlisted in the army as an engineer about a year after I was born. He would have liked to remain on the coast, surfing and knocking around with his mates, but he did what was expected of a new husband and father back in that era, and no doubt felt the pressure all the more for having hitched up with a seventeen-year-old Aboriginal girl. We moved down south into a fibro-board house in the western Sydney suburb of Holesworthy. Reportedly, it was a rough and peculiar place at the time. Dad was often away, either at barracks or out bush on exercise, leaving my barely eighteen-year-old mother to care for me and my younger brother alone. Perhaps because of this situation, my paternal grandfather, Jack, used to drive the seven or eight hours it then took to travel from the mid-north coast down to Sydney to collect me and take me back to my grandparents' home in Kendall.

In the late 1970s, Kendall was a village caught in a time warp. Before the Second World War, my grandfather Jack had come across the mountains from Wauchope to wed my grandmother, Stella Magdalene Steinmetze, who had lived in Kendall all her life and whose father had been influential in the founding of the village. My understanding is that Stell's dad – whom she always referred to as 'Father' – was a tyrant who forbade all his daughters to marry. Stell defied him, but over the next decade or so, he and others within Stell's family continued to meddle in her marriage

138

and, due to this, Jack eventually relocated his family from Kendall to Port Macquarie. Not long afterwards, my teenaged father started mucking around with my even younger teenaged mother.

I can't pinpoint precisely when I learnt I was Aboriginal, but I'm sure I've been aware of it from early on. Certainly Jack and Stell, my father and his older brothers, and the rest of Stell's extended family were aware of it. It's my guess that I picked up on their sentiments towards my mother: feelings and attitudes that were occasionally prejudiced, but generally not expressed openly if I was within earshot. There were the expected incidents of cultural difference. One story involved my mother cooking Jack a meal of pippies for the first time, and Jack – a keen fisherman – protested that she was trying to feed him bait. Eventually, after sampling the gravy, Jack admitted that pippies tasted okay. Nastier expressions of intolerance were directed at my mother from beyond Dad's immediate family, but as a young boy I was spared exposure to them.

I consider myself fortunate to have almost always known that I am Aboriginal. I've also been lucky enough to have family who have maintained connection to our country, despite the varied and numerous violent interventions since England's redcoats invaded Guruk. Many mob – increasingly, younger urban mob – haven't had the same opportunity in terms of connecting with their First Nations heritage from early on.

For a good while growing up, I simply aspired to be more 'authentically' Aboriginal, an interpretation based on a nostalgic imaginary assembled from the depiction of blackfellas in popular television, film and print. I wanted to know all about bush tucker, to spear kangaroo and fish, daub myself in coloured ochre and shake a leg. I wanted to learn all the magic of the clever fellas, break the weather with secret dances and point the bone at my enemies. My biggest wish was to speak traditional lingo. I'd memorise words from general compendiums of Aboriginal language found in local bookstores and libraries. One day I heard that an uncle was in possession of a bunch of words and phrases from our traditional Birpai nation. I pestered Mum for years to get a copy of those from him, but it never did materialise.

Well before all my gazing mystically beyond the horizon while posturing on one leg, my parents and brother returned from

Sydney to Camden Haven (I was more or less already living with Jack and Stell in Kendall by then), and soon afterwards my mother began taking my brother and me to visit her side of the family. My dad and his eldest brother were already close with Mum's side, largely due to gambling on card games alongside them during their period of living in Port. We visited regularly. There were large gatherings, often two-day- or three-day-long parties, and I was always the kid with the big ears under the table, or laid up and playing possum nearby, listening in as they yarned about all sorts of things deep into the night.

That's how I heard about the card games at the Royal Hotel, sometimes called a *bucket-of-blood*. And it's how I heard about the older euchre tournaments, once held in tents at the camp along the breakwall, in the days before King Neptune's Park. I heard about a life of picking peas and tomatoes and cucumbers, of opening oysters and gutting fish. I heard stories about domestic service and girls' homes and life on the missions at Burnt Bridge and Green Hills. I listened to daring escape stories too, and tales of jungle warfare and fist-fighting, and about famous footballers, boxers and singers. And invariably, at the end, there was always an intricate recounting of who was related to whom, from where, when and how, until it sounded as if I was woven into the bloodlines of just about every blackfella I could imagine.

I lived in two immediate worlds – and at least several fanciful others.

The time warp of Kendall was starch-white. Originally plundered for red cedar by European invaders in the 1840s, the area had been logged continuously since. By the early 1980s, any swathe of land that didn't belong to the forestry department was cleared, predominantly for dairy farming. Consequently, the village was tranquil, sedate and orderly. The farmers herded and milked their cows morning and evening; the smoko bell at the local sawmill segmented each day; and there was the regularity of the railway that cut across the foot of the village.

Port Macquarie was the opposite. Port was wild with pubs, taverns, desperate living and occasional violence.

I lived in those two worlds always proud of being Aboriginal but progressively aware of the social realities of each. As I grew older in

Kendall I was privy to some views about blackfellas that were reprehensible in their bigotry. At the time I simply ignored them, but more out of naivety than virtue. Meanwhile, over in Port there existed all the problematic issues often present in our communities. This is the ground where my other fanciful worlds bloomed.

In my first fanciful world, I was a descendant of the valley's first people. The oldest stories of the rivers, lakes and mountains were an integral part of me, and I felt I was an integral part of them. I could sit along the riverbank and feel the deep connection that comes with knowing that one of my relatives sat in precisely the same spot in the millennia before I came along. Whenever artefacts like stone axe-heads were found, or when significant sites such as shell middens were unearthed by new urban development in the area, I felt they were mine to reclaim. At school, when the other kids joked about my family eating witchetty grubs, I told them I loved the flavour, but not as much as the taste of snake and lizard and bat and any other creature that may have featured in the diet of the 'authentic' blackfella I was striving to reproduce.

I was aware of the bigotry, the constraints and the denial of basic rights that my elders experienced, but my scenario, by comparison, was idyllic, privileged. As a young fella I was never quite cluey enough to square that broader picture with my own glimpses of racism in the day to day. At school, towards the end of primary, the other kids decided that I ran fast and was good at football because I was 'abo'. It never occurred to me to be outraged or indignant. Nor when my Grade 5 teacher and the nuns, who were the school's administrators, interrogated me for half a day about where my brand-new red Walkman came from – a gift from my dad's aunt who had visited Hong Kong. Nor did I fully recognise the nuns' judgemental preconceptions when I fronted up to school covered in scabies – the result not of parental neglect, but of my crawling under derelict houses looking for antique bottles.

In January 1988, the year before I entered high school, I went to Sydney with my parents for the bicentennial anniversary of the arrival of the British First Fleet. My dad's cousin had won a ride on one of the replica boats, so we went to wave from the banks of Farm Cove before heading back to Redfern to visit Mum's aunty. Along the way we joined the black protestors returning from Hyde

Park and ended up at the Empress Hotel in Regent Street, Redfern. Later, the party relocated to a terrace house that my great-aunt shared with numerous other activists and radicals. I'd like to say I was aware of what was going on, but I was puzzled by all those blackfellas talking so passionately about politics and political disruption and what it was to be Aboriginal.

Around Easter that year, I was invited to an all-Aboriginal student camp. It was to be held further up the coast and would provide the opportunity to meet cousins from all over the mid-north coast. I was keen to go but had to plead my case to one of my dad's aunts, who was paying the fees for me to attend a private Catholic school in Port Macquarie. That was the first time I personally heard anybody use the term 'niggers'. At the time, the word itself sounded ridiculous. I'd heard all the usual pejoratives, but 'niggers' was foreign to my ear; 'niggers' was imported – it was the barb behind the evil white hand flaying the backs of slaves in films about America. But there was still enough venom behind it to sting. I was incensed, but just as immediately confused by the extent of my anger. It took a little while to realise that my great-aunt's awkward, cruel words were intended to divide me from myself – that is, to dislocate me from my own identity.

I was one of two Aboriginal boys at my high school, but I was good at football and therefore didn't hear too much about my background. Bigoted attitudes were ever-present though. I was accused by a so-called friend of thieving money from his house during his birthday party. His accusation was based on the reasoning that none of the other kids there needed to steal such a paltry amount. There was also minor mocking of my Aboriginal physical features (the heavy brow and thick lips) – the sort of rubbish that made no good sense, considering most of it came from white kids who idolised black performers like Public Enemy, Ice-T and NWA.

The most hurtful prejudices were always those asserting blood quantum: a lingering evil from the White Australia policy era, which remains with us to this day. I was assigned fractions of identity, varying between one-quarter blood and one-eighteenth blood. It was like a lunchtime schoolyard game, and was sadly also fostered by certain teachers within the classroom.

Around this time, I discovered the book *Baal Belbora* by Geoffrey Blomfield, a historical account of the dispersals and massacres of the Birpai and Dunghutti nations since European invasion of the Three Rivers region. I was intrigued by Blomfield's research into accounts of my ancestors' contact with the white occupiers. Historical records from an early commissioner at the Port Macquarie penal colony described my forebears as 'the most daring and atrocious of any I have ever known'. Obviously his evaluation wasn't intended as a compliment, but that's how I read it, proud that my people caused him grief. There were also historical accounts of the old ones engaged in guerrilla resistance, repeatedly burning down buildings and plantations, raiding resources of livestock and hardware, and selectively thinning out the invaders in defence of our nation.

The white reprisals against the Birpai and Dunghutti came in the form of numerous calculated massacres. Blomfield's work traced a lot of them, but there was one that my great-grandfather knew of that remained undocumented at the time. At Blackmans Point, a finger of land located at the juncture of what are currently named the Hastings and Maria rivers, the colonist forces perpetrated mass murder on unsuspecting men, women and children. The crime was part of the same savage dispersals that Blomfield brought to light, all aimed at driving all 'daring' survivors up into the falls country at the top of the valley to either starve to death or submit and surrender. My great-grandfather had knowledge of the atrocity through oral accounts passed down through the intervening years. As I read about this history, I placed it alongside the contemporary accounts I'd heard first-hand about the role of the missions around Kempsey, of domestic servitude and forced removal to the 'homes' at Kinchela and Cootamundra, and it dawned on me that the dispersals didn't end with those early colonial times.

I finished my high school years in the northern rivers, living with a Gunbaynggirr uncle and Minjungbal aunt at Pooningbah. I enrolled at Kingscliff High, where, for the first time during my schooling, I wasn't one of only two blackfellas in the schoolyard. I was also able to take Aboriginal Studies for the first time. Looking back at my results, it was the only subject I excelled at.

My uncle and aunt were involved with the local cultural museum and their home was filled with traditional art. My cousins and their mates along Letitia Road welcomed me, and I felt part of the community. Their connection to culture was far more tangible than I'd experienced before. But I drifted away, falling in with a crew who were skipping classes and running amok.

I moved to Bogangar to live with mates, and things deteriorated from there. One day my mother appeared in tears at the front door of our lair, terrified that the welfare department would come to place me in a home – a hangover from her own experiences and anxieties growing up Aboriginal. I scraped through high school, completing my HSC exams while camped out on Cudgen beach in front of where Casuarina is built today.

As a beneficiary of an early 1990s initiative to increase the number of Indigenous tertiary enrolments, I then blundered my way through a few years at Griffith University's Gold Coast campus. I tried to balance out the cultural wasteland of the Gold Coast with tutoring kids in an after-school program back down the coast at the Minjungbal Museum. My intentions were sound, but the effort didn't last and I finally buckled and dropped out of uni at the end of 1996. At that time, unemployment figures in the Gold Coast region resembled the high national figures during Australia's early 1990s recession, with long-term youth unemployment, in particular, sitting above 16 per cent. This scenario was combined with an absolute market saturation of very affordable amphetamines. After collecting the dole for seven months, and with my future prospects hurtling in the same direction as my weight and mental wellbeing, I was gifted a job as a sites officer with the Tweed Byron Local Aboriginal Land Council. On reflection, the role was crucial in getting me back on track and was undoubtedly devised as such by the Minjungbal Museum community.

The job at the land council principally consisted of making sure the NSW Roads and Traffic Authority's new highway bypass didn't disturb or destroy any culturally sensitive sites. Every morning our three-man team headed down the road to observe the work being done at sites outside of Brunswick Heads, Murwillumbah, Byron Bay and Ballina. Uncle Roy Gordon, chairman of the Bundjalung Elders Council, was our lead officer, and it wasn't long before he had us scooting off-site into the Big Scrub, or down to Lismore, Coraki, Tabulam and the Square at Baryulgil to check all kinds of other sites and meet various characters. We worked with numerous renowned geologists and anthropologists along the highway bypass route, but it was Uncle Roy and the covert excursions further afield that left a lasting impression on me. He was fluent in lingo too, and I bugged him to start teaching me, but we never got around to it properly. Instead, he imparted a different knowledge, teaching me to question the political expediencies of all sides, particularly any groups aligning Indigenous interests with their own.

When I went back to university to knock over my degree, one of the final tasks was to complete a sustained piece of writing. I got a letter from my great-grandmother and great-grandfather authorising me to write our mob's stories, all the yarns I'd heard with my big ears under the table, and the histories I'd gleaned from elsewhere. I set about writing. It was a frustrating enterprise. The material couldn't have been richer: the adolescent trysts of Pop and Nan Josephine at a segregated theatre in Kempsey; life on Burnt Bridge and Green Hill; Pop joining the army to fight in PNG and the lack of veteran compensation on his return; having the Aboriginal welfare board take away his daughters to Cootamundra. There were so many powerful threads, but I struggled to weave them together.

After following a girlfriend to Melbourne and setting up house in Fitzroy, I decided it would be clever to reduce the mess of work I'd written down to twenty-four neat haikus – one for each of my years – that told the story of a young fella dispossessed, living rough but with a remnant of song back to his culture. I wandered Fitzroy's backstreets, searching for Charcoal Lane, tried to imagine Gertrude Street as it would have been in the 1960s, 1970s, 1980s. I near drank myself to oblivion in the suburb's famous hotels, and immersed myself in those reveries, consumed with unwritten, little-known histories. My girlfriend went and left me. I couldn't afford the rent. It was lucky I'd never got a dog. I kept working that big, bristly manuscript down, though, reducing elaborate, serpentine yarns and intricate characters to taut lines and compressed revelations.

When it was done, I borrowed some money from a local criminal and had hundreds of small chapbooks printed, then left handfuls of them at all the significant landmarks around Fitzroy and Collingwood: the old health centre, the Builders Arms Hotel, the Fitzroy Stars gym, the corner of Moor and Smith and, curiously, in all the self-service laundromats along Brunswick Street, of which there were a preposterous number back then. It all seemed very purposeful at the time, and in the immediate years afterwards it was easy to make fun of myself for having ever considered it so meaningful, but later (almost too late) I realised there was more going on, something serious that I'd overlooked.

There's a bit in a song written by Tom Waits that goes, 'If you get far enough away, you'll be on your way back home.' I'd lost sight of the ethos of those stories in reducing them down to the dispossessed individual. In my fixation to reveal a crux, I'd isolated myself from community. This tension between two opposing embedded social imperatives is constant, and the cause of much despair. I'd inadvertently travelled a long way down one road – having set off from high school, then university, and from some point of personal ambition. But I was alone, and getting fretful and sick because of it.

I handed the last three chapbooks to Jimmy Little, Archie Roach and Ruby Hunter in the green room of the Corner Hotel in Richmond after they'd finished a gig one night. I asked Uncle Jimmy if he really knew my nan from the euchre tournaments at the old campsite along the breakwall, and told Archie and Ruby about my headful of yarns, about haikus and conceptual art, about wandering city streets. The three of them were kind-hearted and patient enough to listen and talk with me. They knew. They'd seen it many times before along the same roads.

Black bum

Celeste Liddle

Black bum: these two words mark the first time I realised I was different because my difference was pointed out to me. I was five years old, in my first year of primary school in Canberra, and this small barb was thrown at me by another girl in my class. It hurt me emotionally and so I decided to hurt her back. I pushed her, and she fell to the ground. My five-year-old brain didn't record what happened next, though my Kindergarten school report – which still exists in my mother's albums to this day – outlines a girl who showed advanced capabilities in most subjects but who needed to learn how to 'control her temper'. I think it's reasonably clear to work out who was seen as the problem in this circumstance.

Prior to that point, I had thought everyone had an Aboriginal dad and a white mum. I thought everyone went over to 'Uncle's' place to watch black men talking politics or hear a few country and western tunes being played on the guitar. I thought everyone had seen Aboriginal flags flying everywhere, had gone to protests, and had spent time visiting the Tent Embassy. I didn't realise that most people did not regularly go up to Alice Springs to visit family. In fact, even now, nearly thirty-five years later, I still get shocked when I meet people in this country who have never been to the Northern Territory.

Yet those two words, to this day, remain burnt in my memory as the first time I can recall being told I was different, and that this difference was somehow wrong. It is also the first time I can recall responding to an intended racial slur. It seems so young. I have nephews that age now. While I am yet to hear them being exposed to – and responding to – racial slurs, I have already had to have stern words with them regarding their early signs of sexist thought. It shocks me that these ideas of difference equating to 'wrongness' get ingrained in the minds of children at such a young age.

Following that first instance of playground racism, my schooling seemed to be a mixed affair. I was, and remain to this day, quite introverted. Due to my lack of social engagement, I was put back a year to give me extra time to develop. I spoke with a mumble because, like many Aboriginal kids, I had problems with my ears and therefore I spoke how I heard people. Apart from that, though, I recall many subsequent times where it seemed that if it wasn't my race being pointed out to me as a negative attribute by another kid, it was my gender. So much so that at eleven years old I started acting out against these gendered pressures, but without pushing anyone over. I cut my hair short, resisted wearing a bra (I had received one at that age from a relative) and adopted quite neutral clothing. I therefore have always conflated my struggles as an Aboriginal person with my struggles as a woman. I believe that these early instances of having it pointed out to me how both attributes were wrong led to this heightened awareness.

It's fair to say that I grew up in quite 'white' areas – initially in Canberra, then Melbourne – and that my schooling reflected this mostly. I remember one day when I was still in primary school (but a few years older), my teacher showed us a video about Aboriginal people. All the kids in my class were laughing because the men were walking around naked. Due to the reaction of my peers, I felt embarrassed and as if they were laughing at me. I went home distressed that day and asked my father what I should do. His answer was that I should ask the teacher next time to pause the video and confront my classmates with: 'What's so funny?' I didn't really feel up to doing that. It's telling, though, that as far as learning anything about Aboriginal culture in school, this is the only occasion I can really remember from all those primary school years. It's possible that we did learn more but, if so, it hasn't stuck in my memory. This leads me to believe that if additional engagement did exist, it was merely a token effort. It was never going to overcome the impact of being called a 'nigger', of hearing the joke 'what's an ABC?' (Aboriginal bum cleaner) or of being told that I could give 'the rest of *them* a bad name' in the playground on a regular basis.

Overall, those younger years just left me feeling distressed about an identity that I continually had to defend, but had a limited vocabulary to draw on in order to do so. It was also an isolating experience; I mainly felt as if I was alone and my teachers didn't understand. Yet, back then, Canberra was this thriving hub of Aboriginal political activity, and myself and my younger siblings were engaged in life constantly. Most of the Aboriginal adults we met were public servants. One of the key political moments I remember my family taking part in was the massive convergence on Canberra of land rights' activists when the new Parliament House was opened. It felt as if I was continuously engaged in a precarious balancing act: on one side was full Indigenous immersion and on the other was complete isolation.

If Canberra was a challenge, moving to the outer beachside suburbs of Melbourne was in another league entirely. For years I had heard about the multicultural and progressive nature of Melbourne, yet when we moved there, we managed to end up in possibly the least-diverse area of the city. There seemed to be only a few other kids in my school who stood out due to their heritage, and I was the only openly identifying Aboriginal kid (at least for the majority of my high school years there). Interestingly, many years later I found out that I wasn't actually the only Aboriginal kid there at the time. There were others – they just weren't 'out there'. I didn't have much choice. I was clearly brown enough to never be mistaken as being just white and, despite any grief it had caused me in my early years, I never considered not identifying. I'm thankful for that because it clearly demonstrates that I have always had strength in my identity, regardless of what society thinks about it.

But what was the source of this strength? I couldn't speak Arrernte because it wasn't passed down to me. My grandmother had been Stolen Generations. My father and some of his siblings went to a Catholic boarding school in Alice Springs as kids and any language apart from English was forbidden there. Beyond what I was immersed in through fractured family connections, my culture was more social and political than it was traditional. It was also partly an 'outcast' culture – the culture developed because you are always different and society will remind you of this. There are only two choices when confronted with this phenomenon: you either assimilate and don't make waves, or you rebel. As the type of kid who showed a strong will from a remarkably young age and questioned pretty much everything, I chose the latter on nearly every front possible.

It's interesting, but I believe that my non-Indigenous mother was the catalyst for this more than anyone else. My mother remains to this day a person who questions everything and almost always takes the 'road less travelled'. She married my father against the wishes of some members of her family, which, as a working-class woman in the 1970s, was in itself a bit of a statement. She had attended anti-war marches, had taken her parents for a drink at a known gay-friendly establishment without telling them first, and had some very strange ideas about raising children relative to the era. For one, she really didn't like her girls being given dolls as she believed they promoted the 'training of mothers', and she didn't see that as a necessary goal for us. She also wouldn't let toy guns in the house because she felt they promoted violence and war, much to my brother's dismay. From the time I was little, I was fed a steady stream of feminist thought without even realising it. As I grew older, Mum would expand that through literature: girl- and women-centred stories where females were the heroes, and non-fiction books on feminism and Indigeneity.

Mum was also the one who ended up having to go down to the school when one of her kids had experienced racism. While Dad would be the victim of racism due to his heritage, it was Mum who we'd more often see fighting it. It wasn't an easy gig for her and, at times, must have broken her heart to see her kids struggle in the system. When I was sixteen, I remember both Mum and Dad having to meet with my Year 10 coordinator after a racially based incident had occurred. It was relayed to me later that while the coordinator had shrunk away from the sheer sight of Dad, Mum had been left to mitigate the situation. I'm the eldest of four, so I can't imagine how many times Mum had to do this for each of us. I only know that with her will and strength, combined with Dad's culture and family, rebelling against the people and systems that were trying to make my life difficult was the only real option.

Another huge influence in my life has been music. Though I avoided that old country stuff my Arrernte elders were so fond of, I have long been a grunge, punk and rock aficionado. I remember the first time I saw the video clip for 'Let's Dance' by David Bowie. It was the first time I had seen Aboriginal people and issues displayed in a music video and, given it covered everything from Maralinga to indentured servitude as a way of making a statement about how this country treated its First Peoples, it really packed a punch with me. From there, it was things like 'Beds Are Burning' by Midnight Oil – a song that mirrored the very issues I had heard chanted about at those childhood protest rallies. When Yothu Yindi's 'Treaty' came along, and suddenly people were dancing to Yolngu Matha while hearing our views on politics and the way forward as a country, the statement was intense. I still go back to political music often, for that knowledge, comfort and ability to permeate the social subconsciousness. The fact that music can convey these messages to a sometimes unsuspecting audience is truly a gift. While I never had any real talent in music myself, it was what drew me to writing and the performance arts as a means of political and self-expression.

Let's return, then, to that very white high school, in that very white suburb, all those years ago. When I was in Year 9, I was quite isolated. After a difficult Year 8, I had withdrawn and spent most of my time in the library. One day a teacher approached me asking if I would participate in a 'multicultural assembly' the school was organising, so I said yes. At that assembly, I gave a speech and then chose to read out a poem by Oodgeroo Noonuccal called 'No More Boomerang' – a confronting piece about the process of colonisation and the things it had stolen from us as Aboriginal people. I don't think many in the audience knew quite how to take this poem. Indeed, I barely remember their reactions. I just remember afterwards individual people coming up and congratulating me for speaking. Not all at once, but randomly and over several days. Perhaps I had stirred something for them. Perhaps Oodgeroo's words had hit home. What I know is from that point I stopped being quite so withdrawn and started speaking out more and more. My views and opinions ended up being my saving grace in that isolating environment, and my inability to fit in became my greatest asset.

It exploded when I went to university over the other side of town. Suddenly, I had freedom in the knowledge I could sift through and acquire. I was surrounded by others with enquiring minds who encouraged me along that journey. I had a community through the Aboriginal centre on campus, where I met people who continue to inspire me to this day. I also acquired valuable new tools such as political theory, which helped me better shape my fights, or at least contextualise them within a continuum of struggle.

It was at university that I wrote my play 'Not One Nation'. This was a piece on Indigenous identity based not only on my own experiences but also stories I had been told by other Aboriginal people. I framed these within the political narratives of the time: Hansonism and Howardism – a period when Aboriginal people were again being demonised socially and culturally, and when our history was being erased for political gain. The play not only explored the erasure of language and knowledge via policies which led to the Stolen Generations, it also highlighted historical narratives and took apart the white Australian misconception that Aboriginal people all looked the same, thought the same and had the same story. It dealt with 'intersectional identities' before that became a millennial buzz-phrase, by having an Aboriginal feminist, socialist, atheist, vegetarian lesbian as one of the characters. It was this piece that helped me graduate university with a first-class honours degree, and I am forever thankful to those who helped shape it by sharing their experiences of Aboriginality with me.

If I am honest: as I push the boundaries of my thirties and head into my inevitable forties, I still feel like I am 'growing up Aboriginal'. On a daily basis, I am still fighting those exact same racist struggles that I faced as a kid with a cultural background deemed 'undesirable' by others. It's just that the fight has shifted over the years from individual battles in a playground to larger social justice battles on the streets in the struggle for liberation. I'm still learning my Arrernte culture and language and considering how this was taken from the generations that came before me,

I feel this will be a lifelong journey. I'm still carving out my path as an activist and, as the years go by, rather than mellowing and taking a step back, I feel that focus sharpen. This has particularly been the case as I see so many extended family members still struggling under imposed governmental policies and huge economic disparities. I continue to speak out as I learnt to do at fifteen, except now I have a recognised voice and reputation with which to do so.

However, until this country finally 'grows up Aboriginal' itself, and starts not only being honest about its history and the ongoing impacts of colonisation, but also making amends – for example, by negotiating treaty settlements with First Peoples – I don't feel I will be able to completely grow up Aboriginal myself. I wonder if I will ever get to be able to in this lifetime. I hope so.

Recognised

Mathew Lillyst

David Unaipon, Albert Namatjira, Evonne Goolagong Cawley, Oodgeroo Noonuccal. These are names that are legendary and inspire our people – faces that are recognised by all.

The teachers at my high school were well and truly aware of the Lillyst name. My mother worked in Catholic education and won their hearts through transformative cross-cultural presentations on Aboriginal spirituality. My brother also earnt their affections with his charisma and exceptional musical talents. When I joined the school and staff discovered my surname, they would immediately ask: 'Are you Jayden's brother?' or 'Are you Delsie's son?' Although I was only twelve, it was obvious that many more questions were on the tips of their tongues, but their manners stopped them from investigating any further.

Over time I established myself as a diligent student and developed a passion for social justice. Given that my teachers considered me a role model, I was invited to a reconciliation network day at the Treacy Centre. At the start, all of the boys from our brother Catholic schools sized each other up and made fun of the bright colours and bizarre patterns of the inner-city school uniforms. After fifteen minutes of mutual judgement, we were ushered inside for the day to begin. The main speaker was introduced: I remembered her from Aboriginal events around Melbourne. We had been introduced to each other a number of times over the years, and I was relieved to see a familiar face.

Given that the audience was predominantly non-Aboriginal, she gave a general outline of Aboriginal culture. We are a proud culture. We have a strong connection to the land, our mother. We all have different songs and dances. We are not all drunk and troublesome. We don't all stand on a rock with one leg up and a spear in our hand.

To ascertain the impact of stereotypes on the attitudes of the general Australian public, she posed a question to the audience: 'When you think of Aboriginal people, what do you think they look like?' No one answered. 'Go on, you lot, no need to be shy.' She smiled as she gazed around the room, but no hands went up in the air. Everyone's lips were firmly sealed.

I had sat through this exercise a million times and knew exactly where it was headed. It was comforting to know that today I would not be asked if my mum or dad was an 'Aborigine', or what fraction of my heritage was '*In-digger-ness*'.

'You there.' Her hand opened towards the group of boys who sat with me. 'What do you think Aboriginal people look like?' I stared at the back of the head of the person in front of me and waited for his response. His waxed blond hair had a shine to it, but it was obvious he'd bypassed the shampoo and conditioner that morning.

'No, no, you there.' I turned to the person behind me, but he nervously shook his head as if to point out she was not referring to him. 'You there, with the glasses. I mean you.' I turned back towards the front and her eyes met mine. My heart stopped. She didn't recognise me! 'Don't be shy. What do you think Aboriginal people look like?'

I looked at her.

She looked at me.

I looked at her.

She looked at me ... waiting.

Thoughts were scrambling through my mind but failing to make any sense. My brain was like a CD stacker set to shuffle and someone kept pressing the skip button every five seconds. A stuttering noise broke the silence. The air rushed back into my lungs. Thank god! Someone else was taking the heat and answering the question. Then I realised the stuttering noise was me and the air vanished as quickly as it came. One hundred and fifty pairs of eyes were still fixed on me ... waiting.

My favourite member of the *X-Men* was Jean Grey. I was obsessed with her telekinetic powers and ability to read minds. This obsession escalated to the point where I thought I was psychic too. My eyebrows would furrow as I psychically instructed the person in front of me to tell me my hair looks good today. I would stare, waiting, mentally telling them to repeat after me, 'Mat, your hair looks good today ... Come on, you can do it ... Mat, your hair is looking good today ... Say it with me ... Mat, your hair looks good today.' Although the empirical evidence was not favourable, I was convinced my abilities were real.

In this moment when one hundred and fifty pairs of eyes were focused on me, I realised – yet again – that my special gifts were non-existent. The speaker ignored my psychic messages for help.

Ah well, I thought, here goes nothing.

'Well ... ah ... I'm ... I'm ... I'm Aboriginal too ... so ... uh ...'

Her eyes widened. The awkwardness was filling up the room but only drowning the two of us. My feeble attempt at mastering the English language was just enough to hit the ball back into her court and gave me a chance to compose myself.

Moments later, a smile appeared on her face. Any signs of discomfort had vanished. The authority and control returned to her stance. 'Yeah, but what do you think they look like?'

The world stood still as a sense of calm and ease swept over me. My ancestors were with me now. Their gentle voices broke the silence and assured me everything was okay, that it wasn't my fault. I drew upon their wisdom and strength, and took a deep breath ... I hoped they were right.

'Well, Mum has dark skin and has black hair ... so I guess that's what most Aboriginal people look like.'

'Yes! That's what most people think blackfellas look like. Not many people would've even thought this fella was Aboriginal.' She rushed towards the group on the other side of the room and quickly went on to outline the activities for the day. The momentary glitch in time was over and all was well in the universe. I guess she really didn't remember me.

On the bus ride home I looked at the window. The ghostly face staring back at me seemed unfamiliar. My eyes were still the same. My nose was still the same. My lips and chin were still the same. I searched the maze of pimples and creases but got lost in the details. A few blond streaks were quietly glowing. The gloomy weather outside accentuated the reflection of light off my skin and I looked whiter than I ever had before.

David Unaipon, Albert Namatjira, Evonne Goolagong Cawley, Oodgeroo Noonuccal, Mathew Lillyst. A name that does not hold the same regard as the legends mentioned. A face that may not be recognised by others. But a name and face that are important to me.

Just a young girl

Taryn Little

When I was a young girl, my uncle told me and my older cousin about our family. He told us that family is the most important thing in your life; he told us about our history, our family and who we are as people from the Wiradjuri tribe; he told us these stories so passionately. To me, these stories were the small mustard seeds that we – the next generation of the Wiradjuri tribe – grow to be strong trees and branches that can withstand challenges and hardships. My family has faced many challenges: losing my grandmother and my great-aunty; my grandfather being diagnosed with diabetes; my cousin being born with autism; and another cousin being crushed by a motorbike and breaking her leg. Even through all of this, my family never changed: it stayed the same; it stayed beautiful, like a peaceful butterfly.

I remember being twelve and running around at our family friends' cherry farm. Chasing my cousins with old cherries, smashing them in my hand and smearing them all over their backs and then running away before they could catch me. We had so much fun at the farm – it was an endless adventure. My uncle would stare out over the open plains, watching the clouds roll over the hills, like little children racing each other. He would smile and watch the children of his family running around and dancing in the soft rays of sunshine.

I remember sitting in his lounge room, with all my family around me, and telling them all about my first year at high school, about how great my classes were, how many friends I had made and how well I had done with all my assignments. They all told me that I was a smart girl and that one day I would do great things. Then I told them about all the Indigenous programs I had done that year, about the dancing workshop, the 'talk our language' project, and the Indigenous story I wrote for an English assessment task. My uncle and grandfather were so proud of me – their smiles were the only reward I needed.

Later that evening I felt certain that our ancestors would be so proud of me, that my grandmother would have loved all my hard work and effort, that I was a strong young woman, and that I had made my family proud. When this thought wandered into my head I started to tear up; knowing that my grandma would've been so proud of me had made my heart skip a beat and I could feel it pounding in my chest, ready to jump out.

Now, at thirteen, I wish to tell more non-Indigenous people about the original custodians of this land, about our dances, our food, our culture. I am proud to be Aboriginal, and growing up in an Indigenous family is such an amazing experience. I love my family with all my heart and try to learn as much as I can about our history.

Stranger danger

Amy McQuire

It has become one of those family anecdotes: the time a stranger thought my dad had stolen me.

Dad was walking around a shopping centre in Liverpool, where I was born and lived for a few months in infancy, when a perplexed man came up to him and asked, 'Is that your baby?' The implication was that he was worried I had been kidnapped.

I don't know if that sort of lunacy would take place today, given how diverse western Sydney is now, but back then it must have been a shock to some to see a black man with a little white baby encased in his arms.

But it shouldn't have been. My mother is non-Indigenous, and in terms of genetics my South Sea Islander and Darumbal father never got much of a look-in. I came out with paper-white skin, black hair and blue eyes, which eventually turned green.

But despite what I now know about genetics, the confusion of that man in the shopping centre in many ways spilt over into my own life. A few months after I was born, my dad got a job in his hometown of Rockhampton in central Queensland, and our little family moved back home, where the majority of my family lived. My mother had grown up in a small town called Morven, about an hour's drive from Charleville, and much of her family were now spread out across the state, so I grew up predominantly around my large extended South Sea Murri family, although we visited my maternal grandparents frequently.

Despite this, I always had a complex when I was younger, and it was complicated by the fact that all of my dad's siblings were light-skinned. I was incredibly socially awkward growing up, and painfully shy. I was the type of child who would take books to parties and soccer games and hide under tables while my sister made new friends, and sometimes I think a part of this awkwardness came from a feeling of being an outsider and even a fraud: feeling black but looking white.

I remember lying under our big poinciana tree in the backyard and trying to come up with theories about why I was so pale and freckled. I can't remember many of them now, but one does stand out: that I was white and my dad was black, because I had been born here, in this country. I thought if I had been born in Vanuatu, I would have taken after my father.

Now I know that hypothesis doesn't make any sense at all, but to have imagined it as a child shows that, even at a young age, my developing brain was undergoing the colonising process, teaching me to consider the country I was living in as a white one. This is the continuation of settler colonialism at its most insidious, how it targets our children and feeds them ideas of white supremacy from an early age.

Another reason my childlike musings didn't make sense was because Dad wasn't born in Vanuatu, and neither was his mother or father. In fact, on both sides he had great-grandparents who were kidnapped from their homelands of Vanuatu and the Solomon Islands and taken to Australia, and on his mother's side, a grandmother who was a member of the Stolen Generations, and who was forced into a form of slavery on her own land near Shoalwater Bay, now a US military training base.

I didn't know of this heritage growing up, even though we had lived near the base of the mountains in the area known as 'Nerimbera' (*nerim* meaning mountains and *bera* meaning people) and our lives were interrupted by the flow of the river Toonooba, and even though we walked daily through the massacre sites where our ancestors lost their lives.

I knew nothing about this – all I knew was that we were black. In fact, I only began thinking about the concept of country when I visited Vanuatu, not here in Darumbal country.

I have been going to the island of Tanna since I was nine, when my family first made the journey after we reconnected with our cousins. I always remember my first trip, and I revisit these memories every time I go back. This is how it goes: We get to the village by riding in the back of a ute, dust flying around us as we drive up the steep mountain range, dipping into small valleys surrounded by banyan and banana trees, and passing locals walking to their gardens.

I always get this burst of excitement when we are nearing the village because after we pass a school the country smooths out and to my left I see a dusty soccer field and the familiar faces of children who have grown a few feet taller since I was last there – and maybe some of them are in school now or have morphed into teenagers. They yell out, and then we take a right turn into the *nakamal*, a large meeting place with grass huts and sitting men, and in the middle a looming banyan tree with its exposed roots. We drive straight up to it, and to the right of us is my grandfather Pop Youse's land, with a cement block built by our cousin, and our family runs out to greet us, including my grandmother Mama, who never looks different and is the strongest person in the village. This is how it happens every time we go back. Some things change but, for the most part, it stays the same.

But I'll always remember that first time we went to the village, when I was nine and my sister was six. On that day there was a big ceremony welcoming us back. My memories are a bit hazy now, but I clearly recall sitting on a mat with my family near the banyan tree, watching the dancers. And then somewhere in the midst of this ceremony, the chief got up and gave my sister and me our custom names. From that day on I was known as Tohou Lidia, and my sister is Narlin Selina. A hundred years after my Pop Youse was stolen off a volcanic beach and sent to the pastoral properties and sugarcane fields of Queensland, we had returned.

It was a few years after that ceremony, on another trip, that I began to realise the importance of country, and how land is not just a thing to be bought and sold, as Western society views it. We were at another village on Tanna, at a place that had been named after a specific event – the killing of a white missionary – and I looked around the area and kept thinking: 'This is what land rights is.'

Land holds stories, and within those it contains the people both of the past and the present. You can't just sell it to the highest bidder. In this country, land held so much more.

My Pop Youse left behind a twin on Tanna, and his portion of land is still there. It has been saved for his descendants, and the family he left behind and his twin's offspring cannot give it away because they'd be giving away a part of them, a part of their story and history.

I have always thought of this as I write stories and campaign for land rights back here in Murri country, where the scars of invasion run deep. To me, being Aboriginal, being Darumbal, means being in connection with country. This is the essence of our identity.

Growing up, I didn't know what it meant to be Darumbal. I didn't know that during the killing times, central Queensland was an incredibly violent place where blackfellas were cornered on cliffs and sent to their deaths. I didn't know that the river Toonooba, which cuts Rockhampton in half between the north and the south, was a boundary line that blackfellas couldn't cross during curfew. I didn't know that in this area there was an unofficial licence to kill, and that neighbouring tribes were also decimated, but still survived – the Jiman, the Goreng Goreng, the Birra Gubba peoples. I didn't know that this land holds within it tens of thousands of years of history, that it retains the blood memories of the past, and that in order to heal ourselves we have to heal this country.

And so, growing up, I equated my identity with the colour of my skin, and in my head assessed myself against a barometer constructed by white Australia, which was designed to breed us out. It was only on my other homeland of Tanna, that I began to realise just what my identity meant, and how important it was to hold on to the stories of our ancestors, to know exactly who we are.

It's taken a long time to realise that that stranger in the supermarket, like white Australia, knows nothing about us – and that we must hold our children close and ensure they grow up in the strength of who they are, not what they look like.

Grey

Melanie Mununggurr-Williams

Black. White. Grey.
Too dark. Not dark enough.
Chocolate. Shit skin.
Exotic. Ugly.
Indian. Fijian.
Cultured. Incestuous.
Unique. Different.
Say something in 'Aboriginal'. You can't talk 'Aboriginal'.
You're lucky you got colour. You're lucky you got a white nose.
Dumb. Smarter than ...
That's real black. Stop acting white.
Sister. Second cousin.
Abo. Half-caste.
Girl. Animal.
Black. White.
Grey.

I once had a friend who said to me, somewhat confused, 'If your mum is white and your dad is black, then why aren't you grey?' I was ten.

I laugh sometimes when I think of that remark, not because it was humorous but because, funnily enough, that's how my life felt most days. My world was often grey. Every area was a grey area, because of who I was: a grey Aboriginal.

I was second born to two very strong parents. My father: a leader, a diplomatic Yolngu man, a pillar of his community and his family, peacemaker, dancer, and a man so rich in his culture, so proud of his bloodline. He's also dark as night.

My mother: a resilient woman hailing from Ireland, and the Campbell clan in Scotland. She is the epitome of an independent, hardworking mother: unique, always willing to give her last penny, minute and tears for my happiness and success, and ever optimistic that one day she will find the other side of her family, her central-Australian Aboriginal heritage. She's also white as clay.

In my life, and life in general, there always seems to be a contrast. Always a comparison. Always a grey area. It never was, and never will be, black or white. It's a good thing I don't mind the colour grey. Well, not anymore at least.

I distinctly remember a feeling I often had. Pride. Pride in my culture, pride in my kinship, pride in my language and pride in my connection, so deep, to my land. Today I look back at when I felt the most pride, and it upsets me that such a strong and powerful feeling – one so passionately held – would often be questioned, becoming yet again, another grey area. During times of racism and torment towards my Aboriginality and what that meant, I would still feel pride. Some days, however, I was afraid to feel that way. My pride was shadowed, as if it had been shaded with grey lead, and I was ashamed of it. At that time, I caught myself wondering and questioning: how is that possible? How is a child, a teenager, able to feel pride and at the same time feel ashamed of that very pride? As I say. It's grey. Everything is always grey. There are no black or white answers. There never have been.

But there is a grey answer. The grey answer is everything and nothing, all at once. The grey answer is an Aboriginal child born of a mixed heritage being equally proud of it all. The grey answer is me as a grey Aboriginal child being taught in school that my ancestors came into existence in this country through migration from Asia. It's the subtle defamation of the creation stories that passed delicately through the lips of my grandparents to ensure they stayed alive.

The grey answer is being a thirteen-year-old who, at that tender age, knew and believed with every fibre of my being and of my spirit, that we don't own the land, that the land owns us. It's having my beliefs not only questioned but slammed as being wrong by a classmate in Grade 7. It's being told I need to learn my history, before she tells me in her teacher-like tone that our Dreamtime is merely a myth.

To be ashamed of your pride is a strangely unique, somewhat empowering sentiment. For if you can be ashamed of your pride, then surely you can be proud of your shame. Empowered by it. Being a grey Aboriginal has taught me that.

I was labelled many things growing up. Called many names. I was ridiculed for many things, and complimented for the same things I was ridiculed for, and this confused me. I often found myself having to defend my pride for my culture and my identity. I constantly needed to explain things, even though it was often my understanding that most of the things I was required to explain were nothing more than common sense. Was it really that difficult?

For example, my mother's skin is white and mine is caramel brown. I became less alarmed each time I was questioned by my friends about my skin colour and how it came to be – but the first few times came as a shock and felt, to me, like stupidity. I could not understand how difficult it was to put two and two together and come to the conclusion that, obviously, my other parent has dark skin. Apparently, it's not that simple. I was asked so many times if I was adopted, and compared to other kids who were. What do you answer as an eleven-year-old when asked if you're sure you are Aboriginal and not Indian? Or how you know your mother is your real mother when she's white and you're not? These were not unusual remarks for me to face. These were common.

White Australia questioned my identity, regularly. But they weren't the only ones. I was twelve when a young relative on my dad's side screamed in horror as I tried to pick him up. His toddler speech was developed just enough to cry in language, 'Whiteman! Whiteman! Nooooo! Whiteman!' I cried in my room for hours, for this boy was my blood. Each time I was questioned about my skin colour, or reminded of my difference, I learnt that there was something important about my skin that I needed to work on. Its *thickness*.

I grew up a half-caste, yellafella, brown-skinned chocolate on one end of the grey spectrum, and an *Abo*, coloured, tanned nigger on the other end of the grey spectrum. But of course, regardless, I'm still Aboriginal, still Scottish and still Irish.

Each taunt and slur cut deep and at times I found myself gasping for air, scared and alone in my big grey world. Would the name-calling, the judgement, the racism towards this grey Aboriginal ever end? Despite my pride in my heritage, I would find myself interrogating the world about why I was the way I was. Why wasn't I just black or just white? Why did I have to be alone in the grey? But somewhere in that grey time, though I'm still unsure of where, I found my air. And with every fresh crisp breath, the wounds that had been inflicted by people who were yet to understand my grey world, would start to heal. Each scar was a piece of armour that would strengthen me. Thicken my skin. Prepare me for battles yet to come.

Throughout my entire childhood and over the next twenty years the greyness would inevitably continue. My pride would be endlessly questioned, my culture suspiciously looked down upon, and my identity scrutinised, stereotyped, ridiculed and judged. As with everything grey, however, other entities would arise. My grey Aboriginality would similarly, contrastingly and comparably be a source of success. The grey Aboriginal that I had accepted in myself would be admired as someone who can walk in both worlds, who understands and writes both sides of the story.

In the later years of high school, I would be commended on my ability to connect with people. I would be rewarded for my citizenship. I would be friends with everyone, and enemies of no one. You see, living grey means living black *and* white. Living traditional and mainstream. Grey is not just a colour anymore. It's a face. A black face in a sea of white, and a white face in a sea of black. And a grey face always. A grey face that has come to find acceptance in a world that is greyer than it has ever been.

From the beginning the lines were blurred, the boundaries clear as mud, yet somehow amongst the gloom and the grey, a flower bloomed. It broke through hardened souls and darkened spirits, tore down barriers and continued to bloom in this world of adversity.

A strong, independent woman, wife, mother, daughter, friend. Growing up grey has given me the strength to become this, for it has been many things. It was darkness in the beauty of mainstream neon lights. Difference, like spots amongst stripes. Walking alone in a crowd and swimming against the current. Being grey meant life would be a struggle. It meant that I would forever be neither. But as I grew and understood the beauty of colours, I realised that being grey also meant I would forever be both.

Different times

Doreen Nelson

I am a Noongar woman who was born in the central wheat-belt area of Western Australia in 1947, at a town called Kellerberrin. It was a very hard life for Aboriginal people at that particular time in the past. We did not have the choices and opportunities that our young ones have today in society. When I was growing up, government policies made living conditions very difficult for us. The protection and segregation policies forced our mob to stop speaking our language and practising our culture, and separated and isolated us from the main towns. The authorities expected us to adapt to the European lifestyle and abandon our traditional way of life. The effects of these policies had a devastating impact on our lives, and many of us still suffer from the effects today. I hope by telling my story it gives the younger generation a better understanding of how different things were for us in the past, compared to how it is for them now.

Growing up on the native reserves was difficult at times. These areas were allocated by the government and were located some distance away from the local towns, and we had to walk to get supplies. In the early 1930s there were no basic essential services, like running tap water or proper toilet facilities. I grew up in a large family made up of eight brothers and two sisters. There were four other girls in our family, but they died very young. My dad and mum were Patrick and Christine Jetta, and my mum's maiden name was Yarran. I have family connections in the Whadjuk, Balladong, Yued and Nulla Kala Boodja areas of Noongar country in the south-west of Western Australia.

I remember whenever we came into town to get food or see the doctor, we would stay at the 'dinner camp'. This was an area with a bit of bush and trees just across the road from the hospital. Noongar families would stay and have a feed at this place before returning home to the mission. As a child I spent a couple of occasions in the hospital. For example, I had my tonsils removed when I was only about six years old and I didn't like it there because I was put out on the verandah. I hated being alone at night because the verandah had creaky old wooden floorboards and it frightened me when someone walked on them.

While we were in town there were special rules we had to abide by. There were separate toilets for us natives and we were not allowed to sit down and eat or drink in the shops. Our people were not allowed in the hotel to buy alcohol unless they had their citizenship certificate. Noongars had to be out of town and back on the mission reserve before six p.m., otherwise we could be locked up by the police for the night. There were lots of restrictions, but our fathers and brothers were very hard workers and there was a lot of mutual respect between them and the farmers they worked for in the area.

My earliest memories of my childhood are of living on a native reserve at the Duyring mission, which is about five miles outside of Kellerberrin. This place has great cultural significance and is still a very special place to our Noongar families. Back then there was plenty of bush tucker available to eat, and the elders would teach the young ones to track and hunt for kangaroos, rabbits and other small animals in the bush, and they would show us which bush fruits and plants could be eaten and which could not. As they passed on this important knowledge, they would also tell the Dreaming stories and how they connected to the animals and the bush foods in the area. This was a very happy time in my life and I will never forget these good times we shared with others. We were too young to understand the things that made life hard for our mob.

For a number of years there was a mission school that we kids attended, but then it closed down and the authorities notified the Aboriginal people that they could now send their children to the state school in Kellerberrin. This was a big change for us mob. All of us would catch the bus into school, and it took quite a while to pick up all the kids from the different farms. It was a long trip on the bus, or so it seemed to me, because I was only about six years old then. The day was long too because we didn't have money to buy a lot of things for our lunch and we were very hungry by the time we got home in the afternoons.

Sometimes when Dad worked away on farms we lived nearby in little bush camps. I remember one farm where we stayed there was a big tank or copper that we used to swim in to keep cool when it got too hot during the day. Living conditions were very hard in the bush. Sometimes there were no proper shelters for us to stay in. However, our parents provided for us in the best way that they could.

Aboriginal families suffered a lot trying to cope with all the changes that took place after the arrival of the white man in this country. They had to use all their knowledge of the land and environment to protect and care for their families. Their cultural values and survival skills helped them through the bad times, and I am so thankful to all these old people who worked so hard in very difficult situations so that we could have all the things that we have in our lives today.

Many Noongars had a large number of children in their family and they always had to share and make do with whatever was available to them. There were eleven surviving children in our family, so Mother used to make her own yeast to make bread. She would prepare the yeast, put it in a bottle and keep it for a while before she used it in the flour to make dampers. The dampers were cooked in the camp oven on the open fire and were very tasty. While we were out bush, much of the food was cooked in the camp oven, including stews and baked rabbits.

At mealtimes the family would sit on wheat bags that were sewed together by Mum, and we would eat the stew and rice that she cooked in big pots, and it was so lovely. After the meals were finished in the bush, the bags would be picked up, dusted and then put away for the next meal.

These bags were used for a number of different purposes: as blankets to cover us in winter when it was very cold; to sit on in the bush for protection against the insects; and as building materials to line the walls in the old camps to keep the cold air out. Our mob never wasted anything in those days; one item could be used for a number of purposes because we never had the money to be able to buy a lot of things that we needed.

In the early 1950s we moved to Doodlakine to be close to our grandmother, Hannah Yarran. Doodlakine was a small town about nine miles from Kellerberrin on the Great Eastern Highway. We lived there in camps over the road from the main town site. The camps were designed and made from materials similar to the camps at the Duyring mission reserve. Things changed a lot in the late 1950s when I started going to school. My family settled down, and we stayed around the Doodlakine area for a number of years. When I first started school, I had no idea about this new learning environment. My parents couldn't tell me about it as they never went to school themselves. My father only learnt to write his name while he was in the New Norcia mission, and Mother never went to school at all.

In the beginning I loved going to school and learning with all the other children. I loved to write and enjoyed reading. I was reasonably happy throughout my school days, although there were some sad times when we were made to feel inferior because of our differences. The white kids would often call us names like *niggers* and *boongs*. As I got into higher grades at school, the information became much harder for me to understand and I felt like a failure because I was not able to cope with the work. Little did I know at that time that I had no chance of achieving any academic success because the Western education system was then – and still is to some extent – not appropriate and does not meet the needs of many Aboriginal children.

We stayed at the Doodlakine campsite for a couple of years until we were told to move on up to the Quarry. The Kellerberrin shire council said we had to move because there were no proper toilet facilities at our site. Some other Noongar families were already living at the Quarry, so we all moved up there. When we first moved to the Quarry there was no electricity so we had no lights at night, only light from the open campfires. We would sit around the campfires at night and listen to all the yarns being told by the old people about long ago. Sometimes we would burn old car tyres to light up the area so we could listen to music and dance.

By the early 1960s I knew I could not compete with the white kids at school so I left as soon as I turned fifteen, which was then the legal age one could finish. I didn't get any certificates and I never achieved any academic results. I had no other skills, so the only jobs I could do were domestic duties. I worked for farmers' wives for only $2 a day, and they would give me some extras like eggs and milk. I also worked at the Kellerberrin hospital as a cleaner.

I first met my husband, Grant Nelson, when he came down to the Quarry to visit his relations. He was so handsome and also very popular with all the gang. Grant was very young when he left school and started working with his grandfather, William Nelson, who was known to many as 'Buffalo Bill'. While working with his grandfather, Grant would listen to him tell the Dreamtime stories about Noongar country and the traditional ways of doing things. Later in life he would tell his family about these special times he spent with his grandfather. After his grandfather passed away, Grant got a job on the Australian railways. Like many other young Aboriginal men at that time, he put his age up to sixteen years so that he could get work on the railways. Grant was a hard worker all his life and he would have a go at any type of work to get money to assist with his family.

I was very young when I started going out with Grant. He was so good-looking and I was crazy about him. I got pregnant soon after and, because I was under the legal age of sixteen, I had to stay with my mother at the Doodlakine reserve. During my pregnancy, I had regular fainting spells. I went to my doctor and he said I was anaemic and prescribed some iron supplements for me to take.

My first baby was born on 29 May 1963. I named her Denise Donna Jetta, after my brother Dennis. I had no money of my own so I couldn't afford to buy many things for her. I took her around everywhere to show her off to family members and friends. It was winter, and my mum used to tell me not to take my baby outside in the cold too much, but I didn't listen to her. I was so young and inexperienced at being a mother, so I didn't realise what could happen. At only two weeks old, our little girl got very sick with pneumonia and she passed away. Antibiotics were not available to us back then. Grant and I were devastated.

In time, we got married and we would travel around different towns for Grant's jobs. I was nine months' pregnant when we travelled to Kalgoorlie with my sister Dorothy and her husband for a family member's funeral. We stayed with family up there, and it was at this place, hundreds of miles from my home that I gave birth to our second daughter, Lesley May. She was born on 4 June 1964.

In 1965 we moved to Merredin and stayed on the reserve in one of the government houses while Grant worked as a plant manager for a company that built wheat silos. However, things didn't go very well for us over the next few years. Grant played football for one of the local teams, and after the games he would go to the pub and drink with his mates. Grant began drinking alcohol too much over the next few years and his behaviour got him into trouble a few times. With the drinking came some domestic violence issues, and I began drinking alcohol too. I couldn't manage things very well at that time and I thought by drinking alcohol it would make things easier for me, but I was wrong as this only made things more difficult. I was pregnant again and our daughter, Cynthia, was born on 7 July 1965 at the Merredin hospital. She was born premature and was a very small baby.

Over the following months our little girl didn't gain much weight and always seemed to have an upset stomach. I was not coping very well in my life without my family support. Grant kept on drinking and getting into trouble, so we decided to move back to the Quarry to live. My baby continued getting sick and went into the Kellerberrin hospital. They said she wasn't gaining the amount of weight that she should have for her age and wasn't being cared for properly. Native welfare got involved and our little girl was made a ward of the state and was taken from us. I guess this was one of the lowest points in our life, because we had lost another baby and it was very hard for me to cope with everything.

Our little girl was placed in foster care and we could only visit her at certain times. We missed her very much, and tried to see her as much as we could so that she would not forget us, but it wasn't easy. It seemed that native welfare and the foster parents didn't really want to work with us, and there were always excuses when we tried to make contact with them.

Things didn't change much over the next few months and we realised we needed to do something to change the way we were living. Grant was always a good worker, so he decided to go away up north to find work. He was successful in getting work with a road maintenance company and worked in different towns, such as Port Hedland and Dampier. Grant bought a little Hillman Hunter car and came home after a couple of months and then got a job with the shire council of Westonia. The shire provided a house for us but, as I was nine months pregnant, I didn't go out there until after I had my baby. I stayed at the Quarry with Mum until I gave birth to our youngest daughter, Michelle Anne, who was born on 19 October 1966 at the Doodlakine Quarry. There were no vehicles available on that night to take us to the nearest hospital nine miles away in Kellerberrin. There was also no telephone at the Quarry, so Mum had to walk down the road to a farmer's house and get them to ring for the ambulance. It didn't arrive in time so my baby was born in Mum's house at the Quarry. My grandmother, Hannah, delivered my baby and I wasn't scared because I knew she was an experienced midwife and had delivered many babies over the years.

After we came out of hospital I stayed with Mum for a short while then went out to Westonia with Grant. It was really nice to finally have our own place to live in. I loved doing the housework and some gardening, and we planted some of our own vegies to eat. We contacted the welfare on many occasions, writing letters requesting visits to see our little girl in Perth. She had been fostered out to a white family, and I believe they thought they would be keeping her forever because they weren't too keen to make appointments for our visits.

Grant later got some work with the shire council in Kulin so we moved out there. It was a nice little town and the local people were very friendly. I had always loved playing netball so I joined the local netball team. However, the town was very isolated from other towns and it was hard living away from Mum. It was a long way from the Quarry and I was always homesick, so we didn't stay there long and moved back to the Quarry to be with my family again.

After we moved back to the Quarry, Grant got a job as a farm labourer, and we moved into an old farmhouse not far out of town. We settled into this place well and things became stable for a while. Various family members came to live with us at different times and this is part of our cultural ways. These were very happy times for us because our little girl Cynthia was returned to us for good, and we were a happy family again. It was also at that time that Grant's sister asked us if we could get her children, Wayne and Sonia, out of the Norseman mission, so we applied to foster the children. Our request was accepted, and they both came to live with us. All the younger children went to the Doodlakine Primary School, the same school I had attended many years ago. Our youngest daughter, Michelle, was six years old when I got pregnant again and, on 30 March 1973, our son Grant Junior was born.

In the 1970s all the native reserves were closing down, and Aboriginal people were encouraged to move into the small towns in the area. Grant had decided to go back to study and he was accepted in the Aboriginal bridging course at Curtin University in Bentley, then called the Western Australian Institute of Technology (WAIT). He completed the course and then got a position with Homeswest as the inaugural chairperson of the Aboriginal Housing. In this job he got to travel all over Western Australia, working with his Aboriginal people to improve the housing situation for them. I was approached by the educators at WAIT to see if I was interested in looking after some of the children while mothers attended the bridging course. It was great living in the city – so many things to see and do and we all loved it. We lived in Perth for about three years before we moved to Alice Springs in 1983 and stayed there for ten years. In 1993 we moved to South Australia and once Grant passed away in 1996 I moved home to Western Australia.

Through all my travel, I gained a lot of knowledge, experience and understanding from the different people I met. This helps me now as I continue to work with different stakeholders in the community to improve the health and wellbeing of our Aboriginal people, supporting them to create a better life for themselves. It is important for our younger generations to know these stories and understand the attitudes and beliefs of the early settlers, and why we were not allowed to continue our traditional way of life.

Still we have survived and continue to revive our culture each day by passing on our Dreamtime stories, songs and dances to our younger generation, but still a lot of healing needs to be done. Some things in life can be forgiven, but they can never be forgotten. I know I will never forget those hard times but I remember the good times too, and I want to share these beautiful memories with my family and others. It's so important for us elders to tell our stories and encourage others to write about their experiences and how they have come to terms with the past. As Aboriginal people we may never have the material wealth of our fellow Australians, but I believe by recording our stories we leave behind a wealth of knowledge and a rich and important legacy for our future generations. Young people will then know their identity and cultural connections to this country, and be proud to work towards making a significant contribution to the destiny of their people.

When did you first realise you were Aboriginal?

Sharon Payne

When did you first realise you were Aboriginal? I remember the first time I was asked that question, just after the Stolen Generations report had popularised the notion that those of us who didn't look 'black' were stolen or the children of those who had been. Certainly there was no concept or idea that we grew up Aboriginal; our appearance apparently constituted our identity.

My initial reaction when asked the date and time of my cultural epiphany was to ask in return 'When did you realise you weren't Aboriginal? When did you find out you were "white"?' Mostly that just put people's backs up and they got really defensive, while others became ashamed as the silliness of their question dawned on them. And when I understood that (for the most part) they weren't being nasty or negative but were genuinely interested, I just said 'always' after that.

Anyway, it prompted me to reflect on my life growing up Aboriginal in an overtly racist world where people (thinking they were doing me a favour) would assure me that 'you don't look Aboriginal'; where I was privy to the realities of white privilege (soon taken away when I announced my cultural sympathies); and where when I was in trouble at school ('rebellious'), it was attributed to me being Aboriginal.

The first time I remember getting a hint there was something 'wrong' with me was in Grade 2: we were sitting at our small metal desks after little lunch and Susie Whitegirl (not her real name) stood up. She announced to me and the class: 'My father reckons your mother's just a *nigger*.' I had no idea what she meant – I thought it was a surname or something; we never used words like that at home. The snickering from classmates was another hint.

Anyway, when I got home I asked Mum, 'Mum, are you a *nigger*?' She didn't bat an eyelid and calmly asked where I'd heard that word. I told her the story and she, using a few choice profanities about Mr Whitegirl's manhood, soon relegated him (and his daughter) to the slimy depths he was spawned from. So that was that ... or so I thought. The next holidays she had me tell Nana what 'that girl at school' had said, so I faithfully and innocently repeated the story word for word, until I said the 'n' word and Nana fired up. If I hadn't already got the message, I did then.

Following that, though, Mum did take to warning me 'not to tell anyone you're an Aborigine or they could take you away' (this was the early 1960s so the threat was still real, at least in her mind). I guess I should have had a moment's insight then and there (and realised I *was* Aboriginal), but I was still trying to put the words 'Aborigine' and *nigger* together in my mind, so the opportunity passed.

As I grew older there was plenty of other evidence that I was raised with very different values and experiences. Once when walking home with my cousins, we were stopped by the police, who told me to 'piss off home or we'll tell your parents you're hanging around with *boongs*'. I dared them to and got into trouble for being a smart-arse. But this was my life and, like everyone else, to me it was normal.

If I'd had to think about it, I would have said that what made me different made me special, but I was focusing on other things. Collectively we were becoming politically aware and starting to see the injustices that many of our mob suffered: from having to sit on crates in the back alleyway at the pub to being written out of history. Then there was Vietnam and stuff, so we kept busy in our small-town version of an anti-establishment, underground, youth counterculture movement where Aboriginal rights still had some gloss left over from the Wave Hill walk-off and the 1967 referendum.

After high school I moved to the big city. Whitlam's first year as prime minister would mean big things for this little black duck. Although I hadn't actually completed my high school certificate, I applied to go to uni (at the urging of housemates who said I was 'too smart to study art'). I had the nerve to apply, thanks to them and the Aboriginal Tertiary Assistance Scheme. Even though it was mostly the same as the other new scheme, just having the word 'Aboriginal' in the title seemed to speak to me, invite me in, and I had nothing to lose – it was free.

For me, studying at uni was living the good life. I was the first one from both sides of my family to attend university, as well as the university's first Aboriginal student. Even when I had to personally report each fortnight to a public servant to confirm that yes, I had been a good girl, and yes, I had been doing my assignments and attending lectures (something not required of non-Aboriginal students), I just accepted it, even though my housemates were outraged.

So I've never really had that goosebump moment of realisation, that spark of knowingness – it's just part of who I am. I guess the real answer, then, to the question at the start of this piece is: 'I don't know.' I haven't got a clue when it dawned on me that I'm Aboriginal, but I'm so grateful that it's true.

'Abo Nose'

Zachary Penrith-Puchalski

I am Koori – my tribe is Yorta Yorta.

I didn't know I was black till I was seven years old. I didn't know that people would eventually cross the street to avoid walking on the same path as me. I didn't know that people would define me as 'not looking *that* Aboriginal', as if it were a compliment. I never foresaw that people would think they understood my story before they heard a word pass through my lips.

My mum and dad would tell me how I believed Mum was chocolate, Dad was vanilla and I was caramel. Me and my sister were half-Koori and half-Polish – black Poles, as my mum and dad lovingly referred to us.

A boy named Shawn told an *Abo* joke while we were in Italian class in primary school. I laughed along with the joke because I didn't know what that word meant and I didn't want to appear stupid. I had never heard that word before so I eventually asked my teacher what it meant and she became agitated; she scolded him and threatened him, but still I never knew what this word '*Abo*' meant.

I grew up in a very affluent area where there were white people with million-dollar houses. I grew up in the smallest house on my street. Commission houses with red bricks: everybody knew the red-brick houses meant you were a poor commission-housing kid. If our tiny house wasn't obvious enough, the faded second-hand clothes made it clear.

Me, my sister and the other commission kids formed a group and would play at the park till Mum shouted from our backyard, hundreds of meters away, 'Kyrrah, Zack, DINNER TIME!' We would ignore the first call but the second one we would *definitely* answer, otherwise Mum would walk to the park herself and we would all cop it. All the kids were scared of my mum. She is an unapologetically black woman with all that alludes to. She embarrassed us deeply. I wished she was less aggressive and more gentle in order to get more white kids to play with me. No white parent understood her defiance. Every black parent did.

My mother is Indigenous, and my father is Polish. He drove taxis, and she was an artist. I had always noticed the way that people looked at them: my mum – a visibly black woman with her dark hair, dark eyes, dark skin and even darker beliefs about the world – paired with a very white man who had blue eyes and blond hair and who was very passive. Sometimes people would ask how they 'ended up' together, as if she was a last resort and somehow trapped him. 'That's the story white people predict,' my grandmother would eventually tell me as an adult. 'They don't see us as beautiful – they're trained not to.'

When my mother told me I was black, after me repeating the *Abo* joke I heard at school, she explained that some people would just hate me because of the colour of my skin. My grandmother chimed in with, 'Well, now you know', as if it were a secret they'd resisted telling me. I knew it wasn't a secret and I realise now that they must have wondered how long they could hold off addressing it. They'd predicted that a nice white area would mean a ten-year delay. I'm sorry that Shawn took that away from them.

I didn't believe my mother when she told me that people would dislike me because of the colour of my skin. It seemed so outrageous to my seven-year-old brain. I got angry and stormed out of the room, but she was right. I don't remember the joke but I remembered the word '*Abo*'.

By sixteen I would wear sunscreen religiously and avoid going into direct sunlight to keep my skin as pale as possible. I was only half black so was lucky to be able to be mistaken for Italian. I wouldn't walk around barefoot. I would never wear trackpants outside of the house and I would pretend to be lost if I ever had to set foot inside

Centrelink ('but while I'm here you may as well give me the forms to fill out'). During the course of high school I had heard every *Abo* joke ever to exist; I had also been told I was a faggot because it was spray-painted on school property somewhere. That's about when I realised I was queer. Thanks, random graffiti wall!

Other than me and my sister, there were two or three other Indigenous kids at my high school. One of the other Indigenous boys would actively encourage *Abo* jokes, and would tell some himself. I couldn't imagine doing something like that, and it made me feel he was beneath me, till I realised he was just trying to fit in. He was applying sunscreen with his words, reducing the cost of being black by engaging in the jokes. He was doing the same as I was but with different tools.

It's rough to be Aboriginal and proud and stick up for yourself when it means having no friends at all. All white people in my school would laugh at every *Abo* joke they ever heard while simultaneously being nice to me. I engaged with racist jokes about other cultures in the hopes it would prevent them talking about mine.

By the age of seventeen I had made a solid group of friends, yet I never stopped having to deal with racism about my Aboriginality – and then I'd have to decide how to react. Consider the occasion when I met my best friend's new boyfriend for the first time. We were all looking at photos of a girl we went to high school with, and her boyfriend said, 'She has an *Abo* nose.' I could feel the tension. He realised he'd said something terrible – and I realised he was attacking my identity. One of us had to react eventually, right?

I could tell my best friend wasn't so much pissed off at what her boyfriend had said as concerned about how I would react. 'You don't have an *Abo* nose,' the boyfriend quickly exclaimed, as if it were a compliment, as if it exonerated him. To be honest, there was a time where I would have taken it as a compliment. There was a time when I would encourage this compliment. I'd believed that between the sunscreen and these 'compliments', I could maybe build a fantasy life in my head.

I didn't know how to respond so I left the house and went home. I was pissed off. How could my best friend do *nothing* to prevent this? How could she just sit there and not get mad on my behalf too? Who the fuck was this person I called my best friend?

When I got home and explained to my parents what had happened, they seemed well versed in this exact experience. My dad rolled his eyes and patted me on the back while explaining to me that my friend and her boyfriend weren't trying to hurt me. 'It's common for white people to think that way. They think the goal is to look less Indigenous and appear white.' It was not a good enough answer for my angry ears, but his logic was flawless; it can also be applied to my being gay: people had often told me, 'You're not one of *those* gays, though', as if that were a compliment too.

Later I got a text from my best friend, who turned out to be angry at me for creating a 'scene'. She told me I was a drama queen and was overreacting. And that wasn't the first time or the last time I heard such comments when it comes to experiences like that one. Suddenly becoming that other Indigenous guy in high school seemed reasonable, the one who made *Abo* jokes along with white people; it seemed easier. I understood it more and more with every comment about my blackness that I wasn't permitted to speak about or react to.

I forgave my friend for not reacting or defending me, and I apologised for overreacting. We aren't friends today, but back then I was very desperate to keep the friends I had, so I often apologised even though I didn't know what I was sorry for. Was I sorry for being black? Maybe. I sure acted like it was worth being ashamed of. I was most sorry for myself that this was what I had to endure just to keep friends. Friends that I realised weren't worth it in the end. My identity was assembling.

I don't speak to anybody I used to know from high school now. Evading situations is still deemed as a scene to people. There will never be a correct way to react in their eyes unless it's me saying, 'I'm sorry.' I'm tired of being sorry that I exist. I know I make white people uncomfortable. I'm uncomfortable around them too.

I know that you have to think about the way you speak, and it's like treading on eggshells to be 'normal' around me, but this is not my fault. It isn't entirely your fault either. This is how we've set up racism in Australia: where you think it's okay to make race-based jokes, and I get called a drama queen if I dare react to anything you say. I question myself every time something like that happens and wonder if my reactions are appropriate. I worry more about how you take my reaction than I do about my own feelings. I'm used to questioning myself – it's almost a sport.

There are still parts of me that are afraid of white Australians. I bought an Aboriginal flag t-shirt and I've never worn it in public yet. I intend to, but for now I'm too worried it'll attract negative attention and commentary from strangers. This is similar to the reasons why I don't leave the house on Invasion Day: I know somebody will identify me as Aboriginal and want to tell me something. I don't owe you an explanation for my existence.

Identity is a strong word when you've had to fight hard to keep one. It took years of questioning myself to get to who I am now – I can't let it go. I'm stubborn like my mother now. The qualities that my mother had that used to be embarrassing are now the qualities I admire in myself. Unapologetically black is where I want to be, but just black and questioning myself every now and then is a progression from who I used to be.

I go into the sun a lot without sunscreen now. I enjoy every shade my skin has to offer. I'm twenty-six years old, and I walk to the milkbar down the street barefoot, in trackpants. That's the furthest I've gone. For now.

Too white to be black, too black to be white ...

Carol Pettersen

What's it like growing up Aboriginal? My gawd, how well I remember.

Some of my earliest memories come from the time I spent in a native mission. All I wanted was to hug my big brother – my hero; my world. I just wanted some comfort from him. I couldn't stop the tears that rolled down my face. I was not allowed to talk to him, even though we were in the same mission. I was six years old, for goodness sake, and couldn't understand why they wouldn't let me touch him. This is when I first remember an emotional hurt, a hurt that stays with me forever. I got a belting that day from the missionary lady for trying to hug my brother.

You see, our father was white and our mother was black, and we had four shades of skin colour in our family. The mission people, following government requirements, had to segregate us into separate castes based on the colour of our skins. I was one of the lighter-coloured siblings, while my hero big brother was quite dark like our mother. Even though we walked past each other many times daily, we could not talk or hug each other. I've often asked myself: how many times a day can you break a little kid's heart?

Little did I understand back then that the government of the time had created the caste system because they thought light-coloured kids like me had to be protected from becoming 'contaminated' by 'natives' such as my dark-skinned brother. It sounds unbelievable when I talk about it today, but it did happen to us – it happened to me!

My sister and I had to sleep in a separate, small two-bed cottage and were not allowed in the other girls' main dormitory as, again, we might become 'contaminated'. We came across this information later in obtaining our files. The other girls must have been told not to encourage us into their rooms because since then, and over the ensuring years, most Noongar people, including our own families, have referred to us as being 'whitefullas', even though they know of our Noongar family background. So it really was the government that contaminated us, segregated us and alienated us.

At different points in my life I've tried ways to forget what happened at the mission. I tried booze … I tried pills … I've tried so many therapies, but nothing helps to erase the hurtful words and the internalising of being called a *worthless boong*. Nothing erases the abuse, be it physical, emotional or sexual, of being told that being black is filthy and that 'they' owned you and could do anything to you, such as the sexual abuse from the missionaries' sons and the ever-hurtful taunts from the missionaries' daughter. I used to wet my bed, and she used to call me a *filthy boong*. I'd wet my bed because someone came into my room and … well, you can imagine what happened next. These words and actions were so hurtful that, in order to protect myself emotionally, I have learnt over the years to trust no one with my feelings.

One day at the mission I spotted my mother outside the compound: the image of her that day will stay with me until I die. She was all dressed up and wearing a white wide-brimmed hat and white gloves. She was walking up and down the outside fence and, when I realised who it was, I ran screaming towards her, yelling 'Mummy, Mummy …' But before I could get to the fence, the white missionaries' daughter grabbed me and took me back inside, with me kicking and screaming for my mother. I remember standing and crying near a window, watching the missionary lady talking to my mother. With gut-wrenching sobs, I watched as my mother walked away without me.

I learnt later that 'they' wouldn't let her in and all she wanted was to see her three children: me, and my older sister and brother.

How she must have missed us! I've often wondered how many tears she cried that day. You know, over the years, I had a love–hate relationship with my mother and I could never fully embrace – nor endear myself – to her, although I loved her dearly and still do, even though she has been gone more than forty years.

Later in life, when I sought out counselling, a practitioner identified that I had a long history of suppressed anger and, in assisting me to work through my issues, we discovered that all these years I've held great anger towards my mother for leaving me that day. I was finally able to resolve my negativity towards her and understand that it was not her fault that she could not hug me or take me home. I have now forgiven her and hope she knows that.

Later Mum and Dad were able to get us out of that mission and take us home ... such a joyous occasion, due to the power of a white man. Our father, being white, was able to influence social changes for his family as he had a work contract with the government. When he applied to get married to my mother, he had to sign a 'contract' to ensure that his wife and family would live as 'whites', otherwise their marriage would be revoked and his children taken away again. When he was discharged from government service, he was able to join his family who were safely hidden in the bush and get us out of the mission and then into a small school. We felt so safe with our dad around to protect us.

However, sadly, it was in these following years that we kids got more exposed to the ever-hurtful taunting from the white kids. We were the only Noongar kids in a small county school. '*Nigger, nigger, pull the trigger,*' they would taunt as they pointed make-believe guns at us. '*Pooooo, boongs smell,*' again the taunts, as they held their noses. My brother would lash out, but I protected myself by going off and curling up in a sheltered spot with a book. It really was confusing 'growing up Aboriginal', as black people treated us as white, while white people treated us as black. So confusing, and all I wanted was just to be a kid! This is where I learnt an attitude and behaviour of resilience in order to cope, which is cemented in my heart and my spirit.

As I was a light-coloured kid, I became a kind of passport for my mother. When she went out in public, she would take me with her to prove that she was a respectable married woman, married to a white man, and she had her kid to prove it and her wedding ring, which she showed off proudly.

At the age of twenty, I was engaged to be married, and I'll never forget the day my fiancé and I sat in a small country-town tearoom. We waited for service as we watched other customers come in, eat and leave. Getting frustrated, my fiancé called out for service and was told loudly, 'When you get your *gin* out of here, you might get served.' I was filled with nausea, shame and humiliation. I thought that my man was going to leave me stranded for creating this situation. I felt that he would not want me after hearing that.

That humiliation stayed with me. I held the image of myself as dirty and ugly, as that is what I'd heard about *gins* all those years: 'Natives are good-for-nothing, dirty, worthless, and the ugly *gins* are like animals.' Before the tearoom incident I felt good about myself. I was engaged to a white man, I had a job, I had money and I was dressed to kill, or so I thought.

You know, I rarely looked purposefully in a mirror and I have only a couple of photos of myself from those days. At our wedding I did not organise a photographer, but other people took a couple of photos. Some forty years later, I came across my wedding photos and was shocked to see a very pretty, almost-white girl staring unsmiling back at me. I was told that I was a *gin* and yet here I was looking at a beautiful bride on her wedding day. How could they say I was dirty? Why am I not smiling? It was my wedding day! Don't brides smile on their wedding day?

Over the years, I strived to overcome the negative images that I imagined both the white and black public held of me. There were times when I did not know where to situate myself. I had trouble trying to identify myself for the public's perception. I was caught up in a world of 'too white to be black and too black to be white', and given that my maiden name was Gray, well, I was happy to concentrate on being just that shade: a Gray with firm principles and values! That suited my personal identity fine. I could get on with life and strive to fulfil it.

I took up tertiary studies and learnt of the unfair treatment by successive government towards the original people of this county. I was drawn to activists such as Michael Mansell in Tasmania, to give my anger some justification. I soon became known as a local activist myself. I have been defined by the government and the public as a *native*, then a *native-in-law*, a *boong* and a *coon*, *Aboriginal*, then *Aboriginal activist*, *Indigenous*, oh, and then a *trouble-maker*. I have adjusted and adapted to whatever label they threw at us.

My mother had instilled in me our tribal identity and told me to 'never forget who you are and never forget where you come from'. I guess she was afraid that we would lose our tribal place in an attempt to appease the public's prejudices, or maybe she was afraid that I would 'rise' above who I really was. Maybe she was afraid that I would lose my tribal shroud. But I never will, Mother! She taught us to claim – and identify with – our tribal clan names. She taught us our totemic systems and to understand our roles in our society. Mother fought hard to ensure we never forgot our Noongar background, while Dad fought equally hard to give us an understanding of the responsibilities of being a law-abiding citizen.

Today, white people value my 'Aboriginality', but now I find that it is certain blackfullas who are the perpetrators of racism against me. These are blackfullas who dump the negative on their own people. Blackfullas who call me a 'coconut' and try to bring me down, but I long ago learnt strategies for resilience. I'm now being subjected to what I call 'lateral violence' from some Noongar people, so I find I am still a victim of prejudice because of my skin colour: a skin colour given to me by my loving parent.

What's it like growing up Aboriginal? It's very confusing and often involves a sense of powerlessness and wishing all the time that things could be different. Why do people have to find labels to tag you? This is what instigates stereotyping or the creation of minority grouping. My story is just a part of whole story that takes in the Stolen Generations, reconciliation, shared history and heritage, and is deeply rooted in the consciousness of Noongar people like me. The memories of these events are deeply entrenched and etched permanently and so will remain vividly alive. For my family this history is very much alive: our memories of 'growing up neither black nor white, but Gray' are valued and cherished.

Living between two knowledge systems

Todd Phillips

I grew up an Aboriginal Australian from the north coast of northern New South Wales – we refer to ourselves as Kooris. My great-grandmother Kathleen Kelly, a Gumbaynggirrr woman, was born and raised on a tiny Aboriginal mission outside of Nambucca Heads called Bowraville, locally known as 'Bowra', deriving from the Gumbaynggirrr place name Bawrrung. My grandparents Iris Kelly and Earl Skinner were born and grew up in the regions adjacent to the Clarence River in Bundjalung and Gumbaynggirrr country. Like my family before me, I grew up on the far north coast of New South Wales, and call the regions of the north and south of the Clarence River – the Bundjalung and Gumbaynggirr nations – home. It is the place where my ancestors walked before me, where my relatives reside today, and where I visit frequently to walk on country to reaffirm my identity and learn to be a Bundjalung and Gumbaynggiirr man, a Koori, an Aboriginal.

As a Koori living on the north coast with a big mob, I was privileged to be taught both Koori and Western knowledge: by the banks of the Clarence River for the former, and in public schools, TAFE and university for the latter. Bundjalung *Yanha* and Gumbaynggirr *miindalaygam* are exceptionally unique and highly complex. *Yanha* is the Bundjalung word for traditional ways of learning and *miindalaygam* is the Gumbaynggirr word for traditional learning or education processes. They are deeply embedded within the Bundjalung

191

and Gumbaynggirr lands either side of the Clarence River and hold significant epistemologies from these nation groups. They are firmly rooted in understanding how my ancestors lived and their ways of knowing, being and doing. They continue to influence and pave the way for future generations of Kooris to live by today because these stories of the past remain closely linked and relevant to the lives of Kooris currently and are vital for our lives, success and respect of country.

Bundjalung and Gumbaynggirr knowledges derive from within the context of the region and focus on what my people know to be true about the land. They are generated from deeply rooted experience produced through spirituality and ceremonial training that is passed down through the generations. As a young Koori boy, when I was taken to the river to fish by the older men in my community, I was always told by them that our ancestors once fished in the same place. It was here that I was given my totem – the *Jalbaranay*, also known as the spotted goanna – and was told of my responsibility to care for this monitor lizard. The spotted goanna is a sacred symbol of my tribe and believed to represent descendants of my ancestors in totemic form. It has relevance to the local area, and I have a cultural obligation to care for the goanna to ensure its longevity.

The knowledges that the older men hold about fishing and the water systems are passed down. When I learnt Koori meanings of words, I was told that these were the same words that my ancestors used to describe the environment that I would see around me, and it was this language that was used by our ancestors to communicate with other members of our tribe and was used widely throughout the region and still is today. When I sat by the riverbanks of Clarence River and listened to the stories of the past and to various teachings, and participated in smoking ceremonies, I learnt that our ancestors sat in the exact same places listening to the same stories and participating in the same ceremonies and teachings. The banks of the river, our learning place, are linked to a strong connectivity to country and are valued because they provide connection to the world for many Bundjalung and Gumbaynggirr people. These regions are enormously significant for sharing, supplying and embedding knowledges from one Koori person to another.

For my family, my extended family and for many Koori people who reside in the regions that surround the Clarence River, it serves as much more than a place of recreation, a fishing spot or a place to have a scenic picnic. This historic area along the Clarence River holds great significance. It is a border where several nations meet, including Bundjalung, Gumbaynggirr and Yaegl. Numerous Koori communities are positioned along the Clarence River: Baryulgil, Ngaru Village, Malabugilmah, Muli Muli, Hillcrest and Jubullum.

Members of my family and extended family – my father, uncles, brothers, cousins and my grandfather – would take me as a young boy along the banks of the Clarence River to a place where I listened to the stories of my people from the past and learnt about the ways things were done in the time before me and learnt what was expected of me as a young man in the future. When we fished along the river I learnt about the land and the importance of respecting the land as it is a great provider for both the Bundjalung and Gumbaynggirr people, north and south of the river. I also learnt that the waters that run throughout the local region could be a destructive force. For example, when the Clarence River floods in particular places it demolishes everything in its path, so from a young age a deep respect for – and a valuing of – the lands and waters were fostered in me, as was a deep sense of connection to the land.

When I was growing up, Camp Bundjalung was a camp where young Koori boys from the region were brought together and given an opportunity to learn more about Bundjalung ways of knowing, being and doing. It was a favourite time for me during high school, as we were empowered and encouraged by our male elders and respected older men within our local community. The camp originated from local Indigenous elders identifying a need to address some of the key issues that were affecting the young men in our community, such as their underrepresentation in completing secondary schooling and accessing tertiary education, and various factors leading to high unemployment and crime, resulting in incarceration. I remember our elders and community members used the camp as a platform to address these critical factors that were inhibiting our Bundjalung young men and becoming a trend.

Up to sixty Koori boys aged between thirteen and seventeen could attend the camp at any one time. Lessons taught at the camp by community elders focused on what it means to be a Koori man and emphasised that this should mean that we are proud, positive, confident and strong. I remember a real standout effect of the camp was the sense of belief that was implanted and the positive impact this had on us by the end of the camp. Camp Bundjalung was not only about providing opportunities for sharing cultural knowledges, but also about encouraging the young Koori youth and giving them a sense of direction and the confidence to achieve success in higher education and future careers.

Bundjalung elders shared how we Bundjalung people are special and possess a unique ability to operate successfully in two worlds: the Indigenous one and the Western one. Elders also spoke to the young men about some of the things that are required to be successful in the world and told us that it starts with believing in yourself and not being afraid to tackle the new and difficult challenges that would be set before us. This was the first time I had ever heard anything like this, and I remember it got my brain going into overdrive as I started pondering the multiple possibilities of life if this were true. There was a strong emphasis placed on knowing who you were and where you came from, and many stories were told about how us Bundjalung and Gumbaynggirr boys came from a strong line of descendants who took care of the region and their families and that is something we should all be very proud of and strive for.

Our elders also told us that to be successful in life we needed to think carefully about who we surrounded ourselves with and highlighted that just because members of your family may drink too much, are in jail, use drugs and that Koori men are sometimes portrayed negatively in the media, that didn't give us the excuse to do or be the same. Finally, they told us to look around at each other, and then they told us that we needed to help each other become successful and that we had a responsibility to each other as countrymen to not leave each other behind.

It was at the camp that many stereotypes were also challenged and I was first told that it was possible to gain a great job, study in any educational course I desired, and maintain a strong sense of

Aboriginal culture and way of life. Could I really study at university and become a school teacher and still be strong in my culture? This was the first time that I was ever told – and began to believe – that I could operate successfully in both worlds, as I had grown up not seeing this first-hand. The influence that the elders had amongst the young boys at the camp was extremely powerful.

Elders would encourage participants to start aiming high in terms of education and employment. They also emphasised that we didn't need to solely focus all our energy on our athletic ability to make it in life. We already all knew that a career as a professional footballer or boxer was possible – and our local sporting stars were frequently talked about amongst my peers and praised – but we were now encouraged to start thinking outside the box, or outside the football field and boxing ring. We were told that we didn't need more professional athletes: what we now needed more than ever was more Aboriginal doctors, lawyers, teachers and other professionals, and this would inspire the next generation of Koori men to achieve great things. Our elders told us that as young Koori men we should start thinking seriously about the type of jobs and studies we wanted to pursue, and not to limit ourselves as we now had an abundance of opportunities available to us that they themselves had never had, but had fought hard for us to have. This was their gift to us.

These words from our community elders held so much more weight and reinforced a stronger belief than any of the advice we had received from our schoolteachers or guidance officers. For many of us, it was also the first time we were ever told that we were role models in our community and we were reminded that our younger brothers and cousins were watching and following us and that expectations came with this responsibility. We knew it was important to start taking the elders' advice seriously. Thinking back, I vividly remember being told by several of my high school teachers that us Koori boys should just focus on jobs as manual labourers since many of us didn't finish school. As a graduate from Queensland University of Technology in Brisbane, with a bachelor's, a master's and a PhD in education, I can't help but smile every time I think back to my teachers' limiting beliefs and comments. If only I had their postal addresses, I would send them copies of my degrees, which hang proudly on the walls of my study for reference!

Throughout my growing up on the New South Wales north coast, my learning took place in two very different settings. One learning environment was the all-too-familiar Western school-based one that took place from Monday to Friday, nine a.m. to three p.m., in the school classroom. The other learning environment was outside of the classroom: the Bundjalung and Gumbaynggirr learning that was quite different in many ways, and not confined to a set of key learning areas and a weekly timetable, nor assessed according to outcomes.

Some of the clearest distinctions that I experienced between Koori and Western learning systems were in regard to a sense of belonging, contextualisation and relatedness within the former. Further, there was often conflict between what I knew of Aboriginal culture and knowledges from being taught outside of the classroom and what was being taught in the classroom. Outside the classroom, my peers and I were experiencing the richness of a vibrant, active and living culture.

The little town on the railway track

Kerry Reed-Gilbert

After many years of travelling from town to town and living in tents, paddock shacks and rented houses, we were finally going to get a home of our own – one that was stable, one we could call home. Our house in Condo had burnt down many years ago, and since then we had been travelling from one paddock to another, one place to another.

When Mummy was looking for a house, she had to think about its location, as we needed a good spot because we had to travel to pick fruit when various fruits were in season. So we were very lucky finding this little house in Koora, because we had tomatoes and asparagus in one direction and cherries in the other. And our fruit-picking paddocks didn't stop there. We could go and do the prunes at Greenthorpe and the tomatoes at Goolagong as well. We felt very lucky because we'd have paddocks surrounding us in three directions.

The big day comes and we're moving: we've got the new house and it even has some acres to go with it. Mummy's so proud that it's ours, and so are we – and the best thing is, we don't have to travel all the time and live in strange places.

The most important thing, though, is the welfare can't get us: we'll have our own house and they can't say anything. When our house got burnt down all those years ago in Condo, Mummy and our family built a shack with a bus for us to live in, and the welfare didn't like it so much and came and told Mummy she had to get us a house or they'd take us to the homes. So we packed our bags and headed for the paddocks.

You see, us four younger kids, we were state wards: two boys and two girls; we came in twos – Paddy and Lynnie, Kevin and me. I'm the youngest and I'm twelve years old when we move to Koora. We have bigger brothers and sisters in our family, but they are all grown up and don't live with us. For us kids, moving to this little town meant that we had a place to call home.

Our house is a bit run-down, but we're happy and I'm in heaven: we have a bath tub but it's got a copper in it – that means we have to light a fire so we can have hot water. I won't mind chopping wood for this fire at all. I run into the kitchen telling Mummy I 'bags' first bath. She turns around laughing at me, saying 'yes' and that she'd even get the boys to light it for me today as a special treat.

Our Uncle Raymond (Mummy's brother) came down from Sydney to help us move; him and Paddy do all the heavy lifting. Mummy helps as much as she can – we all do. My older sister Maureen is here too helping us, but she's big and pregnant; her belly sticks out, making it hard for her to do much.

All the furniture's inside the house, and finally we're done. All we have left to do is pack away our clothes. After all the work is done, Uncle Raymond asks Mummy if Paddy can go up to the pub to have a drink with him, as he's just turned eighteen. She lets him go; it's his first time – he's never been to a pub before. We don't have alcohol at our house, and no one is allowed to bring any home.

Time passes and us kids are playing outside on the road – the dust is flying all around us as we play tag – and all of a sudden we hear noises and lots of screaming coming from up the main street. Kevin runs inside the house, yelling about all the noise. Mummy and Maureen rush out as they know straight away the men are in trouble – they didn't need to be told. Mummy tells us kids to stay put and not to follow them.

We stay and wait but they don't come back. Kevin jumps on his bike and rides to the park so he can see what's going on. When he comes back, he says, 'The pub, the whole pub, are fighting with them.' Kevin, Lynnie and me run to help, and we're halfway there when we meet them coming home. Blood's dripping from a gash on Paddy's face, and Uncle Raymond has blood on him too but he's trying to laugh it off. I think he's trying to stop people worrying too much. The men are smashed up a little bit, but they reckon the other blokes look worse than them. Mummy just wants to get them home.

They tell their story about how some blokes in the pub started making comments about blacks, saying they don't want any blacks living in their town and they don't want blacks in their pub either. Mummy's running around tearing up an old sheet to make a bandage for Paddy's hand – he doesn't know how he hurt it but it has a big cut on it. The kettle is on, and Lynnie and me are making a pot of tea while we listen.

Uncle Raymond tells us how all of them at once jumped him and Paddy. Uncle Raymond laughs and says, 'Don't worry, they got more than they bargained for. Serves 'em right.' A few more swear words come out of his mouth and then he gets even angrier as he calls them 'gutless' because, when Mummy and Maureen arrived, they even wanted to fight them. Uncle Raymond's a returned war hero so he is really furious. He reckons they wouldn't have lasted in the army for a day.

Us kids talk about it later and start laughing. Serves them right – we hope Uncle and Paddy flogged them real good. That'll teach them for messing with the blacks. I hope they got hurt real bad. Mummy tells us to be careful: we are not to go anywhere alone at all; and we aren't even allowed to play out the front in case any of them decide to come down for another round.

Paddy comes and sits with us younger ones outside under my favourite tree; we all talk about what happened and we get pretty fired up about the people in the town. We all agree we can fight with each other and that's alright, but no one else can fight with us. We hate this town already; we've only been here a little while, not even a day, just moved in and already they're causing us heartache. Tears form in my eyes as I realise this town isn't going to be our little slice of heaven after all.

But even after all that, our spirits couldn't be squashed, because it was still wonderful to have our very own house. Days go by and soon it's time for me to be enrolled in the primary school here. Lynnie and Kevin head to Young High School: they catch the bus every day; it's a long way for them to travel back and forth.

Mummy's still worried about what happened at the pub so she walks me to and from the school each day; I tell her I'll be alright but she doesn't listen. She may be able to protect me outside the school, but she can't once I'm inside. I get teased and taunted every day.

Some of the kids write my name in the dirt and write things about me there. They make sure the teacher's not around, and when I walk out of class there's a message calling me a *gin* and saying other things too. I fight with them. I have punch-ups with the boys when they say things to me. I ain't scared of no one.

After a few punch-ups, though, they leave me alone because I can beat most of them at fighting. I have a best friend named Heather, and she's white and pretty cool. I hate school but I don't tell Mummy what's happening there.

The grown-ups in the town are real mean – they hate us blacks. Even the policeman, Constable Saunders, is as bad as the rest of the town. He ran over our dogs for no reason, and they were only little ones. And people did terrible things to the rest of our animals: we had some pigs and one day while we were away somebody came and shot pellets into them, even into their teats. I wonder how can people do mean things like that?

They even shoot at Mummy one time. We have a cow called Mini Moo – she's named after Lynnie – and she had a baby, and one day Mummy went to feed them and the lady across the way shot at her. The bullet went through Mummy's hair. Mummy goes to see Constable Saunders and he says he'll talk to our neighbour. He comes back and says to Mummy that the woman thought Mummy was trespassing on her land and he does nothing more. She knew it was our land; that's just an excuse. I hate this town.

Mummy wants her charged. 'She could've killed me!' Constable Saunders still doesn't want to charge her. Angry and determined, Mummy drives the seventeen miles to the police station in Cowra and gets her charged. They go to court and the woman gets about two hundred hours of weekend detention. They should make her rot in jail for months as far as I am concerned. Mummy feels sorry for her because she's a little bit *gwarnnee* (gone in the head) and she has a new baby. I don't feel sorry for her. I hate her for trying to hurt my mother.

The people in this town persecute us. They stalk our house at night-time; we can hear them outside, laughing and talking, trying to scare us into leaving town. Mummy walks outside, sings out to them, calling them cowards and telling them they had better watch out if she catches them. She tells them she has a gun, but she doesn't really.

None of us kids are allowed to go anywhere outside after dark by ourselves. We can't even go out to the toilet at night: we gotta go in twos, and Mummy stands at the door and watches. She has a big *bundi* ready in case there's any trouble. But if it gets too late and we gotta go to the toilet, we've got a bucket inside to use if we need it. Terror is outside our door, and we can't do anything about it.

Constable Saunders is more racist than the whole town put together. He harasses us kids, even when we go to the shop or the disco that they have at the town hall. He comes along and lets the tyres down on Kevin's and my pushbikes. We start arguing with him, telling him 'he has no right to do that. What about the other kids' bikes? They're standing right beside ours. Is he gonna let them down too?' He never touches anyone else's, only ours.

After he leaves, we swear about him and call him names. We've gotta walk our bikes home now. When we get home we tell Mummy. She goes after him – she won't let anyone harass us, even if it is a policeman. He tells her he's the law and he can do whatever he wants and she can't stop him from harassing us all the time.

She's had enough of him and one day she decides to write to his boss and put in a complaint. She tells him about being shot at, about Constable Saunders not charging our neighbour – how she had to go to Cowra to have the woman charged. How he deliberately ran over our dogs, killing them. How the townspeople were shooting our animals and stalking our house at night and how he picks on us kids whenever he sees us up the street without her.

Constable Saunders is in big trouble and he doesn't like it. He comes to Mummy and asks her to withdraw the complaint and he will change his ways, but Mummy says, 'No.' She has a favourite saying – 'a leopard doesn't change its spots' – and I think that suits him down to a tee. He's never going to change.

Constable Saunders is sent elsewhere and we're happy to see the back of him and hope there's no blackfellas in the town he's going to 'cause we know they are gonna cop it real bad. Soon our life settles down, and the majority of the townspeople start to accept the blacks living in their town. The kids become our friends, but my special schoolgirl friendship with Heather will always be the guiding light of what true friendship is about, as she too took on the town when she decided that she would be my best friend.

Looking back, Koora was a hard town to live in, especially when you knew that most of the people in that town hated you not because of you as a person but because of who you represented. I often think of my mother trying to keep the welfare from our door, a roof over our heads, clothes on our back and food in our mouths. We grew up trying to stay out of white people's sight, but our Aboriginality made us the target for every man and his dog who wanted to hate us on the basis of race.

When people say to me 'you mob live in the past', I say to them, 'No, the past lives in us, because if I can stand in front of you and talk about the segregation and apartheid that I've experienced in my own country, it can't be the past because I am very much living.'

A story from my life

William Russell

I'm an old fella and have gotten used to being called 'Aboriginal'.
I accept Indigenous too; I don't argue, since the two – Aboriginal
and Indigenous – are very close synonyms. Any fine distinction
between the words is lost on most whitefellas anyway. I have seen
myself in different ways at various points in my life, given the different situations I found myself in – but always, somehow, still
Aboriginal.

And it isn't just how I might see myself, but also how individuals or the world at large insist I should be seen. I've lived in
Queensland and been a Murri; in New South Wales, the ACT and
Victoria and been a Koori; and in Western Australia and been a
Nyoongah. I've been *Abo*, *boong*, *nigger* and worse – and over time
have learnt not to take on the cruelty and pain of it. Though I've
never gotten used to: 'Hey, you're fair-skinned enough to get away
with being white', or 'How much Aborigine do you have in you?'
And, if you don't disclose your Aboriginality, you are seen as
deceiving people, and I've lost jobs, relationships and friendships
that way; and anyway, I feel and am Aboriginal.

My features are rather unmistakably blackfella. My identity is
in my spirituality, my moral values and culture – and all of those
are Aboriginal. I'm not a modern Aboriginal; I was lucky to have
traditional culture and languages taught to me in childhood by my
great-grandfather and the old people. I am not half one thing and

half another. If I define it further, it is *Ya-idt'midtung* (that's the name of my language group/nation). I reckon us mob are all different; and when we start telling each other how we should be or think or talk, or even perceive ourselves, we are getting and showing the symptoms of too much whitefella disease. They've spent generations telling us what to be and think. We've all got our own mind – and each one of us should be allowed to flower in our own unique and individual way.

So am I Australian? Now there is a more complex question: I know I'm Aboriginal and that is who I want to be anyway – but Australian, I'm not so sure about. I have served this nation (the first two years of that service was before the 1967 referendum, so I wasn't really even Australian in Australian eyes: I served for six years). I served an ideal drummed into my head; but the reality of that ideal never eventuated. It never even came close. I am ashamed of how this nation has abused my kin, my family, my country and myself; and for the way it has treated those who served with me. I am ashamed of what this nation has become internally, and on the world stage. I'm ashamed of what it is doing to my country, my land; and I'm ashamed of what it is doing to our children. And I'm ashamed of what it does to the armed services personnel, and subsequently to ex-service personnel.

I've tried to live outside of Australia for protracted periods in some sort of voluntary exile, and when I did so my Aboriginality and my beliefs were mostly respected by my host nation. But I felt disconnected from my own country. If I go to my own country, I feel pain seeing what 'Australia' is doing to it. When they dig up a world you know intimately – the stories of it, and the place it has played in the whole coming together of your identity – the loss simply cannot be described. It destroys language and the very core of your being. How can you go back there? It is gone.

I fought for this nation in the armed forces. I have fought as a leader in the Aboriginal political world; I have fought for land rights, cultural education and more; and I have spent most of my life attempting to build a bridge over the chasm of ignorance that divides 'Australian' and Aboriginal cultures. But, at my age now, I have come to realise there is nothing I can do that will put things right; all I can do is work at helping us towards an understanding with whitefellas through my writing. An understanding that may help achieve some sort of realisation for Australians. And to help them develop some sort of ownership: to the *koona* (shit) of the past; and towards some sort of respectful inclusive future. The worst thing about whitefella Australians – the world as a whole, I suspect – is this lack of respect.

Thank you, readers, for allowing my rant – I feel a little better for it. This collection and its editor seem to have opened a door in my frankness that I rarely open. I don't ever submit my work directly for publication. I'm a damaged old man who writes powerful and sometimes beautiful poetry. Not all of it Aboriginal, but all of it William Russell. And William Russell is a black, fair, ex-serviceman with PTSD, blind and with a severe hearing impediment, and a long list of other physical problems from military service. But that beautiful and powerful poetry is the flower amongst the thorns: perhaps I'm a warrior poet.

*

A Stranger in My Own Land
I felt like a bit of a nong, sitting on the side of a suburban roadway looking down on a patchwork of backyards, front yards, and the tiled roofs of houses. And, to make things even more bizarre, I was about to unwrap a corned beef and pickle sandwich and open a thermos of tea. A car pulled up behind me, and I heard the footsteps of two people walking up.

'Odd place for a picnic, sir.'

I knew who it was before I bothered to look: *djoonkars* – policemen. I thought of a dozen answers I'd *like* to give: 'I'm practising my whitefella picnicking skills' or 'Pull up a pew – the show starts in a minute.' Instead I turned to the voice and looked up.

'Interesting day, this. I came up here naively thinking I'd see bush; then, once here, I stupidly assumed that the sight of a *boong* sitting on the side of the road with sandwiches and thermos would be seen as an assimilated Australian needing to eat.'

'There's no need to be defensive, sir.'

'Spend a couple of days in my skin and tell me that you don't develop calluses.'

'Right. Well, would you like to tell us what you are doing? We've received several calls from nervous residents.' The voice was coming down to my level as it spoke – its owner was squatting.

'See those houses down there' – I pointed to the houses below us – 'they are built over a creek. There used to be a rise over there, but it looks like it's been bulldozed. Probably used to fill the creek.'

'You an insurance agent?' The other voice was thin and reedy.

I turned to see another officer, tall and thin and angular as his voice. 'Nope. I'm a writer. I used to live over near the top of that mountain over there, and we used to get our drinking and washing water from this creek.'

'A long way to walk for water. That must've been a few years ago.' The voice of the first policeman was a little deeper than average – though higher than mine. He was solid; my build thirty years ago.

'Half a century, plus.' I grimaced. 'The population of that town down there was twenty: fifteen if you excluded my family – and the locals did. There were other Aboriginal families strung out through all these hills: all on the edges of the towns. None of you fellas. The nearest *djoonkar* – police officer – was sixteen miles over that way, and fifteen miles by road over that way. The roads were all dirt, and the *djoonkar* over that way would take an hour plus if he dropped everything and came. The other cop'd take forty-five to fifty minutes. But the reality was they'd mostly come to any call in the next day or two.' I took a sip of my tea. 'I'd offer you some, but there wouldn't be enough. And the creek's buried, and the trees have all been cut down, so making a fire to boil a billy is out.' I poured the tea back into the thermos and screwed on the lid. 'I'm here to get a feel of where I grew up so I can write about it. But I can see that I'm not going to get what I want, so I'll stop scaring the locals and go.'

'That'd be a pretty good idea,' the thin reedy voice said.

'When I was about four, the population of the town had grown by a few – six or eight – and the locals wanted to get rid of the *Abos*.' I looked at the police who were both watching me. 'Dad worked down in the city and only came home for a couple of hours on Sundays. One night – about nine or ten on a Friday – all of the men in the town came up to our house. They stood there yelling out, demanding Mum come outside. Eventually Mum, realising they wouldn't go away until they saw her – and hoping that the sight of me at her side and my baby brother in her arms might coax them to be a little respectful – went out to them. "What do you want?" she said. I'd seen Mum scared before: the authorities came to take my brother and me away not long after my brother was born …'

'Why?'

'Haven't you heard of the Stolen Generations?'

'Oh. Yeah. Sorry.'

'Well, Mum and Dad won on that occasion 'cause we went bush. This time, these men were drunk and violent. And as I said earlier, there were no cops, and no way of contacting them. The only phone was at the railway station, and the station master held the authority to control that, and he was in hospital in the city and his replacement was standing with these other men and he was carrying a cosh. "We don't want niggers in this town. You and the kids and that old man who lives somewhere up this track can pack up and get out. Tonight!" These blokes were itching for this to go wrong so they could use violence. One or two might have wanted an excuse to rape Mum. Mum was beautiful. All the men thought it: even though she was coloured: a *gin*.

'All of the men were armed with something – axe handles, shotguns, iron pipes. One had a cricket bat.'

'That's not cricket!' the reedy cop interjected awkwardly. Both officers laughed.

I ignored the comment and continued. 'A couple had torches and most of the rest had lanterns – hurricane lamps – to illuminate their hate.' I paused. 'Well, they were all yelling and threatening and making demands – swearing – when suddenly, out of the dark behind me, there was a blast from a shotgun. I heard the pellets crash through the leaves in the trees over the heads of these men. All of the men shrugged down and fell silent. "Any of you *moomakung* ever killed a man?" The voice came from the moonless ink and there was my great-grandfather, Bab. He was a dark-skinned fella, so you couldn't see him in the black of the night. Mum said (in our language): "*You were slow coming here.*"

'He stepped out of the dark and into the lantern light of the men. He was, as always, naked, and he had taken some time to paint himself up in ochre and kaolin and decorate his hair with feathers. "You fellas know of me. I'm that old mad blackfella who used to be a bushranger back in them olden days. An' you'd know I killed people. Even killed a couple'a whitefellas in my time. This other barrel of this gun, he's got a live one in it, so I think I might kill me another *moomakung* whitefella and make it three. Three's a good number, what'da'ya reckon? Don't reckon the court'd mind me defending little babies."

'All this time I watched as the men in front of us pulled back a yard or two, and a couple slunk away back down the track: pretending they'd never been there. One of the men levelled his shotgun at Bab and said, "You only got one shot left. I got two." But Bab just laughed out loud and cocked the hammer of his own gun. "Yep, you got two, and I got one. But there's only one of you, ya silly bugger. And I've killed people and you haven't. You try and pull on that trigger. You gunna find your finger won't move." The fella cocked his gun and said, "I fought in the war." But Bab just laughed again and said: "Which is an effin' bluff, because if you'd killed anyone in the war, you'd'a said: I killed people during the war. Anyway, you can kill me, and this woman here, and her little kiddies, but on Sunday the kiddies' father comes home. And yer think I'm a problem? He is a bigger problem than me. Now you all go home to your missuses before some silly-pugger gets hurt." And they all, sheepishly, turned and started to leave. Bab emptied the other barrel over their heads, and they ran.

'Silly old bugger. He'd never killed anyone in his life. He was a tough old coot, and hard, and he fought like a demon; and he had been a bushranger and he'd hid a lot of bushrangers; but he'd never killed anyone in his life.'

'Wild days.'

'Sure were. Hard. Too wild maybe. Dad came home on Sunday. He went down into the town and knocked on each door. If the man came to the door, Dad thumped him in the mouth; and when their wives came running out, Dad said, "When he comes to, missus, tell him to stay away from my wife." If the woman came to the door, he simply said: "Tell your husband to stay away from my wife."'

Both policemen were laughing.

'Then he went to the local priest – who had been standing in the back of the mob that had come up to chase Mum and us kids out of town – and he said, 'You want your big red-dressed mate in Melbourne to know you incited the men in the town to get rid of us Abos? Or are you going to get the ladies in this town to look after my wife and kids when I'm away working?"'

I let the story hang a moment. Neither cop moved.

'Well, I dined on cucumber sandwiches and scones, jam and cream for morning and afternoon teas for a couple of months after that. Every lady in the district invited Mum to their morning and afternoon teas.' I looked down on the forest of houses. 'But it's all changed now.'

'Yep. Well, we'd better go or the sarge will be on our backs. Sorry to have disrupted your memories.'

'Tell the complainants that I'll be heading off in a few minutes. I'd really like to finish this sandwich and tea before I leave.'

'Sure.' Both men walked back to their vehicle. 'Lots of luck with the book. Sounds like you've got a lot to write about, anyway.'

*

Mrs Farquhar always served a sponge dressed in passionfruit and thick, fresh whipped cream. Mum dressed us up in the best clothes we had – bought especially for the morning and afternoon teas – and spent days repairing her two sun frocks so they looked presentable. Then she'd 'paint up whitefella way', as Bab would say, lipstick and rouge and powder for dark-skinned people that her sister had bought from an Indian woman in the city. She had scrimped and saved for enough money to get a pair of stockings and a suspender belt to hold them up.

My brother's hair and mine would be held in place with strong black tea. 'Now, don't make pigs of yourselves, but remember that this will do for your dinner tonight. Don't go straight for the cakes: sandwiches first. Sit still, and no fighting.'

I learnt more about etiquette in those few months than most white kids ever learn. We had to be perfect. If we had done it wrong, it would have proved everything these redneck women believed about Aboriginal people. We had to play their game better than they did. And Mum schooled us well.

So Mrs Farquhar made and displayed her superb passionfruit sponge dripping in 'mouseshit and snot', as I teased Mum. Mrs

Farquhar's daughter, Jane Stewart, always brought a custard tart and sandwiches. Mrs Turner from over the railway line always brought scones – hot and draped in a gingham tea towel – and jugs of whipped cream. The vicar's wife brought jams and sandwiches – always with their crusts removed (which pleased my brother and me, as it would all small boys who didn't believe in the myth that crusts gave you chest hair).

There were roses stuffed into china vases on the sideboard, framing a plate of fairy cakes peppered with hundreds and thousands – possibly courtesy of Mrs Chandler; a plate stacked with the obligatory lamingtons, either from Mrs Rose or Mrs Perry; and, as Mrs Farquhar's soirées were in the late afternoon, a forest of sherry glasses gathered before a long-necked squat, fat-bellied crystal decanter of cream sherry at the far end of the sideboard. There were cups and saucers and plates: all fine and prettily decorated china. Small china jam bowls, whipped cream piled like wet snow in dessert dishes, and a bowl of boiled sweets. Everything sat on crocheted doilies.

Mrs Farquhar's sponge always had pride of place in the centre of the coffee table, flanked by plates of crustless cucumber sandwiches. Sugar was in cubes. There would be cordial in a crystal jorum for my brother and me: red or green. My brother would be draped in a huge bib and sat on a large towel. Though often after a sandwich or two he'd fall asleep, and I would be forced to eat for the both of us.

It was all another world, for me. Bab and the old people sitting and making trinkets for tourists and telling me stories of my country, talking our language; the sound of the lyrebird singing; and the smell of tree-fern and mountain ash – that's where I felt at home. The wall of Mrs Farquhar's lounge room was papered with a repetitious print of improbable or exotic blue birds perched on a recurrent vine with flowers that superficially resembled roses (with a touch of passionflower and chrysanthemum tossed in for effect). And there was a painting in an elegant and elaborately carved gold frame. It was of an English pastoral scene.

Cronulla to Papunya

Marlee Silva

Everywhere in Papunya is a road.

Hot winds, camp dog packs and bare feet with the night-surveillance truck forming crop circles in the burnt sand outlining the town's boundaries. From the sky, the connecting curves and faint lines resemble a *tjupi*, or honeyant, an insect that looks like an everyday ant from above but with a swollen amber abdomen that is said to taste like a sweet treat. It is the animal that has represented the Dreaming for the area for over sixty thousand years.

On the outermost ring of the community, closest to the rest of the world, live the out-of-towners: the youth workers, the teachers, the owner of the convenience store, the floating professionals living in a government building, the occasional tradesman, a nurse or two, and volunteers from a charity who pass through for a picture and a story.

The inner circles of red dust have a higher density. A dozen or so identical Lego-block houses sit side-by-side, overflowing with brothers and sisters and mums and dads and aunts and uncs and cuzzies and mutts and fleas and nits. They hug the final ring of buildings at the centre, where you'll find the shop that sells $15 bananas, the Centrelink office and the church. And, most importantly, the town of three hundred's beating heart: Papunya School.

The school awakens at 8.15 a.m., before the forty-degree heat sets in, with a school-provided breakfast and trips to the face-washing station. There's a covered basketball court surrounded by classroom buildings, and those silver playground tables that seem to be the universal symbol of all schoolyards.

The median age for Papunya dwellers is twenty-two; one hundred of the residents are students at the school and, aside from two paid positions at the store, the only other employer in town involves a tin shed that has been converted into an art space, where the older ladies paint stories onto canvases and sell them to people far away from terracotta-coloured earth and honey ants.

It's tough country out here, arid and still. The people who call this place home are not unaware of their disadvantages, but instead choose to focus on the parts of each day that sparkle in the Territory's everlasting sun; and I'm starting to think that they've got it all right.

*

Less than a thirty-minute drive (on a good day) south of Sydney's CBD, 200,000 people live alongside a stretch of sand and sea as white and blue as most of the occupants' skin and eyes. Cronulla, the pearl of the Sutherland Shire, is the only place I've ever known as home. My ancestors came from Britain and Germany on one side and, on the other, northern New South Wales, Kamilaroi and Dunghutti country in Moree and Kempsey, far quieter towns and far blacker than the one I've grown up in.

I've always known that I'm Aboriginal. But for a long time I knew it in the same way that I knew I had a sister; that my postcode was 2228; that I was given the name Marlee Jade Silva on 15 September 1995 in a hospital room in Kogarah after fourteen hours of labour, two weeks before my father would score the last try in the NRL Winfield Cup and win a premiership with the Canterbury–Bankstown Bulldogs.

For a long time my Aboriginality was one fact amongst many.

I started my first year of secondary school at Port Hacking High in 2008, two years after the race riots that brought my hometown to the world's attention, and three weeks before the prime minister of the time, Kevin Rudd, made his national apology address to the Stolen Generations. Port Hacking High is a collection of red-brick buildings that have inhabited a corner block in the suburb of Miranda since 1959. It took the length of one song on morning radio to get from my childhood home to the school's main entrance along Kingsway, which stretches almost the entire breadth of the Sutherland Shire. There was another way in, off Wandella Road, which was the most popular exit point for truanting students, who'd brave the long driveway that weaves from the back of the Maths block to a great black iron gate.

By my second week of Year 7, I'd found the courage to forge some friendships with my classmates. When I get nostalgic with the high school friends I still have today, we can all recall vague memories of first impressions: how we bonded over a shared love of *Harry Potter* or playfully argued over whose favourite footy team was better. There's only one of these encounters, though, that I remember in intricate detail, almost word for word. One girl – blond, tall, pale skin, not unlike many of my other friends – gave me a story that will remain with me for the rest of my life.

We struck up a conversation after a Science class, when she'd called someone else's name and I'd misheard it as my own. She seemed like a very suitable friend choice although, admittedly, anyone who was willing to talk to me at this point was appealing.

Soon I found out she was the granddaughter of a priest, had two younger sisters and a labradoodle called Tango, and she was the first person I'd ever known to compete in triathlons, which also meant she was the first person my age I knew who was on a strict diet. Later in the year she'd insult my mum at my thirteenth birthday party when she refused to take anything from the cheese and cabanossi platter, because she couldn't consume something called 'trans fats'.

On the Friday of the week we first became friends, the final bell of the day rang at 3.05 p.m. and the sky opened with a summer afternoon storm. It was a torrential downpour, the kind of drenching that comes from a storm that turns the sky so grey it looks green and blasts thunder so loud it deafens the squeals of hundreds of schoolkids as they run or skip or dance through it. My new triathlete friend and I left via the truants' driveway, towards the bus bay south of the main gate, where disgruntled bus drivers would encounter parents who came looking for their children there, when unable to find a parking spot.

We took a moment at the beginning of the driveway, under the final bit of awning, before exposure to the rain, and said goodbye to the comfort of dry uniforms; then we were running and giggling towards the gate, happily welcoming fat water drops on our cheeks all the way.

As we got to the end, I went to say what would have been an awkward but sincere *See ya later! Add me on MySpace!* kind of farewell, when I was stopped by a deep voice calling out my name. I peered up to find a man waiting at the exit.

Wrinkling a smile in my direction, he wore flannelette shorts, white with navy pinstripes, a grey shirt with a dried coffee stain in the centre, stubble that a younger me might have called a 'scratchy beard' and heavy bags under his eyes – all perfectly paired with bright-blue shin-high gumboots.

The rain, which had soaked through my cotton school shirt, danced around his four-person umbrella, but I didn't dare approach it. My face burnt and shoulders hunched; I clenched my fists around my bag straps and turned my attention to the asphalt below.

It was my dad. He called out to me again, only this time he didn't say Marlee, but screamed 'Mooky!' (a nickname nobody else had used since I was five) and waved with excitement as I mistakenly made eye contact.

I hoped with all my might that my new triathlete friend hadn't realised he was addressing me as I turned to quickly say goodbye to her and moved in the vague direction of Dad. Weaving through the sea of uniforms and regulation black-leather shoes, I made it to the passenger door of our white Honda Civic without indicating any connection to him.

In hindsight, it was very kind of him to brave the rain to make sure I didn't get wet, but at the time I was convinced my father was committed to totally destroying my chances of developing a social life. After refusing to talk to him on the drive home, I cooled down and refocused my energy on crossing all of my appendages throughout the weekend, hoping that anyone who witnessed my mortified moment would have completely forgotten about it before rollcall on Monday.

However, in second period on Monday the following week, I had Science with the triathlete again. Her blond side ponytail sat at the desk ahead of me, and as our teacher left the room to photo-copy worksheets, she swung it around to ask the dreaded question.

'Who was that who picked you up on Friday? In the gumboots?'

I felt my face blush and my heart sink all over again. I remember attempting to laugh it off as I admitted the gumbooted man in question was my dad. But where I'd been so sure that she'd laugh at me or embarrass me further, she surprised me with a response I could never have imagined.

'Is he your stepdad? Or your *real* dad?'

At first I figured she was hoping to spare me from biological relation to his shamelessness, laughing through the discomfort once more, 'Um, yeah, he's my real dad.'

I can still see the way she tilted her head and squinted her eyes slightly – she looked quite like my border collie would when we'd ask him *who's a good boy?* – before she expressed the single most defining question of my life: 'Why is your dad *black*?'

So in 2008 I had someone paint colour into my world for the very first time. Sure, Mum and Dad had always been different in the degrees to which they tanned in summer, but that meant nothing until I had a twelve-year-old peer categorise them to me as opposites: 'black' versus 'white'.

Soon after, I explained to her that we are Aboriginal, to which she responded, stunning me once more, 'No way! I've never met an Aboriginal before!'

Then it felt as though I'd been found out by my whole school, and I was instantly confronted with an onslaught of questions and reactions that I was in no way prepared for.

'Do you believe in the Dreamtime?'

'Like, how much Aboriginal are you though? One quarter? A sixteenth?'

I was ashamed when I couldn't come up with the right answers, so, very quickly, I became obsessed with building myself into a spokesperson of sorts for Aboriginal Australia to my white friends and even whiter school environment. I collected every story I could from my family, read every bit of history I could find, and emerged as someone who was bitter about the injustices we had faced and continue to face, but also determined to be a leader and a positive representation of my people.

A few years later, even though my confidence in who I was strengthened, my frustration with other people's misunderstandings – and my teenage angst in general – grew. By this time, the people who existed in my school context had got all their burning questions and wonderings out of their systems, with mostly innocent motives, but the outside world wasn't done with me yet, and the strain on my emotions began to show.

One day, in response to someone (not for the first time) telling me I wasn't *really* Aboriginal because of my fair skin, I broke down. In amongst our daily ritual of family catch-ups over dinner, tears dampened my lasagne as I succumbed to the pain of that question over my identity. I'd been fighting so hard, but nothing seemed to be changing. I remember the sadness bubbling in my gut, rising as fury and erupting to climax with an exclamation of, 'I *hate* white people.' I felt Mum wince, Dad told me to watch my mouth and remember I am the product of two cultures, but I just spat back at them that I wished I wasn't.

Dad called me to the kitchen the morning after my meltdown and I found him at our bench in front of two ceramic mugs and a carton of milk.

'Come watch this.' He gestured at me to look into the mugs: they were both filled halfway with black coffee. His callused hands picked up the milk and poured an inch of it into one of the cups, turning its contents a creamy brown.

'Tell me what you're looking at.' I shrugged, but he urged me on. 'They're cups of coffee, right?'

'Well, yeah, I guess so ...'

'No. No guessing. No doubt. They're coffee. Both of them. It's what they've always been and what they'll always be. This one' – he gestured to the lighter-coloured liquid – 'is no less coffee than the other. It doesn't matter how much milk you add: they'll never *not* be coffee.'

I still carry that image with me today, as a shield. One which brushes off brows that furrow when I wear a t-shirt with my flag on it to a music festival; or eyes that pop when someone spots the tattoo on the back of my ankle and is greeted with the knowledge that the *yurrandaali*, or tree goanna, is my family totem; or even ponders out loud that if my self-proclaimed race is true, does this mean I receive government handouts for everything?

Never not coffee, never not coffee, I think over and over, but no protection is completely indestructible.

*

Back in Papunya, Caleb is probably ten, but he never confirms this with me. When his twig fingers clutch the nook of my arm, his head reaches my lower rib cage. He lives in a Chicago Bulls basketball uniform and, although his reading and writing skills are some of the best in his class, his favourite times at Papunya School are spent outside getting sweaty.

One lunchtime I take a rest from running about in the heat and slump in the shade beside the basketball court to eat my fifth muesli bar of the day. Caleb sits beside me, and for the first time ever he hesitates from begging me to rejoin the game in front of us. He notices the red, yellow and black braided bracelet on my wrist and begins running it through his fingertips. His rich umber-toned skin seems to bleach mine further as they graze one another, sending Dad's coffee analogy echoing through my mind.

I tell Caleb that I am Aboriginal too, just a different shade of Aboriginal. He just continues to fiddle with the worn threads of my homemade jewellery in silence, before turning his focus to my outstretched legs. He places both of his hands around the lone, brown mole on my right knee, making a diamond shape. He stares at it, craning his neck closer, before finally poking at it with a curious index finger.

'What's this?' his chocolate eyes meet my blue ones with a frown.

'That? That's a mole.'

'You hurt yourself?'

'No.' I laugh, and Caleb proceeds to try and pop it. 'No! It's not a pimple!'

I laugh harder and four other students come over to stare at the alien mark. 'I've had it for a long time. It's just a spot on my skin from the sun – no big deal.'

It's obvious that they've got no idea what I'm on about, but sweet giggles gurgle and overflow from their mouths anyway.

Then, within seconds, someone's said the word 'basketball' again, and Caleb's tugging at me to get up.

I was twenty-one and a half when I decided to volunteer in remote Australia. I'd spent my entire adolescence spewing passionate words of equality and justice for our nation's first people onto deaf ears; I'd worked for an Aboriginal organisation from the moment I left high school and was sure that I knew just about everything about everything. By twenty-one and a half I was confident that I'd invested enough time into knowing my own Aboriginality, that I knew other people's too.

Now I am twenty-one and three-quarters and realise: I am wrong.

I once lived in a colourblind world, but in a blink so much of me became obsessed with blackness – *my* blackness. What it is, what it means, how it dictates who I am, and how I can prove to other people that it does in fact exist, if only below the surface.

Then suddenly here I was, in Papunya, a place that's arguably one of the few communities left in our country that hasn't been irreversibly severed from our traditional ways of living, language and customs – and nobody cares what colour I am. They care only about *who* I am. Sure there is some question of why I have strange spots on my body, but there's more around whether I'm someone who can be their friend, can make jokes, tell stories or, most importantly, whether I can play basketball.

We hear so many stories about the difficulties and the heartaches from this part of the world, but this microcosm of hardship and resilience seems to have achieved the unachievable. Here exists a group of young, vibrant people who see others as, quite simply, fellow human beings. I don't know why it's taken me so long to realise, but now it's so obvious that underneath the invisible barriers and expectations we have constructed and placed on each other, we are all brothers and sisters; we are all just pink flesh and bone.

Letterbox-gate

Liza-Mare Syron

Balmain is traditionally an industrial Sydney suburb. Before Cook, Gadigal and Wangal people lived on the bush landscape now known as Peacock Point. My great-grandfather Daniel Syron moved to Balmain in the 1920s after the First World War to find work on the wharves. He is a Birripi man from Cape Hawke on the mid-north coast of New South Wales. I have no memory of ever meeting him. I have seen photos of him stuck in an old photo album held together by broken silver corners. He was a tall man, black and handsome. All the Syron men are. He was a light horseman and a returned soldier. Although Aboriginal people weren't allowed to enlist in the Australian army at that time, he must have slipped through. Daniel met his wife, Elizabeth Murray, an English migrant from Manchester, on his return from service. Elizabeth was a tough cookie having survived working down coalmines as a child. She thought Dan was your typical bronzed Aussie. Together they had eight children. Their firstborn is my grandmother, Catherine Mary Syron. Cathy's eldest son, Frederick George, is my father. He was also born in Balmain, as was I and my two younger sisters. My mother came from the now well-to-do eastern suburb of Waverly and her family heritage includes the First Fleet Irish convict Henry Kable. However, I didn't know all this about my Aboriginal history when I was growing up.

In 1979 I was sixteen and living with my parents and two sisters; we had just moved to another house in Balmain. We moved a lot. It was nothing fancy. My mother and father had decided to reconcile their five-year separation. It was the same year that Neville Bonner, the first Aboriginal parliamentarian in Australia, became Australian of the Year. There was a fire at Luna Park, and the film *Mad Max* made its Australian premiere. It was also the year that my father passed away. He was thirty-eight years old.

It was a January morning and I was fast asleep. My two younger sisters were trying to wake me up. 'Dad's dead!' they yelled, running up and down the corridor from room to room. I thought it was a prank. Mum was already there performing resuscitation, pushing her breath into his mouth. 'Come on, Freddy!' she screamed. He was lying flat and lifeless like a rag doll on the bed, his body responding only to her physical interventions. I wanted to help so I started pumping his chest with my hands. I didn't know what else to do. I looked to my sisters, then eleven and twelve, who watched in horror from the foot of the bed, as his stomach loomed large like an inflated balloon.

In a panic I tried to move his body onto one side. Coma position. There was a second of hope. We waited. Then slowly from the corner of his mouth a trickle of blood gently fell onto his pillow. This was the final mark of his body. That day 'Little Freddy', as he was affectionately known, became just another statistic: another Aboriginal man who had succumbed to the modern curse of cardiovascular heart disease. He was the one in four, a rate of death fifteen times higher for that condition than other Australians face. He was on the waiting list for a bypass operation – he missed out on it by just one month.

'Little Freddy': a handsome man, cheeky grin, wavy dark hair, side burns, green eyes, big smile and false teeth. He was a grumpy old fart, just thirty-eight years old. He liked a drink and loved to dance. Man of the hour. Smoked too much and gambled everything away. Sat down on the lounge every afternoon and drank tea – no milk. Farted a lot. Had a quick temper. No one messed with Freddy. You could always count on him in a fight. He loved women – maybe too many. He wore red and yellow polo shirts, with pants and leather shoes. He always had coins in his pocket for us to pick whenever he fell asleep. A kind man. He swore a lot, all the time – although he did try not to by clenching his teeth:

'Freekin' hell.' His favourite song was Englebert Humperdinck's 'Please Release Me'.

Everyone loved Little Freddy, so-called because his father was a monster of a man. Six foot four. Dad was five foot ten. He had his faults: he was a flirt and a womaniser. Most of the women he had affairs with were Aboriginal. He had two children to one woman during my parents' separation. The girls were at his funeral. Dad's aunties had brought them along. My mother refused to have anything to do with them. I wondered if they would be there and I looked for them. They looked like Dad. I wanted to say something to them, but I kept close to my mother, protected by a cloak of shame. I never saw them again and I didn't try to.

Funerals: a gathering of people and relatives, some of whom you have never met. They offer condolences or extend promises of assistance, but they disappear as quickly as they appear, each relative searching for their own solace. After the blur that was my father's funeral, our home became a shell. My mother empty, as my sisters and I ploughed our way through what seemed like an eternal darkness. You learn a lot about people during such events. Once we were a family: a Syron clan. Not anymore.

My mother never spoke to those relations again. Nor did she ever pay her respects at their passing. Many faded into the background of our lives. Only a few remained.

It was during my final year of high school – a time when little seemed to dispel my growing sense of futility about life – that my father's uncle came to visit me. He was my grandmother's little brother and an important man in our family. Like his father, Daniel, Brian Syron was also handsome, a male model, but he was not so tall and not so black. He was well known in his later years as a human rights advocate, a teacher, an actor, a writer, a stage director, and Australia's first Indigenous feature-film director. In the early 1980s he held acting classes in a small studio on William Street in Darlinghurst, Sydney. He boasted such students as Helen Morse, John Hargraves, Lydia Miller and Rhoda Roberts. His specialty was the 'American method', something he'd learnt from many years studying under Stella Adler at her New York City school in the 1960s. During his time in America he returned only a handful of times to Australia.

It was warm on the day Brian visited. We walked together along the top hockey field of my school, not really saying much to each other, when, without warning, he suddenly turned to me and asked, 'Do you know you are Aboriginal?' What an odd question. 'No,' I replied as I shrugged my shoulders in confusion. Once he said the 'A' word, however, many things started to make sense to me. Like why my mother screamed hysterically the day my father brought home a letterbox covered in red, black and yellow stripes emblazoned with a shield and spear, a gift from his mates at the electricity commission. It was a joke. But it was much more than that. I was only twelve at the time, as I sat with my two sisters wondering how an ordinary thing of such little significance could cause the storm of emotion that was coming from my mother, who wanted 'that thing' out of the house. It was, as I later came to understand, an object of identification painted in the colours of the Aboriginal flag, with its crest a symbol of a pre-colonial existence. It represented something my mother seemed ashamed of: my father's Aboriginal heritage. It was less than ten years after the referendum to include Aboriginal people in the census, and my mother still wanted to shelter us from our identity. Was it really that bad? My father didn't think so. He thought it was very funny.

Nothing more was ever said about that letterbox, but it did take pride of place on top of my parents' wardrobe, where it remained looking down on them both until that night my father passed away. Mum laughs now when we remind her of the whole saga, a sign perhaps that she has moved on in her thinking and is more accepting of the past.

Brian told me that day that 'they' would pay for me to stay at school. What he actually meant was that I could be supported by a small government allowance provided by the federal government to assist Aboriginal disadvantage. It was 1979, and I received three dollars a week. My mother accepted twelve dollars a fortnight for me to stay on in school. I went on to finish my Higher School Certificate the following year.

When I was twenty-four years old I packed a small bag of clothes and headed to Melbourne to study acting. I had nothing to lose, literally. I only had a small inheritance, a track to a greater world that Brian had left me, a life where anything seemed possible. But that world has rules. Brian always said to me, 'Life is a game and I had to learn how to play.' Melbourne was as far enough away from the distractions and temptations of Sydney in the 1980s. I was never going to find my way out of my misery at the bottom of a hangover or a dance floor.

Drama school was not something that life had so far prepared me for. There were exercises that opened me up physically, mentally and emotionally, plus hours of improvisation in close proximity to others. In my family, intimacy was like a disease, something that you might catch if you got too close to someone. A hug from my mother was a headlock, and kissing was always on the cheek as a sign of respect. Tough love. To be fair, Mum has a family history too. Her mother grew up in a girls' home. I don't know which home, because my grandmother rarely spoke about that time or how she ended up there. What I do know is that my grandmother was certainly affected by her lack of mothering in ways that only my mother would understand.

Over the three years of drama school I studied approaches to acting that were informed by Canadian improviser Keith Johnson, English director Peter Brook, and Polish theatre maker Jerzy Grotowski. Aboriginal theatre and history were examined only briefly. It was 1988 and a number of Aboriginal plays were in commission as part of Australia's bicentennial celebrations, plays that now form part of the Aboriginal theatre cannon, such as those written by Jack Davis, Bobby Merritt and Kevin Gilbert. Back then, however, there were very few Aboriginal plays in circulation. Aboriginal theatre and actors in the late 1980s were a new phenomenon for Australian stages. Although actor training brought me closer to my physical and emotional self, I felt no closer to a sense of self. Something was missing.

In 1993 I returned home to Sydney and attended Brian's funeral. I was hungry for much of that year, literally. I could not find work. I finally found myself an agent; he was old school and he'd known Brian. One the first auditions he sent me for was a role in a Sydney Festival show called *Shark Island Stories*. The play by Mary Morris was based on *The Flying Emu and Other Stories*, a children's book written by Aboriginal writer Sally Morgan. Shark Island is the first island you encounter as you enter Sydney Harbour and a popular local picnic spot with native trees and shrubs. The island's Aboriginal name is Boambilly (Boo-am-billy) in the language of the original inhabitants, the Gadigal people. I was cast in the role of the Magic Pouch and also played Marni, a young Aboriginal girl.

What did I know about playing an Aboriginal role? Sitting on a ferry next to two cast members on the way to the first week of rehearsals, I was asked a similar question by one. 'What do you know about your practice and history?' The other woman had piercing green eyes that stared right through me. She was about to be the first Aboriginal woman on *Play School*. Behind those beautiful eyes, however, was a sadness that she rarely spoke about. She was a child of the Stolen Generations, removed from her natural family when she was two years old and placed in a home before being fostered out to a German family. She seemed unsettled, yet she sat quietly as the other woman spoke strongly about her opinions on what it meant to be an Aboriginal performer. That woman had grown up on country, in a community with her Aboriginal family. It was an uncomfortable journey, and I felt a growing unease about the line of questioning. She went so far as to question my identity. 'Are you Aboriginal?' At the time I didn't feel it was necessary to prove my identity to her. Brian had told me I was Aboriginal and that was enough for me. Or was it?

In the early 1970s Brian had been involved in the Black Theatre in Redfern. I was front row with my dad at the Bondi Pavilion production of Bobby Merritt's *The Cake Man*. It was 1977. I was fourteen. My dad and Brian were very close, and it would have meant a lot to Brian that he was there. *The Cake Man* is about a time in Australia's history when Aboriginal people were moved from their traditional lands onto state- or church-run missions – something at the time I knew nothing about. This was my first-ever play and it was a black play about black people living on a mission in Cowra, New South Wales. After the show, Dad and I were escorted back to the dressing room where I met a tall magnificent-looking woman. It was Justine Saunders, a Woppaburra woman from Queensland. I was embarrassed. She stood there in front of me almost naked, a tall slender black woman wearing four-inch cane-wedged sandals and sporting a magnificent afro. Everyone had afros back then, even Brian, who had just played the lead of Sweet William in the production. Aunty Justine played the female lead of Ruby. They both looked like gods.

This memory was all I had to offer the women that day on the ferry. I had placed myself in the room during a significant time in Aboriginal theatre history – something I knew very few other Aboriginal people could claim. I was related to Brian, who was a formidable Aboriginal man and moved in many arts and political circles. I told that story in the knowledge that I was – and still am – protected by his legacy. Where is the shame in that?

Over the course of rehearsing *Shark Island Stories*, I did learn something from those women, and that is: my life would always be a contested one. Like that letterbox, I will not always find my place in life nor be embraced by everyone I meet. Some people may validate my Aboriginality, while others may not. My identity is, however, mine to know and for other people to discover.

When I was young, I did not know what I did not know. I did not know that I was Aboriginal, but when Brian told me I kind of knew, yet also didn't know. For a long time I thought that knowing was enough, but the women on the ferry harshly yet generously reminded me that in fact I did not know much at all. Their questioning did, however, awaken in me the awareness that while, at that time, I did not know a lot about our culture and history, I did know something about what it was like to be an Aboriginal person growing up in Sydney during the 1970s, 1980s and 1990s.

I am who I am today because of these experiences and I now understand that I come from a long, long time ago, well beyond where I am today. When, like now, I return to these experiences, I try to make sure that I brush my present life, work and family realities with those soft bristles of the past.

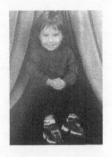

From Marree to the city

Frank Szekely

My name is Frank Szekely. I am a proud Adnyamathanha and Arabana man; Adnyamathanha from the northern Flinders Ranges and Arabana from Marree and Kati Thanda (the scared name for Lake Eyre, the flat saltpan that was formed after the skin of a kangaroo was spread over the ground). The most beautiful thing about the Flinders Ranges is how green and amazing the view is; it makes me proud seeing the reactions on tourists' faces when they see the ranges – it's also a really good spot for camping and hunting. When I first saw Kati Thanda, I was actually shocked by how beautiful it was. The lake goes on so far you can't even see where it ends – and how the sky and clouds reflect on the lake is really amazing. Again, seeing visitors' reactions makes me feel proud. Places of importance to me will always be Port Augusta, just because I grew up there, and also the Flinders Ranges and Marree region.

Growing up Aboriginal in Australia has been both a hard and an exciting journey for me, because there are sad (but also great) memories and experiences that will stick with me forever. The fun memories always revolve around my cousins. Going to the park and kicking the footy, eating lollies and laughing all day long, hunting and building cubbyhouses at the beach – happy days and nights that I'll always remember.

For me, life is about people and place, and the love I have for both. The most influential people throughout my life would be my mum and two older brothers. Mum is loving, caring and funny as. She always jokes around and she has a job at Australian Red Cross, working towards closing the gap. Mum (and what she does for the community) makes me feel proud. She's always willing to put herself out for others, and she has a strong religious faith that she has passed on to me. My oldest brother, Wade, is quite serious and a positive role model for me. He is twenty-eight years old and I'm proud of the work he does as the Aboriginal community development coordinator at the Port Adelaide Football Club. He makes sure I work hard at my training, eat the right food and surround myself with good people. Both Mum and Wade have shaped the good person that I've become today.

When I look back on my childhood now, I regret a lot of the stuff I did. I also regret being involved with – and around – the wrong people. I went to Willsden Primary School in Port Augusta from Grade 1 all the way up to Grade 7. Then I transitioned to Port Augusta Secondary School, where I completed Year 8 to Year 10. When I look back on my primary school days, I'm actually mad and disappointed about the way I behaved, especially throughout my early years. I was very disrespectful towards other students and teachers. Sometimes I felt I was treated differently and unfairly – just because I was Aboriginal. Perhaps that's why I was often disrespectful towards them. Some students would make racist comments and that is another reason why I always found myself in fights. But that's not the only reason: I grew up seeing domestic violence nearly every day, which I believe is why I acted the way I did throughout primary school.

When I was in Year 11, I made the move to Adelaide to attend Sacred Heart College – to further my education and footy career. It was really hard for me at the time because I didn't want to leave my family and friends and I felt as if I was being forced to go. My family wanted me to attend Sacred Heart College (it wasn't my decision), and I wanted to make them proud, so I had to make the move. Initially this was a very challenging time. The biggest differences between Port Augusta schooling and the schooling in Adelaide were the workload, and needing to be organised and on time to school and all classes – and the college uniform and tie were also very different

It took roughly a term for me to settle into being a boarder, as I was really quiet and didn't really like being the centre of attention or speaking in front of people that I didn't know; I think that speaking is an obvious struggle for many Aboriginal students going through education – and just generally speaking to people who you don't know. Being able to express yourself and share ideas is hard because we, as Aboriginal people, are considered shy and I, myself, am a lot like that.

My first year was quite difficult – just being away from family. The reason why I'd always feel homesick was because I'd always think about my family every day; I was so used to seeing them in the morning, throughout the day and at night. Not being able to see them for weeks was really hard for me at the time. But in the second term I overcame homesickness by calling my family daily, and eventually I was all settled in.

School's good. Boarding House is good. Everything is good. The place where I'm at now is a good place to be. Every Tuesday I go to Alberton Oval at the Port Adelaide Football Club as part of the Aboriginal AFL Academy. I'm working towards being drafted, hopefully by Port or otherwise another Adelaide team would be good; I'd like, if possible, to stay in the place where my people are from. When I look back on myself when I was younger I can see how shy I was and how much I've grown. Becoming more independent has been a big part of that. I'm looking forward to where my footy might take me and perhaps giving something back to my community and maybe some of the more remote communities, where kids don't always receive the same opportunities that I have been lucky to experience.

I have always enjoyed going camping and hunting with my uncles at the Flinders Rangers, hunting *kungarra* (Arabana word for kangaroo) and sitting around the fire telling stories. The Flinders Ranges are important to me because that is the land of our tribe, the Adnyamathanha people. Although I'm currently living in Adelaide, Port Augusta will always be my home, just as the Flinders Ranges will always be my land. These places are where my people are from and they will always be special to me.

Nobody puts Baby Spice in a corner

Miranda Tapsell

There have been many moments in my life when I've had to take control of my own identity. I think in many ways, some more sub-conscious than not, I've always wanted it to be left up to me.

When I was about four, I really wanted to be a ballerina and I would dance along to Tchaikovsky's *The Dance of the Sugar Plum Fairy* whenever my dad played it. One morning I came into the dining room for breakfast, and he greeted me affectionately with, 'Good morning, Sugar Plum.' Forgetting I had previously pirouet-ted to Tchaikovsky, I turned to him in disgust and said, 'Not Sugar Plum! Am I a fruit?' This four-year-old told him what was what. Women aren't objects, dammit. Another morning I came in for breakfast and he tried to greet me with, 'Good morning, Golden Girl.' I looked at him in confusion and said, 'I'm not a Golden Girl, I'm a Black Girl.' Poor Dad couldn't catch a break.

So as you can see, I've been an intersectional feminist since the age of four. I knew exactly who I wanted to be. And I'm sure you've already noticed, it was something that my parents never censored.

I did most of my schooling at Jabiru, which is 200 kilometres from Darwin in the Northern Territory. 'Jabbers', as the locals affectionately call it, is in the middle of Kakadu National Park. We moved there from Darwin when I was five years old.

My dad was the town clerk of Jabiru Town Council, and my mum was the Aboriginal education officer at Jabiru Area School.

I got to know most of the Indigenous students through Mum. Because of the gap in education between the Aboriginal and non-Indigenous students, it was Mum's job to support the black kids through an intimidating Western education system that often left a lot of them behind. During her time there, she ran the breakfast program, which ensured the Indigenous students didn't skip the most important meal of the day before class started. She got the school to donate uniforms so that they had fresh clothes after they showered. She'd check up on them when they hadn't been to school, take them to the clinic when they were sick. She also made it mandatory for me to attend the homework centre, which was an initiative to assist the Aboriginal students who might not have had the space or the assistance at home to get their home-work done. At the time I hated it and couldn't understand why I couldn't just do mine at home. In hindsight, I now know that because she only got to Year 11 – and really struggled with school-work herself – she didn't have the confidence to help me. She wanted me to take the opportunities given to me in my education that weren't given to her.

Mum didn't have the answers to closing the gap in health or education. When the media ask me about it now, I don't know either. But I grew up without judging anyone who had lived expe-riences outside of my own. Every individual, every family, every community needs different things. But my mum had – and still has – the biggest heart of anyone I know and was there for these students whenever they needed her.

Jabiru Area School was that tiny I ended up being friends with most of the kids in the school. Even though I got on with the Aboriginal students, I still felt like an outsider in the group. While there was an unspoken solidarity between us, I didn't have a lot in common with them. First case in point: I loved the Spice Girls and Hanson; most of them listened to either Tupac or Biggie. A lot of the mob lived and breathed AFL; I had no idea what was happen-ing during the games. I was loud and shameless most of the time; the rest of the Aboriginal kids just played it cool.

It also wasn't my country: my people, the Larrakia, come from the Darwin region, and the traditional owners of Jabiru and its sur-roundings were the Mirrar people. A lot of non-Indigenous people think that because I grew up in Jabiru, I must have come from there. But there were a lot of blackfellas who had come from other places and most know it's like living in Spain if you are Portuguese. I was a weird in-betweener. The one who got on really well with lots of non-Indigenous people, but also the Aboriginal mob.

And because most of them lived outside of town, I ended up making friends with the mining kids who lived in town with me. Now, at this point I should tell you that I was the only black girl in my group of friends. So I think lots of my non-Indigenous friends chose not to see colour. I was just like them. But when they were reminded of my Larrakia heritage, it made them uncomfortable.

The first time I really became aware of this was when I was eight years old. My class were colouring in the same picture of a family in front of a Christmas tree. It a was great time because we were nearing the end of term and there was less homework. Now, normally when I drew or coloured in, I would colour in all the people as blond-haired and blue-eyed. I guess that's what happens when that's all you see in your books, TV shows and movies. Also, I was sitting next to my non-Indigenous friend, Iggy*, who was colouring in the people in the picture with blond and red hair like her family. So, naturally, I was copying my friend.

But then I saw another Aboriginal girl in the class, Jacinta*, colour in her family all brown. That's when it occurred to me that I was whitewashing my own pictures. I thought to myself, 'Why on earth am I copying Iggy?' That wasn't what I looked like. It's not what my mum looked like. So I coloured in my family the same as Jacinta.

In my picture, the mum and kids were brown. I kept the dad white, just like mine. That essentially meant leaving him the colour of the paper. I liked this picture. Sure, colouring the people brown took more time, but something about it made me feel validated. Proud.

Suddenly there were so many brown people in my pictures that it seemed to start bothering Iggy.

'Why do you do that all the time?' she asked me.

'Do what?'

'Colour in all your people brown?'

I was so caught off-guard when Iggy asked me this. All of a sudden I felt really bad. Was I being divisive making people in my pictures brown? I didn't think I was – I thought I was just reflecting the kind of people I interacted with on a daily basis in my artwork.

In hindsight, I should have asked Iggy, 'Why do you colour your people blond-haired and blue-eyed all the time?' Instead I shrugged and said, 'I dunno, I just like it.'

But from then on, whenever we did art, I would draw brown people. I should add here that we did do maths and English at school – it wasn't all just colouring in and drawing. It used to bug Iggy a lot, and she would feel the need to comment on it. It seemed to me that whenever my friends were reminded of my Aboriginality, they wouldn't know how to navigate it. Their uncertainty would turn to anguish, and it would be my fault that I was making them sad or angry.

As I entered my pre-teen years, my friends began to see my colour, and things would still get awkward when they didn't need to be.

When I was eleven, my mum and a few others working at Jabiru Area School organised a Blue Light Disco, and it was fancy dress. At the time, my friends and I were still very much obsessed with the Spice Girls. If you were to ask how obsessed I was with the Spice Girls, I would say to you: does having the Posh Spice doll, the pencil case, their posters plastered all over my walls, every single lyric to all the songs memorised off by heart mean being obsessed? Absolutely not. That's called being committed.

I loved them so much because their songs were about how awesome girls were. Listening to their albums made me feel great to be one. Sure, the songs were heteronormative, but I liked that their songs demanded respect from their male lovers. For those of you who didn't grow up in the 1990s like me, you seriously missed out and need to listen to the lyrics of their hit song 'Wannabe'.

Essentially they were telling eleven-year-old Miranda that if my future boyfriend was not going to treat me like his equal, then I needed to say goodbye. A relationship not built on trust and respect was not worth my time. I had to prioritise my friendships with other girls first and foremost.

My friends and I had decided that we would dress up as them for the disco. So who would be who? I was really into Ginger, but I didn't know how I felt about her Union Jack dress. I mean, slightly problematic for me, don't you think? Everyone in my group was all about Ginger, Posh and Baby.

One of my friends, Corrine*, said I needed to be Scary Spice. Really? I didn't get why I *needed* to be. I didn't *need* to wear that much leopard print. I didn't *need* to stick my tongue out like a frilled neck lizard. When I asked why I needed to be Scary, my friend told me, 'Because no one else is brown!'

Looking back, I wonder if Corrine felt uncomfortable about dressing up as a brown celebrity. I mean, it was the 1990s, and white people still struggled with dressing up as black or brown artists without the added melanin. Let's be real, not melanin – boot polish.

I didn't know what blackface was at that point in my life, but I definitely knew that colour didn't make the costume. Those five female singers had such iconic styles that most people my age would instantly recognise the Spice Girl you were dressed as. With *wigs*. And *clothing*. While I was very proud of the heritage that my mother had passed onto me, I didn't want to dress up as Scary just because I had brown skin like her.

So I started to realise that even though I didn't have much in common with the Aboriginal kids in Kakadu, it seemed I didn't have much in common with the non-Indigenous kids either. I think Spice Girls, Hanson and *Smash Hits* was about all we had.

Thank goodness for Heather*. She was my closest friend in the non-Indigenous group, and is still my best friend to this day. As five-year-olds, Heather and I started school on the same day and have been inseparable ever since. Because the group didn't consider Heather conventionally girly they thought she should be Sporty. Now, Heather was not sporty at all. In PE she would always point out the ball for someone else to get, even if she was closest to it. It was like the opening of the MTV animated series *Daria*. In fact, everyone began calling her Daria. They only cast her as Sporty because she never wore dresses and wore sneakers a lot of the time. I could tell that Heather wasn't that keen on being Sporty, but she was so shy and would rather go along with it than confront anyone. She was less fussy than I was.

Now, I don't have anything against Scary or Sporty, but I couldn't help but feel that they were the two Spice Girls that our group were indifferent towards. I couldn't shake the feeling that Heather and I were given the less favoured choices.

When I got home, my mum asked me who I was going to dress up as. I told her about Corrine, and how much she lost her mind over my objection to being Scary Spice at the Blue Light Disco.

'You don't have to dress up as Scary Spice,' Mum assured me. 'You have a pink floral dress that looks like something Baby would wear.'

I was hesitant about wearing the dress, because I was still worried about what Corrine would think. I didn't want to be hated; I just wanted to have a good night without having to deal with her saying something hurtful. She made me feel awful about wanting to be someone different from whom she wanted me to be.

I began to annoy my mother with this. Don't get me wrong, she is the fairy godmother of this story. But my fairy godmother was strict, and she had overcome many limitations placed upon her just to make a good life for herself. If society hasn't allowed you the freedom to express your feelings as an Aboriginal woman, then god help you when you're granted a daughter who expresses every feeling she has in every single moment of her life!

'Why do you care what she thinks?' Mum asked me, exasperated. 'You can be whoever you want to be.' That's right, fairy godmother just wanted Cinderella to get on with things and go to the goddamn ball.

On the night of the disco, I put on the pink flowery dress, and Mum put my hair up in two high buns like Baby Spice. I even used glitter hairspray in my hair! I really need glitter hairspray back in my life.

Mum was a supervisor at the disco, so I rocked up with her. As I had predicted, my friend saw me and got really upset.

'I told you, I'm Baby Spice!' Corrine yelled at me.

'Why can't I be Baby Spice too?' I asked her.

She moved away from me and spent the whole night sulking. Eleven-year-old me felt sad that my friend didn't want to hang with me. I wasn't dressed the same as her solely to upset her. I think that's how she saw it.

But my mum had taught me something valuable that night – even though I'd continue to care what my friends thought of me.

I didn't take anything away from Corrine, and I shouldn't be made to feel bad because I wanted to be Baby Spice.

Sissy, an Aboriginal girl, came up to me and asked, 'Are you Scary Spice?'

Was she serious?

'No, I'm Baby Spice,' I told her.

I could not believe this! At what point did Scary wear pink or *flowers* for that matter? Did Sissy not collect the posters out of *Smash Hits*?

'Oh, why weren't you Scary?' she asked me.

Poor Sissy, she was conditioned like all of us to believe brown people could only be Scary.

As for Heather, she just rocked up as Sporty Spice in clothes I'd often seen her wear at school. I loved that about Heather. For her it was more about being there and having a good time.

So I went through puberty learning that, unfortunately, there would be a lot of people like Corrine; non-Indigenous Australians who would be disappointed and angry at the fact you wouldn't conform to how they saw you. If it's not having a problem with you being Baby Spice instead of Scary, it's you being Aboriginal instead of being Australian.

As I look back at my childhood, I realise that I wanted to become an artist because then I could take back the control of who I wanted to be. I was tired of the limitations people were putting on me. But growing up I learnt that people aren't always going to agree with how you define yourself. And while my identity is now something that I have some control over, I had to learn to deal with the idea that saying you're Aboriginal is a political act. To paraphrase the Spice Girls' song 'Move Over', I decided to take some heat and go with the flow. Okay, look, out of context it might not make sense, but the sentiment is there. Just have a listen to the song on Spotify.

Thank you, Spice Girls, for giving eleven-year-old Miranda a bit of Girl Power. No one puts Baby Spice in a corner.

* *Names have been changed.*

Daredevil days

Jared Thomas

I was born in Port Augusta in 1976 and grew up on the edge of the bush and the salt lake, looking over the southern Flinders Ranges.

When I was very young, I used to play in the western side of the salt lake that had dried up and formed a crater ringed by dunes. The bottom of the crater was firm, a mixture of sand and salt. Above the dunes the saltbushes and nitre bush (bush grape/sultana) extended towards an oasis of wattles and acacias that covered a red bank of sand on the edges of what would later be my primary school oval.

There was a track that ran from my home to the rubbish tip, and Dad would take me there in his Mini Moke. I felt like I'd fly out of the car as we went over the sand dunes. It was a real joy ride, but one day I arrived at the tip and found myself staring at old Aboriginal people searching for things amongst the rubbish. They were much blacker than the members of my family who I'd met at the time. I asked Dad why the old people were looking for things in the rubbish, and Dad made light of it by telling me that he and his five brothers and two sisters used to find parts at the rubbish tip to build bikes when they were kids.

Lots of people rode their motorbikes in the bush and saltpan. One day I heard screaming across the road and Dad ran over to help someone who had broken his leg. Even before that day, Dad had always warned me about riding motorbikes. But then I started riding a little blue pushbike with tricycle-type handlebars. Mum remembers walking across the road to call me in for dinner one time, and I was sitting on my bike at the top of a sand dune, looking down before I made the drop. Mum kind of laughed it off, but ever since that day I've been making her have kittens with my risk-taking.

Another time I remember an air balloon landing at the top of that sand dune I rode down. It was a bright, crisp day and the balloon was the most colourful and magical thing I'd seen. Mum ran over to stop me grabbing a lift. Later someone ran a ramp down to the bottom of the crater, and next thing I was riding down the dunes and launching myself over old dumped car tyres. I thought I was Evel Knievel.

Around 1981, when I was five, the old car tyres became the edges of a BMX track. My first BMX was a rusted metallic colour; it was heavy and had a pedal brake, but I loved it. It was easier to pick up supplies from the shop on the BMX than on my little blue bike. On my seventh birthday I woke to find a lightweight alloy BMX with a hand brake and three-piece cranks as my present. It was the most amazing thing I'd ever seen.

My dad worked at the power station and Mum worked as an usherette at the cinema. Mum's cinema job was cool because it meant I got to see so many great '80s movies in the Port Augusta Cinema. The cinema, set in the old town hall, had red carpet and velvet seats. As you walked up the staircase to the ticket office and snack bar, there were huge boards with names of soldiers who'd fought in the two world wars. The place seemed ancient and mystical, full of ghosts and possibilities. Stepping into it always gave me butterflies and watching films made me think of all of the different types of lives I could live when I was older. For much of my childhood, surrounded by a huge family that had a great love of music, I wanted to become a famous musician.

I was the oldest of all my cousins until my uncle met his partner, who had a son older than me. After seeing *Spiderman* with my new big cuz, he started to scale metres up the side of buildings. He was a couple of years older than me, and I wanted to be like him. He was always hanging off of buildings and trees and objects, and I saw him break some bones as a result.

I can't remember much about the first couple of years of school, except being very interested in the people around me. It was then that those old people I'd seen at the rubbish dump started to make sense to me. From those earliest days at school I started to hear kids and adults say things about Aboriginal people, with their mouths full of hatred and scorn. I assumed that when they said those things they didn't realise that I was Aboriginal. I started believing that Aboriginal people were supposed to be poor – I knew that Dad and Mum weren't rich, but I felt better off than most of the kids in my neighbourhood. But then there were some members of my family who seemed to have less money and belongings than anyone I knew.

In Year 2 I was lined up with Aboriginal classmates to be checked for nits and, as I stood there with fingers being raked through my hair, I felt angry and embarrassed as my non-Indigenous classmates watched. I realised that someone at the school knew I was Aboriginal even though my skin was fair and that for some reason it was only supposed to be us Aboriginal kids that had nits.

Then Dad got sick with a back injury and was off work for at least a couple of years. Unfortunately, that meant that I couldn't kick a footy with him or have a hit of cricket, not that that really mattered to me much at the time, because I was more into my BMX riding. I'd wake up and spend the weekend riding through the bush and jumping things. I wanted to launch myself into the air as high and far as I could. My mum, meanwhile, started reading books and writing on a typewriter at the kitchen table each night and then she started working as a receptionist at the Port Augusta hospital.

I started spending a lot of time with my uncle and aunty, especially because I wanted to hang out with my new big cuz. He had a suitcase in the shape of Darth Vader's head that was full of *Star Wars* figurines; he could jump off his rainwater tank onto the trampoline, land on his stomach and do somersaults; and he had his own record player.

After football each Saturday my uncle would take my sister Megan and me – and sometimes our cousins – fishing at Hospital Creek or out of town to camp, sometimes by the coast but mostly at Saltia Creek, around the bend from where my great-great-grandmother, Nukunu woman Florence Bramfield was born beneath a tree on the edge of the creek bed. At Saltia I'd sleep by the fire and wake early to fish or check rabbit traps. I'd trudge up and down the hill with a hessian sack full or rabbits or traps weighing me down.

It was hard to keep up with my uncle and big cuz. My big cuz was incredibly athletic. I'd spend a lot of time bowling a cricket ball to him only to be smacked around the backyard for hours and, after we'd watched *Rocky*, boxing with him. He'd always land a few jarring blows on my scone.

By Year 4 I was chubby and it sucked. I think it might have been from all the junk food I ate between races at the BMX track. School sport became a thing and although I'd played club footy since I was five, I didn't realise that being good at sport was such a big deal. I started playing the keyboard, watching *Footloose* and riding my bike to 'Snips' hairdressing salon, where I got my first crop-styled haircut. I was very self-conscious, and the haircuts always made me feel better.

My sister Megan came third in a major BMX title that year and I was jealous – but we still hung out together, playing basketball, running around the bush, watching films and fighting, as siblings do. Although I'm the eldest, I'd always felt intimidated by my sister. Like all of the women in my dad's family they're the most grounded, tough and focused people I know.

We started spending a lot more time at my Pop Rations' place, my dad's father. Pop Rations' name is really Raymond, but Rations is the name people know him by. He lived in Wilsden, near two of my uncles and my aunty. Pop Rations raised his eight kids, including my dad, all by himself for most of their lives. He would get Megan and me to cut up vegetables for ox- or roo-tail stew, and often danced around a lot and played the spoons. He had the oldest house I'd ever seen, with a yard full of weeds and a goat to try to keep them under control. He always had jars of pickled razor fish and blue swimmer crabs in the fridge.

Dad taught me to track in the bushland across from home, as he told me stories about his Ngadjuri grandmother and Nukunu grandfather and the things they had taught him, pointing to the sky or places in the range across the lake. As I got older, especially when I got my driver's licence and would visit home, Nukunu relatives would start to share more stories about places with me.

In summer, when a cool change or a storm rolled in, we'd sit on the verandah and Dad would tell Megan and me about his childhood. He told us about all of the people living in his grandparents' home – mostly the good stuff, like how the white people in the area exchanged fruit and fish and rabbits and things with his family, and how they would go for big community picnics that included a running race on the saltpans. He would talk about how his great-grandmother Florence and his uncle would need to sneak to their place at night to visit the family because the government restricted family members from seeing each other, and how they were very special people.

Often we'd have big Thomas parties and my family would sing along to music spanning from the 1950s to the latest hits. There were always stacks and stacks of vinyl records in our living room, and Dad still has a great music collection. He played in bands and I would go along to his band practices.

My great-aunty spent an afternoon a fortnight doing some ironing for us. She was like a grandmother to me, and often nursed me when I was sick, lying me on the couch in front of the fire and wrapping poultices to my throat. I used to get tonsillitis all the time and often spent nights in hospital with that and asthma.

When I was twelve I smoked marijuana for the first time. I knew it was wrong but the cool kids at school did it and no one had even thought at that time to tell me not to. One of the kids who I smoked marijuana with asked me, 'What's the old *Abo* woman doing in your house?' The other friend who was with us, who was Aboriginal too, just laughed. Although I wanted to pound them both, I knew they'd flog me if I tried. I started to look forward to high school and making new friends.

I got skinny in first year high school. Maybe it was because I had further to walk to school and started to become a handy cricketer, footballer and runner. I started playing piano in a bar and then playing in Dad's band. That meant I had cash to buy things, mostly flash sneakers and clothes.

I knew lots of people at high school and the older tough guys seemed to cut me some slack. I put that down to constantly riding the streets of Port Augusta, and hanging out with kids who lived in both the rough and the expensive parts of town.

I enjoyed Aboriginal Studies at high school, despite learning about all of the terrible things that happened early in Australian history. But one day a classmate said, 'We should put you all on Tasmania and blow you all up.' I was furious and had a few things to say, but then my Aboriginal Education Worker, Russell Smith, realised I was about to pound my classmate and pulled me out of class. I didn't know why I was getting taken out of class and not the other bloke. Russell told me I'd just land myself in trouble if I flogged the kid, and soon after he set me up with band practice with Nunga rock band.

I started playing keyboard in the band That's Us, with Adnyamathanha and Arabunna fellas who were much older than me. We played music by Bob Marley, Coloured Stone, No Fixed Address and Midnight Oil. We even made 'Battle of the Bands' in Adelaide, and Russell organised Levi's sponsorship for us. Playing in a band seemed to help gain some attention from girls, and I was happy about that because even when I was a chubby little fella, I really loved girls.

One afternoon I was called out of school and taken to my grandfather's house. My dad was there in tears, as was my aunty and some of my other uncles. One of my uncles walked through the house to the fridge, grabbed some beers and started throwing them at the back fence. And then he broke down too. Pop Rations' funeral was the biggest I'd seen in my life.

When I was in high school, my big cuz was smoking a lot of pot and he developed schizophrenia. That's been a really sad thing throughout my life. At the time it made me focus on doing well at sport and music and my schoolwork, and has always made me wary of drugs and alcohol.

When I was about fifteen I was set the task of writing the biography of an old person I knew. I chose my grandfather, Jim Fitzpatrick, my mum's father. His life was fascinating: he grew up in Winton, Queensland, with an Aboriginal mother and a pretty well-to-do Irish father. However, my great-grandmother and her kids were exiled when Pop's Irish grandparents arrived in Australia and discovered my great-grandmother, Hilda Dodd, was Aboriginal. Pop had to start working to support his family at a young age, during the Depression.

I asked Pop a lot of questions about racism, prejudice and discrimination. He gave me a glimpse into some of the appalling racism he and his family experienced and then told me to read Bryce Courtenay's *The Power of One*, about Courtenay's life in South Africa. The book is based on his experiences of setting up a literacy program for black South Africans during apartheid and then being exiled as a consequence. I wasn't much of a reader back then, and when I looked at that big book it seemed overwhelming, but I still remember that first taste of being fully captivated by a novel.

A lot of my non-Indigenous friends seemed to take offence that I was more interested in my Aboriginal heritage than my non-Indigenous heritage, which I knew little about, and consequently I felt like I was constantly fighting to justify my choices. I would run for miles each day to subdue my anger and confusion, as well as ploughing through fellas on the football field and trying to bowl the skin off cricket balls. I also found some peace when Dad and Mum took up painting and started to take Megan and me into the Flinders Ranges, where they'd paint pictures of the country.

At the beginning of Year 12 I watched the play *Funerals and Circuses* by Aboriginal playwright Roger Bennett, a play about strained 'race' relations in a rural town. It was the first time I'd seen Aboriginal and non-Aboriginal people working together to address racism, and I knew then that I wanted to write – to write about all of the things my dad and grandfather had told me, all of the things I'd seen.

My Year 12 teacher, Mrs Bray, who had also been my parents' schoolteacher, encouraged me to work hard through my final year and apply to the Centre of Aboriginal Studies in Music (CASM) at Adelaide University. At the end of 1992, a couple of months before I turned seventeen, I gained entry into CASM, but still I knew I really wanted to study something that would help me become a writer.

Dad was reluctant to let me go to study in Adelaide. No one in our immediate family had ever gone to college, but I was asked to trial for Port Adelaide Football Club Under-17s and that softened him to the idea of letting me leave home. Dad and Mum arranged for me to live with two of Dad's childhood friends – brothers who worked in the gas fields. The night before Dad left me at their place, he drove me through the Adelaide hills to show me all the city lights below. It was beautiful and terrifying.

As I was saying goodbye to my mum, one of the brothers slipped me a rose to give to her. I handed it to her and then I was left to look after myself, and it felt like my childhood was over.

Finding my belonging

Ceane G. Towers

It was in the early hours of the morning of 22 December 1972 that my mother gave birth to her 'Little Ray of Sunshine' – Mum used to sing that song to me she told me. I was the first daughter resulting from her marriage to my dad, although she had two boys before me. Mum had finally met the man who would provide her with the security to raise a family and who would love her unconditionally 'til death do them part. Which is actually what happened.

My parents' love and support towards each other showed their family what true supportive and healthy relationships are all about. It was the first real experience of love and devotion shown to my Aboriginal mother that she could remember since the age of three, when the Catholic priest took her away from her own mother, as the church's and Australian government's policy took away every mother before her in my family. With my dad, Mum felt safe to express her feelings, something she could not remember being able to do before, and her love was reciprocated by my father.

He was an apprentice electrician who finished his apprenticeship and ended up joining the railway, eventually becoming the head electrician and working on locomotives. My parents settled in a 'Master' railway house up the road from the 'loco', as they used to refer to the work-shed; the rent was cheap. However, the Master railway house was haunted. Dad was a night-shift worker, and so Mum was home alone with the kids at night, and strange things used to happen that we older kids, Mum, Nan, neighbours and friends used to witness.

Later we moved across the road to the civilian railway semi-detached flats, which is where I grew up for most of my young childhood, hand in hand with the neighborhood children. This was in a valley on the edge of the Blue Mountains named Lithgow. Surrounding Lithgow are the Blue Gum hills, and we grew up with these trees as our friends. We cuddled the hills as we climbed over them; we would use rocks as our chairs; and we'd look across the valley and over the edge of cliffs and that was our television. Eastern greys, wallabies, lizards, snakes, birds with all the colours of the rainbow would greet us there in the mystical lands that called to us each afternoon and on weekends.

We would set off with the neighborhood's children and our pet dog too, carrying a picnic to share and waving goodbye to our mothers who wanted their children playing outside so they could clean up the house and drink tea with other neighborhood mothers. In my memory, this was the most happy and peaceful time in my life. We would sit and picnic on rocks on top of those hills with a 360-degree panorama, drinking from puddles – and our dog would quench her thirst too. Timothy, our female bitsa (bits of everything) dog, would come everywhere with us. I was a child who felt at one with everything, and sometimes stripped off my clothes to roam free on those rocks at the top of the world.

Those hills were a special place indeed for us children, even though we didn't know then that they actually were sacred places for the Aborigines who ventured there before us. Those people were the Wiradjuri and those are Wiradjuri lands. My mother and her children are all Wiradjuri, and we are also connected to the Darug and Gamilaraay nations. The Towers clan – including my seven siblings and I – were born and bred in Lithgow, except for one brother, and connected to all of our history. My father with his European genealogy makes us 'mixed breeds', as they say in Australia. Bitsas, like our family dog! Bits of this and bits of that. Aboriginals were considered in Australia as flora and fauna and were not entitled to vote or classified as citizens until the late 1960s.

As well as exploring the hills on our side of the valley where we lived, we older kids would also go to Hermitage Flats where Mum's adopted mother, Pearl, lived. We used to call her Nan, but we did not know that she was not our real grandmother. Mum was from the Stolen Generations. Me and my best friend Jodie used to make caramel slices at her Nan's house and then go up to the top of the hill above the showground and sit on the highest rock there, which was sacred. One time we both cut our knees with a rock, and joined them together and became blood sisters at a place called Scotchman's Hill. Now we know its original name is Wallaby Rock. That place called for ceremony, and so we shared blood and that connected us to each other and to all the living things surrounding us. I shared this story with my mother years later and found out that she had become blood sisters in the same fashion with her own best friend, named Dianne, in the exact same place.

When school started I was scared – and had every right to be, as it was like nothing I knew. I took my Raggedy Anne doll to comfort me through the assimilation, and off I went to school. Everything about this mainstream culture was about dividing and separating. All I knew about literacy was from the back of a cereal packet as we kids hadn't learnt English by reading books before bed or being read to. We were more inclined to act out our own role plays and yarn to each other in Aboriginal and Australian slang, rather than speak English, let alone read or write it. Once we hit mainstream school, our youth and innocence left us quickly. I learnt I was stupid courtesy of a kindergarten teacher who told me in front of the whole class that I couldn't colour in properly, and everyone laughed and shamed me.

My reading level was low in the early days compared to others, and that classified me as 'not as smart as' the majority, as this environment measured you assuming English was your first language. I failed miserably. The stereotyping and categorising of me became fixed from kindergarten onwards. My own strengths and interests would not resurface until I started sharing with others the 'ceremonies' and 'knowledge' I'd learnt from aunties, uncles and elders and began teaching professionally.

In mainstream school, because of my skin colour, I was not considered Aboriginal, nor was it understood that I had a different way of learning and a different understanding of what was important from my particular cultural perspective. Many Australians back then would not believe my own identity, as I did not look like an Aborigine: I was too pretty and did not have a flat nose; also I did not live up north where the 'real' Aborigines (i.e. full bloods, they'd call them) lived. Yet I was not considered white enough either, as I looked ethnic, which was also not acceptable.

In high school there was so much discrimination. I thought I must have a sign on my forehead saying: *Be racist towards her; she is not good enough to succeed or have friends, or go to communion or confession.* Teachers in the Catholic school would let this torment occur and not put a stop to it, and I would be punished for it. I'd be made to clean all the classroom windows with methylated spirits and newspapers after school each day, and to stay late writing words out of a section of the dictionary before I could go home. This is how I learnt English. I'd often meet my older brother at the office, where he would be given the cane, and I'd be sent for punishment for, say, not wearing fawn-coloured socks under winter trousers. My brother was called *Abo* too, and told he was fat, and he eventually committed suicide. I knew how he felt. I was set to fail from the word go. I was isolated and treated like a nobody.

Throughout my school days I was told by both teachers and students that I was dumb, unworthy, unimportant, dirty, a sinner, not deserving of friendships, not worthy of God or support because I was the lowest denomination on earth: Aboriginal. I was treated as a black person, yet I was also told I was not black enough. Confusing. I did not fit and I went on in life feeling as if I didn't belong. This affected my education, which my parents paid good money for, and they didn't have a lot of money. I never told my parents what was happening. I did not want to disappoint them too!

Life improved for my parents when they got a home loan through Indigenous Business Australia. The mainstream media stereotypes these loans as unfair and we're told that *Abos* get it easy and are given everything on a silver plate, which is so far from the truth. In fact, our people are the least likely group in Australia to own our own homes, and we work hard for the dollars to pay off loans. Now I am the second generation in my family to receive an

Aboriginal home loan. As a single mother it's a hard life paying off a mortgage, balancing family, keeping everything going, but I am committed to breaking the cycle of my history and making my family secure so we can live safely on Wiradjuri country.

I have managed to get a university education, completing a bachelor's and a master's degree amongst other qualifications. I've been successful because I've managed to break the mould and didn't accept others' views of me. My saying in life is: 'Just because a million people say or believe one thing and you have a different opinion, it doesn't mean that you are wrong.' I am a mentor and advocate for the Aboriginal communities in my area. My spirituality has always kept me alive, as has the love of the country where I belong.

My childhood

Aileen Walsh

'I'm not Aboriginal, I'm Hawaiian.' I said this when I was at school in Roleystone. I had got sick of the other kids giving me a hard time about being Aboriginal. I also got asked questions such as, 'Why did the Aboriginal peoples give up so easily?' My answer was that Aboriginal people were non-violent and so that's why. It was odd growing up in Roleystone. It was very isolated, and we lived on a huge block surrounded by miles of bush, with a few houses dotted here and there. We moved there when I was four. I don't have very many happy memories of Roleystone. Mum was one of the Stolen Generations and was an alcoholic; Dad was a policeman and when he wasn't at work he was being a strict disciplinarian – he had an Irish Catholic background, very working-class, but with aspirations to be richer than his parents.

Mum's drinking frames my memories of Roleystone but, in the lulls between her bouts, there were also days of exploration and cultural teachings through the bush, as she taught us how to clean our teeth with charcoal and the green twigs of eucalypts or did milimbi in the yellow building sand. Or how to look for edible plants. Mum was raised in the Norseman mission, halfway between Kalgoorlie and Esperance on the edge of the Nullarbor. My active imagination had filled in how Mum had been stolen: in my mind a government 'protector' had chased her family down on a horse and she had been captured that way. In comparison, the reality seems much more mundane: Mum was taken from her parents at Rawlinna, or possibly Kronie siding; she was stolen by a Mr Carlisle, who took her to Kalgoorlie, where she saw running water for the first time and was clothed, also for the first time. Mum remembers taking her clothes off and hiding them in the bushes for months after she was placed in the mission.

Mum was fortunate that there were other members of her family in the Norseman mission from her mum's side, the Spinifex people. They all knew each other. In particular, there was Mum's older cousin Elsie Lambadgee nee Wogagee, who took my mum under her wing. And there were also family members from her dad's side, so Mum does consider herself lucky.

I grew up with stories of the mission, hearing the names of all the people she was in there with, as well as tales of life outside the mission. Aunty Elsie hadn't been stolen, because she was a so-called 'full blood', so every school holidays she was allowed to go home to her family in Spinifex country.

We always understood, even as children, that Mum's experience in a children's home had had a profound effect on her. While living in Roleystone, we attended the local primary school but also other schools. Mum was always trying to get sober – or maybe she was being made to get sober, I'm not sure – but anyway, when she did go away to get sober we didn't stay home with Dad but had to go to Dad's sister's place in Lesmurdie. So we went to Lesmurdie Primary School, where we were again the only Aboriginal kids. Then, another time, we went to Balcatta Primary School. Here there were other Aboriginal kids, and I fell in love for the first time. I was about seven or eight.

The most traumatic separation we had was when I was eight. Mum's drinking was bad again, and I don't know where Dad was. Oh, that's right: I think that was when he left to go and work up north. (My memory of the chronological timeline is not as clear as it used to be.) So because Mum was drinking again, I rang Nan and Pop Morrow. They were a couple of old people who used to help us out; sometimes we would go and stay with them, and I loved it. I felt safe being with them and they had good food, so I rang them thinking they would help out again. But this time they didn't. This time they rang the authorities and they came and took us. My youngest sister, Megan, and I were quite docile about it and just hopped into the car. But my other sister, Kathleen, didn't want to: she was screaming and crying and hanging onto a tree; they had to forcibly remove her.

It wasn't so strange being taken to a children's home – we'd been moved around so much. We were put in Bridgewater home and given clothes and food. We went to Applecross Primary School, where we had all the books and pencils we needed. It was good in the home, but I didn't feel safe. There was the constant worry that I was going to be interfered with. The bed had this revolting vinyl cover that you were meant to fold back at night. But I didn't. I kept that vinyl cover over me, even though it made me sweat like a pig and it went mouldy on the underside, but I felt a bit safer.

While we were in Bridgewater home, our cousins turned up: Kathi, Hannah and Cameron. I loved having my cousins in the home with us. We didn't see that much of them – they were in another house – but it was just nice to know they were close.

Mum came to visit us, and it turned out she was in a psychiatric hospital called Heathcote across the road. She took us over there, and Mum and I played a game of tennis. I remember that I aced her! Mum had always loved her tennis and played every weekend on the Roleystone courts. I know she liked to think of herself as the local Evonne Goolagong – Mum even looked a bit like her.

I grew up loving tennis as well. Once a week when we lived in Roleystone, I would be given twenty cents to go to Mr Cook's tennis lessons after school. Sometimes I didn't have the twenty cents but I would turn up anyway and Mr Cook would always let me stay.

I haven't told you who my family is yet; I mean, I haven't named them. My mum is Violet Newman, daughter of Len Newman and Marwung. My dad is Norm Walsh, son of Eileen Stanley and Dick Walsh. I was named after my Grandma Eileen, but I'm Aileen. My sisters are Kathleen, Megan and Tara.

Tara wasn't born until 1975, so she didn't go through what us older girls went through at Roleystone. By the time Tara was born, we had moved to Newman in the Pilbara. Moving there was a huge adjustment. We lived on the edge of the town, and across the road the spinifex and mulga bush stretched indefinitely. It was a huge change from the bush of Roleystone in the Darling Ranges near Perth. But I loved it. I walked through the spinifex bush a lot, knowing that it was Aboriginal land. I would imagine how Aboriginal people had walked for generations across this landscape in their family groups, and it felt natural and a part of me.

I also used to run away to the bush when things at home weren't going well. The bush was a refuge, and I would stay out all day. That has just reminded me of a time I ran away into the bush in Roleystone. We had an old black-and-white TV, and the knob to change the channel always fell off; or it was kept hold of by the person who wanted to dictate which channel we were going to watch. On this occasion, it was me: I had the knob. Then Mr Brockman turned up with the delivery of gas that was needed for our hot water system. I used to climb over his truck and this time I still had the TV knob with me. Mr Brockman left and Mum wanted to know where the TV knob was. Kathleen and Megan told her that I'd had it, but I didn't know where it was. Then Mum realised: I'd left it on Mr Brockman's truck. Mum got wild – I mean, *really* wild. Sometimes she used to get the grass tree leaves – you know those long spines of the balga – and she'd grab a handful of those and whip us with them. But this time she didn't use the balga spines; she got her hands on this red length of insulated wire that was lying around outside and she whipped me with that. I didn't stay around to get whipped more and ran off into the bush. I was barefoot and it hurt; the pricklebush leaves everywhere made sure of that.

Growing up in a mining town like Newman was a lovely experience. We had some family out at Jigalong and they used to come and stay with us, usually bringing bush turkey for a feed. They used to come and have the longest showers, and afterwards there would be talcum powder everywhere.

As I was a fair-skinned Aborigine I was very aware of not being acknowledged as Aboriginal, so when at high school they started calling me *boong*, I didn't mind – they were acknowledging my identity. I can remember when I was doing the final of a high jump event in Year 10, all my friends were in the stand chanting: 'Come on, *boong*. Come on, *boong*.' It felt so good to have them behind me. When I think about it now I cringe, but that's how it was back then.

And then there was the time I decided to leave home when I was sixteen. My white friend Stacey's family was leaving Newman to live in Geraldton. I don't know how it happened, but it was decided I was going to go to Geraldton and live with them. We all travelled down to Perth from Newman. I went to visit my Aunty Maureen and when she found out that I was going to go and live with a white family in Geraldton, she hit the roof. She said there was no way I was going to live with a white family and that if I was going to leave home I would live with her. So that's what I did. I went to live with my aunty and my cousins Kathi, Hannah and Cameron. These were the same cousins who had been with us in the Bridgewater home years earlier. I stayed with my aunty and cousins only for a term, and then I went to Pallottine Catholic mission in Rossmoyne, where I had a fantastic time.

A lot of my childhood was spent moving around. At the time I didn't mind too much, but my sisters hated it. The years of the Stolen Generations in Australia have had profound effects on Aboriginal families such as mine. Though I didn't spend a long stretch of time in a children's home, the memory of it is etched indelibly on my mind. And growing up feeling unloved is a terrible feeling.

Life lessons, or something like them

Shahni Wellington

I'm no good at dot painting. I tried my best in dance until the pressure on my thighs became too much – I was always more of a 'lounging kangaroo' myself. Even though I write with honesty and my story is my own genuine account of growing up as an Aboriginal person, I still question whether what I say will resonate with anyone. Whether this account is specific to me and me alone, and my rollercoaster of identity is really a one-person ride. I have never been relegated to the back of a bus. I have never been denied the right to vote in my lifetime. I have grown up with my family, in our own home, with the blood of both my parents in my veins. My struggle comes in different forms, and these small battles feel like mountains some days. I guess that is what this book is about, right? I hope I can contribute in some way. So here goes: my name is Shahni and I am a proud Jerrinja woman.

I'm twenty-three years young and I moved to Darwin just over a year ago. I studied communications at the University of Newcastle, play too much netball, and have a freak ability to seek out white choc and macadamia cookies if they're within a ten-kilometre radius.

While you're reading my story, I want you to remember that I am one of the lucky ones. I was born in 1994 and grew up knowing who I was and where I come from. I am a Wellington and we are descended from the south coast of New South Wales – Roseby Park, Orient

Point. My dad grew up there with his brothers and sisters, and his favourite pastime was playing 'cowboys and Indians' on the hill. My family live by the water, on a literal point surrounded by the most beautiful views you will encounter. As you drive up the first hill, the landscape opens up and welcomes you home; the beauty of the river spreads across the landscape; Cullunghutti Mountain is always watching over us. I do not know my language, nor do I know my totem. My dad does not know his language, and he does not know his totem. And that is the sad truth that we have accepted, unspoken. It's something that many Aboriginal families live with today, and it's a harsh reality that was imposed on us by colonisation, disconnection and – above all – time.

What we do know is family. 'Jerrinja' is tattooed across chests and backs and forearms, and there will always be extra fish cooked at lunchtime in case someone stops in for a feed. We know pride, we know love, and we know that we always feel better by the ocean.

I have what could be called a 'mixed bag'. These days I think this has become more common and should be more accepted – and this does not make me any less of a proud Aboriginal woman. I love my mum and I love my dad. I love all my older brothers: one with brown skin, two who are milky Dutchmen, and one who is not with us anymore. I have my dad's nose, but my mum's cheek structure (so I'm told). I have nieces and nephews who are pasty and beautiful, and they will play on the same hill where my dad, pretending to be a sheriff, chased down his brother Muddy. I have brown eyes, while the boys inherited blue, green and hazel. I always thought it was a bit of a stitch-up, but I tell myself now ... your eyes are beautiful.

Much of my father's family dated my mum's family. They were the pretty girls visiting the caravan park down the road from 'the mish', and Dad and his cousins surfed Crookhaven Heads when they weren't playing football. In a few cases I'm related to my cousins on both sides, which sounds incestuous, but it's really not. So that's me. That is how I have grown and continue to grow up a proud blackfella.

There's been many times in my life when other people have tried to make me question my identity. Friends, loved ones and a long list of systems. It's not always intentional, and it isn't always direct, but you feel it in your throat and you feel it in your heart. You find it in the places where you thought you were safe.

I've decided to summarise my journey with three main lessons I've learnt from key events in my life, and I've kept them in my mental pocket ever since. I find myself taking them out for guidance almost too often, and I hope I can do them justice: that by the end you'll understand the significance they have had – and continue to have. I hope they might help you with your life's journey.

Lesson one: Put your identity first

Seems easy enough, right? Ah, bear with me, young grasshopper. Sometimes you aren't always able to wake up with a vibrant appreciation for culture woven into your life – unfortunately it doesn't always work that way. Like many others, my family moved away from the mission when I was young to look for opportunities. And as you grow up your grasp on traditional ways can shift and loosen. The thing about Aboriginality is that if you feel it, you can find it. If you know who you are, then there are ways to know about where you come from and learn more about that history. I found a lot of mine within the school gates.

I had a support system there, a safe haven in the form of a dingy demountable building that was allocated as the 'Aboriginal Room'. I had another family gifted to me through Aboriginal education workers and officers – more suitably called my aunties. To this day my heart is full when thinking of all those women gave to us. As students we would travel to events and spread this appreciation we had for our culture through didge and dance, performing well in the classroom so we wouldn't lose the opportunity to perform on a stage. I'd watch my brother and my best friends teach didge clinics to children and think to myself that they were planting the seeds for the same love when those kids grow.

Although lesson number one is more of a motto to live by, it was truly tested on the day I was given a choice. I'd always been very into my studies and I knew I wanted to be a writer. A 'storyteller' is more to the point, so I applied myself at school when it came to subjects and assignments. I relied on natural ability more than I like to admit but, hey, we're only young once, right? I had places to be back then. What drove me at school was my competitiveness.

I wanted to finish on top, and so that's what I strove for. This only came to fruition in English-related subjects; Science and Maths were chucked in the bin early on (whoops). This competitive edge that I inherited from Dad transferred into the sporting arena too; I've been a keen netballer since throwing on a bib at the tender age of twelve. I was picked up for representative teams, and for my sweet sixteenth was named in the Australian Indigenous Schoolgirls squad. It was the accumulation of these successes that led to an offer to attend Presbyterian Ladies College in Sydney. I was given a route away from all that Gorokan High School had given me, and I thought maybe this was the chance they had been preparing me for all along.

I packed my super-cool, oversized, regulation backpack and I moved to the courtyards of PLC. It was luxurious and smelt of heritage buildings and all that was expensive. State-of-the-art everything, with tennis courts, swimming pools, amphitheatres and something else that was completely foreign to me: a locker system. Whaddaya mean you don't just carry your books with you? I was the luckiest person I knew. It could have been the nerves of starting a new school, but I remember standing at the foot of that big staircase, looking up at the chandelier with the floor-to-ceiling stained-glass windows and thinking to myself :'Why do I feel so lost already?' I was going to complete my senior years there as a boarder. A newbie to the private school system, a newbie to all-girl education, and a newbie to life without my family – I was freaking out, man!

I made a few friends and got to know other boarders, other people on scholarships and the other Aboriginal girls who had moved there to do their families proud. The teachers were different and the faculties were different. It felt as if I had gone straight into university, the way I was learning, but I did the only thing I could: I adjusted. It doesn't take a social experiment to know that there are many benefits to private school education; it's prestigious for good reason. It seemed I was learning more than I had before, but it was also the first time I was ever aware that I had grown up with less money than the people around me. This place was different, but different is not always better.

It took six months for me to call my mum and tell her I needed to come home. I didn't have a support system at school anymore, and it got to a point where without those connections or aunties to talk to, without a community to share with, I couldn't do it alone. I hadn't only left one family behind when I chose to leave Gorokan High, I had left two.

I returned to my regular school, wasting a lot of good people's time and money in the process, and so I needed to make some changes. I had passed up an amazing education opportunity, and so now I needed to prove to myself that I had made the right decision. I buckled down in school, giving up some of my netball commitments in the process. I decided that my future lay in writing, and I was determined that the public school system would be no disadvantage. It was where I was happy, and I could grow as a proud, strong and educated Aboriginal woman.

I continued to put my passion for culture into my schoolwork, performing across the country with our troop, and doing mentoring with young Indigenous kids about all things, from leadership to enrolling to vote. I took up public speaking and did the keynote address at the NSW Aboriginal Education Consultative Group conference, talking about my experiences and how important it is to have stronger personal support in all schools for Aboriginal students.

I topped the state in the HSC for my results in Aboriginal Studies, a subject not offered at PLC. I re-enacted the 1965 Freedom Rides in my final year of school, making my own video about grassroots thoughts on constitutional change – a project that inspired me to pursue a career in journalism. And all because I felt in my heart that I did not fit the private-school mould and – when I came to a crossroads – decided to remember who I was.

My story isn't uncommon. If you are an Aboriginal person showing potential, people will try to help to enable a brighter future, which is not a bad thing. It might not be in relation to school, but if you come to a crossroads where you need to make a choice, always choose your identity. Take opportunities and scholarships and jobs, and do what you need to in order to have the best possible life, but never sacrifice who you are in the process. I want young people to realise that it isn't always a choice between staying with your family, maintaining your culture and being happy, or leaving that community and kinship to be successful ... and possibly

ostracised in the process. If you keep this lesson in your pocket –
and in your mind every day – your success and your identity will
never be exclusive matters.

Lesson two: Respect and educate

Above, I addressed applying strength in your identity to big events:
such as your education, making decisions about your future, jobs
and growing up, adding to your LinkedIn profile etc. etc. But it
also comes into play in the personal battlefield of dating. As a real
millennial, I'm going to tell you about how I learnt some of the
hardest lessons about choosing to respect and to educate on a
Tinder date.

I used the renowned app quite a bit when I first moved to
Darwin. It's hard moving to a new town, especially one you've
never been to before and where you literally know no one. Just to
reassure my mum, I was swiping left and right on the potential
Tinder matches purely for social purposes. This isn't an in-depth
retelling of any sexcapades: it's actually much less juicy. I was going
on dates so I could meet some friends, get out of the house and talk
to people beyond passing someone on the street and saying 'How
are you?' as they try to avert their eyes. And so the tagline was
born. You know when you add a short explainer tagline to someone's name? For example, if you're telling a friend about a guy
named John who you happened to meet at a Bliss n Eso show, so
when you mention him, instead of just saying John you say 'Oh
you know, Bliss-n-Eso John?'

Well, these taglines came in handy when I would talk to my
friends over the phone. And thus was born 'Country Sam', the
outback cowboy who was no good at texting; 'Tim Tam man', a
US pilot who was in Darwin for a night, so I gave him a tour of
the city and included a packet of Tim Tams for good measure;
and last but not least, there was 'Racist Paul' (Paul is not actually
his name).

I came across Paul during the course of a lazy Tinder swipe, a
young good-looking lad, and those can, at times, be few and far
between. He was dark and handsome, with a short bio about being
from England and enjoying the outdoors, and ultimately seemed
like a safe and normal bloke ... And he was.

We hit it off with banter and I really grew to like Paul. He introduced me to some British terms like 'innit', which I can only describe as being able to replace any word known to man, especially contractions like 'can't' and 'isn't'. We started going on fun dates, involving kicking the football (soccer ball), playing Sudoku, shooting hoops and eating Mexican food. I may have even given him a tour around Darwin, because there's nothing wrong with recycling date ideas.

He was funny and I thought we had a real connection. I don't know at what point it was that I started noticing Paul's racial slurs; it must have been early on. His comments were off-handed and jovial, and he had no idea the way they made me feel. Until of course I told him. Within seconds of him using the word *Abo*, I explained the inappropriateness. He apologised profusely, and I was adamant that I wasn't being sensitive – he was being careless. I thought now that he knew about Aboriginal people and how he needed to show more respect that would be the end of it. But it was a sign of things to come.

I carried on getting to know Paul, and it was great. I really bloody liked him. So you can imagine how it broke my heart watching him and his backpacker friends drunkenly broadcast on Snapchat the torment of traditional owners who were begging on the streets. I watched them mimic their movements and have a jolly good laugh, describing these elders as the 'walking dead' and offering not a dollar, not a conversation. I hate even thinking about it.

I decided that since they were newcomers to our country, possibly the root of all this ignorance was a lack of education. That maybe what we had was salvageable. We spoke about colonisation, and the effect of disconnection from land and kinship. I sent him articles and told him about my upbringing, my family and the history of our people. We spoke about how many of those blackfellas are on the streets because of circumstances they can't control, a system that they don't belong too. And I tried – I really did.

We were driving along the highway a few weeks later when I hit a branch that made a *fud* noise. Paul simply laughed and said, 'Not to worry, probably just a *coon*.' And that was it. He apologised for making the 'joke' and that it completely slipped his mind that he was with me ... Which got me thinking: do you really want someone who has those thoughts to be in your life?

Some people just don't want to understand. Racist Paul was a lesson to me on values and relationships. By disregarding people's ignorance, you can never break a cycle. Respect is about knowing who you are and standing up for it. It's also respecting yourself enough to accept the losses that comes with it.

Lesson three: Keep it strong

There will be times where your trust in who you are wavers. It could come from the outside, but it can also come from inside. Practise your culture and practise your beliefs: you are Aboriginal and you are proud, and you are doing your best.

School, work and social circles are big parts of growing up, and definitely big parts of growing up a blackfella. You can be known as the girl or boy who gets narky about Indigenous issues. Who always turns a light conversation into a debate. But why would you not want to be? Casual racism is at the root of the divide between Aboriginal and non-Aboriginal Australians. Conversations don't need to be an attack; you simply have to let someone know that what they're doing is not okay. Sure, they might make you out to be some sort of social pariah – but *you* are not in the wrong. Calling people out when they say racist and unjust things should make them feel uncomfortable, not you. If something you say makes a person think again about the ideas they are perpetuating then I think that's a win. It starts with you. It isn't always easy.

My journey is my own, and I hope you can take something from it. Learning from each other and telling our stories is how people continue to grow up proud blackfellas, continue the longest-living civilisation on earth and make changes for a better future. So don't forget: Put your identity first. Respect and educate. Keep it strong.

It's too hot

Alexis West

It's hot. It's so fucking hot! The smell of eucalypt bursting from branches fills the air mingled with melting bitumen. The heat from the tarry road cooks the soles of my feet through my flimsy thongs. Two sweaty, grumpy boys cling to each of my arms. I'm cross. I don't want their slick, sweaty hands on me. I want my space. I want them off me. They cling tighter. Ugh! I'm desperate to find us relief, to wander around the shops aimlessly in the pursuit of staying cool.

The heat is making me paranoid – or maybe it was the joint. But people are staring at the black single mother with the stinky, sweaty, bratty kids. We haven't even entered the centre but I know they'll check my bag at the checkout.

The automated, glass double-doors reflect the sun. It glares back at us almost blinding. But we know what's on the other side. Sweet cold air. People bustle by us, racing for the doors. They give us looks as if we're not good enough to be there – like they're blonder than me ... I mean, better than me. But maybe I'm just being paranoid.

We reach the shining surface of the doors and step towards the mechanical eye that will allow us entry. The doors glitch. What! A tall pasty bearded hipster walks towards the exit from the other side, staring at us like we're an exhibition. The doors glide open. I rush us in. We are hit by a blast of cool air. BLISS!

Wendy's hot-pink-and-white sign beckons us! Ice-cold ice-cream! The line is long. I look in my purse, counting out 5-cent, 10-cent and 20-cent pieces. A couple of goldies. 'Just enough for you both to have an ice-cream,' I declare. Phew! While the sweaty boys eat their ice-cream I'll get both my arms back. Maybe.

We move towards the queue, eyes on the sign. My youngest tugs on my arm; I pull away in anger. 'Don't yank on me!' He yanks again and points to an older hairy man; he is dirty, sweaty, smelly and very, very red in the face; his lips are dried and cracked; and he also looks as though he has an intellectual disability or some kind of mental health issue. I don't know I'm not an expert. He is collapsed on the floor against a pillar staring listlessly at the *Wendy's* ice-creamery. People step over him to get their ice-cream, milk-shake, hot dog, whatever.

I'm appalled. My eldest asks if we can help him. We approach, kneel down.

'Can we help you? How long have you been sitting here? Can I call you an ambulance?'

We have attracted an audience. The people who were so intent on ignoring the old man now stare.

Both my sons say, 'Do you want an ice-cream?'

I wave at the blonde *Wendy's* girl who has been glaring at the man who has been spoiling her view. I walk towards her, cutting in front of other customers. 'Can you get me some water, please,' I demand. No one makes eye contact with me; they hang their heads, I hope in shame. She hands me the water. 'Thank you.'

The boys and I sit with the man as he sips his water. We are all quiet, enjoying the cool. My eldest takes the change from my hand. He stands in line waiting his turn. He returns with one big ice-cream. He gives it to the old man who licks it gratefully. My youngest doesn't mind missing out.

We sit together surrounded – and ignored – by others, but for us it's a moment of unity. I don't mind our sweaty bodies touching now. It's not long before the security guard comes to move us away.

Aboriginemo

Alison Whittaker

I couldn't bring myself to do it.

Twelve minutes of solid eye to eye, *ngamu* to *ngamu* contact, my hands trembling at her back. I made my lips heavy. Not pouting. Just them got lush and bloody and present. Her inexplicably long index finger made circles where neck meets spine. On reflection, pouting.

On the other side of this regional hub's Centenary Park, over its fake lake (a jelly pudding of larvae through which ducks gingerly kicked), the NAIDOC celebrations rolled on. We'd come into town to dog internet at the library, share a hot chocolate, buy skinny jeans, but instead this is where we ended up. On the drought-grass, retaining all of its blade shape and none of its give beneath my arse. In the half-shade, fistfuls of my cousins only metres away.

On this eventless horizon, dense with wafts of frying sausage and onion, we played out a boring series of events. Like many boring events, it would weave in and out of my life. This isn't a first kiss story, which is a true boring, consequenceless story.

NAIDOC 2007, and the early-late-capitalism goth spin-off new adults on the internet have come to regret is a bigger kind of boring. It's the story of how I narrowly missed missing-out on the community that was, literally, face-to-face with me – until I learnt to see it, and myself.

264

Like my stupid, boring kiss, I couldn't bring myself to do it. I was too embarrassed that I might be the only one.

*

My first-ever girlfriend tilted her head to look across at the NAIDOC festival. 'I'm Aboriginal, you know.'

I dry-gulped. Made my hands stiff so they didn't reflexively recoil. A miscalculation on my part; they vibrated on her waist.

We should have addressed this three weeks ago. Three weeks ago we started flirting on Bebo through school internet proxies. I assumed there were no other blak emos. None of our internet aesthetics suggested it.

Why would they? How can you get weaving, or etching, or cultja anywhere into high-contrast selfies shot from above?

Basing your DeviantArt screen-name on lyrics by Nine Inch Nails, Placebo, My Chemical Romance was a no-brainer litmus test for whiteness. Them kids reachin' out for the suffering they hope will shape them, when there's no shortage of that suffering in the blak suburbs of this town.

Red flag! We both chose AFI lyrics. *A Fire Inside*? More like *Aboriginal Fornication? Ill-advised.*

I shoulda expected it. In some way it made sense. Red and black and yellow could easily shift a NAIDOC Nan wardrobe into NAIDOC daut teenage ghoulishness, if the yellow was ironic. And Aboriginal emos must exist on a level; there I was, after all.

I saw her selfies anew (*arm elbow-shadowed; it looked like a NAIDOC croc sausage sinking in surrender to the grill*). Blackfulla lines, tracing the bridge of her nose to the centre point of her cheeks. I shoulda seen it. I was thrown by the bisexuality. Confluence of them three things (*Aboriginality; queerness; red skinny jeans*) seemed impossible, unbearable points of difference! But Aboriginemo queers must exist on a level. There I was, after all.

It was so obvious! And I was so obviously a *reckless almost-cousin-fucker*.

Once all these horrifying revelations had played out, I said: 'Me too!'

Her face locked. Her eyes dropped to the valleys that looped from my nose to my cheeks. She read them like an equation. Our faces were mutually reflected in the other's eyes. Mine *wide, nose bulbous, lips big*. Hers *longer, buttoned, thin lips*. She had huge eyes; mine sparsely lashed slits.

The calculation done, I think we both found it a worthwhile, if minimal, risk. Where else (*anywhere*), and when else (*2006–2010*), could you find someone to know you like this – so wordlessly braided to you in life and mind? Don't dwell on how close the braid starts.

Whatever the nature of the braid, it didn't stop her taking me to the trees with those weird thin fingers over the next weeks, to the bushes near my school, and to this park again, where some of my relatives would eventually find us. They expected to pick me up at the library. Surprised to find me at the park. More surprised by the red Os interlocked on my face from philtrum to chin. You know that kind of story.

*

We lost contact years ago. Later, when we were no longer girl-friends (*girls who hated each other; friends; friends grown apart; acquaintances politely ending contact; girls who don't often think about each other*), our Aboriginality done come to be the one thing that wove us. Not long ago, I found a photo of her in an old shoebox. We both held devon sandwiches up to cover our faces. I could make out only my grinning chin and hers. Whatever was so especially funny about even that well-worn blak devon sandwich joke is lost on me now.

I seen new photos. Beyond arm-warmers and eye-curtain fringes, we look alike enough to make me doubt what ancestry. com.au charged me $30/month to know. And I *know*; I paid $120.

I see myself in her and try not to dwell on it. Think instead of her weird, tiny mouth. Wordless slurping and wincing in the park. The nicest, clearest conversation about Aboriginal bisexuality I ever had.

*

Aboriginemo didn't stop there. It grew – too blak too strong – an aberration from the already-aberrant rural emo scene.

266

While rural emos in the eastern suburbs, perched on hills over-looking the rest, turned introverted an' dominated the internet, Aboriginemo thrived in the meat of community. These, them acts of seeing, come braid us all in land.

The isolating expense of internet in 2007, in a township some 50 per cent below the median national income, meant that only two or three in my circles got it. I relied on them to Limewire music when local schools blocked every well-known proxy service.

Internet-ed Aboriginemos become Tamworth's tastemakers. They had vast social media counter-empires on Bebo and MySpace. They curated bountiful playlists. For a costs-only fee they wove ya holographic CD-ROM after holographic CD-ROM. If you had a computer you could siphon these treasures too, you could invest in a CD-RW and take it to them month after month, replenishing your coolamon with blak Internet 1.0.

Where the eastern emos refined and turned inward them own online taste like hill after hill to overlook us – in early modelling of social-media brand – Aboriginemos built that network out like ugly provincial sprawl. Even now I'm struck by the generosity of what it took to build an online blak community almost entirely offline, strung together by homes that acted as modems, their meat byte residents taking songs in and out on a twice-a-day bus route.

*

Aboriginemo was also unabashedly queer. Eastern suburbs emos stuck to their aspirational straightness and its virtue path: date a guy one grade higher in their brother school, dump him, go to uni, marry. I thought it a contemptible waste of the opportunity an all-girls school presented.

In 2009, an old preschool friend got caught on the same offline internet bus route as me. After a half-hour of off-handed updates, she started as if remembering something obvious and urgent. When she turned to me from the seat ahead, her arm was slung coolly over the rubber balustrade separating us. But her fingers gone shaky. She flushed at me in a hushed voice: 'Guess what. I watched Jacob make out with another guy last weekend.'

She described each to me. There was no tone of malice or dis-gust or jealousy. Jacob, her boyfriend: lanky blue hair, wandering flitty hands only touched people with fingertip pulp. 'Another guy': 'black hair, nat-ur-ally black hair, Al, like and all sooty round his eyes and stuff.'

She breathed quick-like, eyes popped. Raisin' her many arm hairs to involuntarily ask the same response of me. I wanted in.

I wanted to touch her cheeks at their tell-tale blak creases only with the pulp of my index finger. See her like see me. Descend me into (extensive birth-certificate checks permitting) that blak pile of squirmy, showy-offy boys and her. I froze my hands; they sweated in my lap.

Before she left the bus at the networked node, she smiled back at me: 'Look, Steff told me about, y'know. Just wanna say sorry things didn't work out with –'

Flung with the bus brake, she gave up on pity, waved and hollerin': 'That cunt gave me ya number, though! I'll call, ay?'

I knew that Steff (stuck living in these suburbs because she was poor and white) told everyone that me and *almost-cousin-fucker* broke up. I knew this because two days before, Steff saw me an' her return things we borrowed from each other (*a silver cross necklace and a white iPod shuffle, both 2008 stalwarts*) at the butcher where I worked. She yelled, over the counter an' loud enough to quiet the whole shops, 'God, lesbians are saaaaaaaaaad!' Waving my friend off the bus, covered in chicken guts and bleach, I was not in a place to contest that.

*

Blak lesbians were saaaaaaaaaaad. Aboriginemos were sad. Wasn't the music, or the subculture of emotional greyness that did it. Them songs and lyrics worlds from ours. I listened to them like a food-poisoning puke: awkward, rectum-clenching, traumatic activities to excise some'un in your gut.

Emo music videos were unrecognisable. All 'em set in middle America where money flowed thick, bedrooms were large and not damp, and curtains – not sheets – covered windows. A longstanding Aboriginemo favourite, Escape the Fate's 'Not Good Enough for the Truth in Cliche', play round at every party. Sweethearts ate into each other's eyes while the video's protagonists, scruffy boy and mascara-run girl, took some unnamed poison because one of them had a plane ticket that moved their family away. It could not be less relatable. Two planes come there a day. Tickets $500. Most craved the chance to leave anyway. Poison, expensive and for those ill-versed in anatomies of violence, was also out.

The remaining emo musical canon valorised the car crash: a contextless, morally neutral youth tragedy. Car-crash memorials lined both highways out, but there was nothing contextless, nothing morally neutral about the context that clad Aboriginemos. There was comfort in watching emo cultural imaginaries where suffering was a throat-hold surprise (*relationship overthought; love gone long-distance; turn taken too quick*) not a slow-burn.

Aboriginemos weren't all sad. There's risk in a nostalgia. Yet, amongst the strategic and paternal bleakness of the stories that get told about blak teenagers I choose to remember this of Aboriginemo: *unparalleled emotional literacy; shameless tenderness; two blak kids in black say'n' 'Yaama' on the main street and in EB Games.* My heart wanna go an' burst. It gone an' burn at the non-event of it all.

*

Eventually, Aboriginemo buckled under its own weight. In bi-monthly gatherings turned performance art spaces, we met to weave each other's music to ourselves. It took almost no time for us to realise it was bad and to devolve into parody.

Grindcore bands at the local Police-Citizen Youth Club (PCYC), with names deliberately woven to offend, lyricised and screamed off the cuff to a dry youth venue (*remember, closing at 10 tonight, guys!*) to highlight the naffness of post-pop punk. Freestyle's terror stumbling blocks met the very worst teenage metal. One such gig, in 2010, is where the Aboriginemo project rolled back.

A band, with a name the PCYC social worker refused to read, played Aboriginemo's last set. Blue-haired blak frontboy launched himself into a throng of sway-jumpin' Aboriginemos. He gesticulated wildly at his thick half-nude frame, requesting touch as stimulus. His friend feigned a leg hump. (PCYC social worker: *Mate, mate, no. That's not on. No, mate, no.*) A stranger tweaked his nipple. (*Mate, no. No, no. Put your shirt back on. No.*) Between the red-faced social worker and the titterring crowd, frontboy hesitated for lyrics, on the cusp between self-deprecation and actual embarrassment. I couldn't bring myself to not do it.

I rushed forward and licked his armpit. (*No, no. Come on!*) It was not clean.

Frontboy bounced back, real cheeky-like, his bad-teeth ecstatic wince. He slapped my hand an' howled: 'She licked my armpit, I'm in love!' He chanted this again and again as the band stood like crabs and tried to keep up lookin' sullen.

All us in the room come down as one in a split belly laugh for the real joke, which was us.

While we did, I saw them Aboriginemo braids unravel. We saw the earnest shame of Aboriginemo for the first time, yet felt none ashamed. After four years, Aboriginemo was over.

After that, and without any malice, we curled away from each other. I cut my hair. Bought a yellow t-shirt. The braid stayed tied at its scalp, where the crimp betrays the binds we used to have.

There! I sawn it. A common crease! Her blakfulla lines sunk into her cheeks; their mix-tape bus-routes; his festy armpit; their blush; her stupid defiance. Bigger blaker kinds of boring.

That and the internet archivin' our *shamejob*! The nicest, clearest conversation about Aboriginality I ever had.

Split affinity

John Williams-Mozley

Like so many Aboriginal kids who were removed from their family under the raft of 'assimilation' policies in place throughout Australia between the 1920s and mid-1970s, I was removed from my mother who was a 'ward of the state'. She was transported from Alice Springs to Mulgoa mission near Warragamba, New South Wales, when she was thirteen. My mother's fate at that time was to spend the rest of her life in domestic service.

My mother was seventeen when I was born and she remained a ward of the state until she was twenty-one, when, after several appeals to the Native Welfare Board, she was permitted to return to the Northern Territory, minus her firstborn child. I had been 'adopted' by a non-Aboriginal couple when I was seven months old and still, aged sixty-five, have been unable to secure a copy of my original birth certificate, which confirms my mother as my mother. Equally importantly, it would also show the name my mother gave me: Douglas Raymond Williams.

I was twenty-seven years old before I was able to locate my mother, my five younger brothers, three younger sisters and extended Western Arrernte family. When I finally located them, my mother and the two youngest siblings were living in Tennant Creek. I travelled to Alice Springs and Ntaria (Hermannsburg) many times to get to know my mother-aunties, father-uncles, uncles and cousins. From those visits, I got to know who I was and where I fitted in Western Arrernte community life and culture. Eventually I was enrolled on the Register of Traditional Owners of Mpulungkinya (Palm Valley), the place celebrated through the watercolour paintings of my 'grandfather', Albert Namatjira. Well before that, however, my mother died of diabetes-induced kidney failure, aged fifty-one.

As it was, I grew up in Charlestown, a small town on the southern outskirts of Newcastle's urban sprawl and a couple of kilometres from the Pacific Ocean. At that time, the early 1950s, most houses were built on a quarter-acre block, and there was a generous sprinkling of fenced paddocks where citrus and stone fruit trees were grown in rows and handfuls of cows were left unattended to graze. I lived in a small fibro house with my mother, father and younger brother. My brother was exactly one year and one day younger than me. His name is Richard, which, for reasons that escape me now, I shortened to 'Dick'. Perhaps the word appealed to my infantile sense of humour, which at that time was heavily influenced by bodily functions and parts.

A few years later, I changed my mother's name also. Her given name was Audrey, which I arbitrarily changed to 'Sam'. That didn't happen suddenly but was an evolutionary process. The catalyst for her name change was a silly American television show called *The Many Loves of Dobie Gillis* that featured a short, emaciated-looking actor named Bob Denver who is probably better known for his role as Gilligan in *Gilligan's Island*. Denver played Maynard G. Crabbs.

Maynard G was my idol. He wore a black beret over a mop of unruly dark hair and had a Dali-like triangle of whiskers protruding from below his bottom lip. Maynard G was a 'beatnik' who truly marched to the beat of a different drum, a beat that spoke loudly to me. Maynard G spoke mainly in monosyllables and called everyone 'Sam'. I started speaking in monosyllables and calling everyone 'Sam' also, but the only person who didn't object or threaten to inflict bodily harm when I took on Maynard G's character was my mother. Long after the disappearance of the *Dobie Gillis* show from TV, I was still calling my mother Sam. I still do, even though she has now passed.

My mother's family name was Williams. Her father was Welsh and immigrated to Australia at the turn of the twentieth century.

He was a stevedore and apparently spent a great deal of time away from home working on iron-ore carriers between Newcastle and Port Augusta in South Australia. After he married Sam's mother, they built a house in Dudley Road, Charlestown, where they raised five children. Sam was the eldest girl and second oldest of the children. Well before Sam reached adulthood, her father died relatively young, and miserably, from coal dust on the lungs. When Sam's older brother married, he built a house next to his mother's house. When Sam and Pop, my adoptive father, married, they built a house on the other side of her mother's house. While Sam obviously wanted to be close to her mother, I don't think Pop shared the same view. In any case, his culture had no formal mores for mother-in-law avoidance and the story goes that he got it in the neck from Sam's mother every other day.

My father's name is George Mozley. No middle name, just Christian name and surname. I remember seeing a Monty Python sketch some years ago where two men reminisce about growing up in absolute poverty in a mining town in England. Each one tries to outdo the other claiming the other lived in 'sheer bloody luxury' compared to his circumstances. In the sketch, one fella says: 'Poor, you call that poor? We were so bloody poor our parents couldn't even afford to give us a middle name.' Pop's parents were born and raised in the city of Lancashire, England, a tough industrial area that had had its halcyon days during the industrial revolution of the previous century. Perhaps the Monty Python sketch did have some truth in amongst all the silliness.

In 1929, when he was five years old, Pop left England with his mother and father and immigrated to Australia. He has only been back to his country of birth once since then. Subsequently, Pop and his four younger brothers were raised in a small wood-slatted house in the suburb of Guildford, just south of Parramatta in New South Wales. Pop started working in a grocery store at the age of fourteen to help his parents put his younger brothers through school. None of them were given middle names either. When he was eighteen, he enlisted in the RAAF as ground crew and served in New Guinea in the Second World War. After the war, he worked as a carriage builder with the NSW Railway. He did so until he retired aged fifty-five.

While Pop doesn't say much about his war service, Sam often referred to the fact that Pop suffered from war neurosis, which manifested in drinking and violence during the early years of their marriage. Perhaps the problem was living so close to Nanna Williams more than episodic bouts of 'neurosis'. Nevertheless, while I have no clear recollection of those behaviours affecting Dick and me when we were growing up, it was only in recent years that Pop found it bearable to attend ANZAC Day ceremonies with his old RAAF mates who, sadly, are now so few in number.

Down the back of our house at Charlestown was a large vegetable garden where Pop grew spinach, cabbage, radish, lettuce, tomatoes and beans. He also had a few chooks and a couple of ducks. According to Sam, duck eggs were better than hens' eggs for cake-making, especially sponge cakes. If my recollections of Sam's foot-high sponges filled with homemade blackberry jam and cream are right, then duck eggs should be mandatory in sponges. Alternatively, they can also be used to make the most outrageous stink bombs.

Beyond the garden was the bush. As I said earlier, we lived next door to my mother's mother, known simply as Nanna Williams. She was called other names, of course, especially when she caught my cousins, my brother and me for alleged swearing. Swearing, in her view, included 'bloody', 'hell' and 'fa-chrisake'. Rather tame by today's standards but, back then, deserving of Nanna's special oral and moral hygiene treatment. In short, you got your mouth washed out with soap. Not with anything as luxuriant as Lux, or as pampering as Palmolive, but a big chunky bar of all-purpose Sunlight soap. I believe it did a fair job on clothes as well.

Next door to Nanna lived my cousins, Pete, Steve and Jimmy Williams. As well as being my cousins, they were also my best mates. Their parents, Uncle Mick and Auntie Brenda, were the type of parents who always seemed to find the time to join in our games in their front yard, no matter what time of day or night it was or whatever else they had to do. My recollections of those early years are of continuous games of 'war' or cowboys and Indians with my cousins and brother in the scraggy bushland behind our house; racing billy carts, made out of an assortment of scavenged bits of wood, pram wheels and the odd bike part, hell for leather down steep bush tracks; stealing apricots, loquats, plums and lilly pillies from near, and not so near, neighbours' fruit trees; and the countless number of lollies sixpence would buy. One of the 'near' neighbours was Nanna Williams. Sam told me many years ago that whenever Nanna Williams discovered fruit missing from her trees, she'd cut the tree down. Talk about cutting off your nose to spite your face! And she grew such great fruit too. I wonder if she thought of her grandchildren as thieves.

When I was about four or five, I asked my mother why I was different from her, my father and my brother. Even though we lived together as a family and had the same surname – Mozley – I knew something was amiss, because I was black and they were white. Little did I know at that time that this type of uncanny deductive reasoning would feature strongly in my chosen career many years later?

For a long time, Sam wouldn't answer my question directly. In the end, my insistence paid off. My mother and father sat me down in the living room one night and solemnly told me that there was something they wanted to tell me. We had just finished dinner, the wood fire was crackling, and the radio was tuned to one of the weekly serials. Pop switched the radio off. This must be serious, I thought. Pop eventually spoke up and said gravely, 'Son, the reason why you're different is because you're adopted.' I looked at the fire and was instantly mesmerised by the orange-blue flames licking around the edges of a gnarled log on the fire. My mother was close to tears in anticipation of what effect these words would have on me. I turned to them both and said, 'So, if you're adopted, it means you're black ... right?'

After several prolonged conversations about what being adopted meant, I realised, selfishly I suppose, that I must have another mother and father, perhaps other brothers, sisters, uncles and aunts too. Not that there was anything wrong with my adoptive family. My adoptive parents grew me up with all the love and material comfort that was theirs to give from when I was seven months old. They loved me, and I loved them as a son should. However, like so many people in Australian society at that time, my adoptive family had little understanding or factual knowledge about Aboriginal people and cultures. Consequently, I had to wait several years before I came to know what it meant being Aboriginal in Australia.

A few years later, my mother told me that when she and Pop went to pick me up from the 'Hillcrest' Salvation Army Maternity Hospital (colloquially called the 'Hillcrest Home for Unwed Mothers') near Newcastle, she was informed by the Child Welfare Department that my natural mother was an Aboriginal woman named Mary Williams. Williams! If Sam's family name is Williams and my mother's family name is Williams, is there a connection here or is it simply coincidence?

The only other information she was given about my natural family was that my mother was originally from Alice Springs and that her father was a policeman in the Northern Territory. Even though I was told my grandfather was a policeman, I still assumed he was Aboriginal. I knew then that when I grew up I was going to be a policeman, just like my grandfather. I was nine at the time and we had by then moved to Sydney. It is only in retrospect that I understand why it was so important, even at that tender age, for me to know who my mother was and where her country was.

Although it took me twenty-seven years to find my family and, thereafter, many years to establish my personal identity as a Western Arrernte man, I achieved my original goal of becoming a police officer like the man who grew my mother up at the Heavytree Gap police station on the outskirts of present-day Alice Springs. After being accepted into the NSW Police Cadet Corps at the age of sixteen, I was sworn in as a constable of police at the age of nineteen. Subsequently, I spent a total of twenty-six years as a police officer, special investigator, federal police investigator as well as serving in the United Nations Civilian Policing Component in Cyprus. During this time I undertook tertiary studies and completed a bachelor's degree and a master's degree and, subsequently, a PhD. After calling it a day in that occupation, I entered academia and taught Criminology to undergraduate students before heading up the Aboriginal and Torres Strait Islander Education Centres at Charles Sturt University and the University of Southern Queensland. I retired from full-time paid employment in 2014.

When I look back to the early years of my life, I can only recall lots of love, mateship, cosy hand-knitted jumpers, fresh food from the garden, home-baked cakes and biscuits, adventure-filled days walking to and from school, playing in the bush with my cousins, and going into Newcastle on the bus with Sam and Dick to wander around the large department stores. They were good days, but I often wonder how different my life would have been had my birth circumstances been different. This isn't to say that I never experienced racism, discrimination or unequal treatment throughout my life. All these things came later, as a young adult in the workplace, in retail shops, real-estate agencies, banks, universities, hotels and motels – the same places and kinds of occurrences the majority of Aboriginal people in this country are all too familiar with.

While I often get sad when I think about the awful treatment my mother, my brothers Kenny, Peter and Paul, and my sister Elna received as wards of the state and, therefore, either being institutionalised (my mother, Kenny and Elna) or removed from the Northern Territory to Western Australia (Peter) or South Australia (Paul), I know that their stories aren't that different from the countless number of Aboriginal children unlucky enough to be born when these horrific practices were in place.

In the end, it is reasonable to state that I didn't grow up Aboriginal in Australia; I grew into being Aboriginal in Australia.

First, second, third, fourth

Tara June Winch

First, looking up, there is the dance. How long ago? A long time ago. Growing up, I knew my father's family came from *a long time ago*. All time, from time travel, yet we were severed from the knowledge of the dance – where the feet go, the arms bent, the hips, the line of spine. We didn't have the *carriberrie* or *corroboree*, nor the song with it. We were living on saltwater country, not freshwater, not from those rivers and lakes where history sat beyond the escarpment in a slouched pose, defeated. There was no dance handed down, it had been cast into the four winds, yet I saw the dance. My cousin is the dancer still and there, that early memory is of her at a family gathering – in one of those blip moments, I am looking up at an impromptu modern dance, fluid, mad, yet articulate. I think she'd just graduated from dancing with the Martha Graham School in New York and returned to our slip of coast. I looked up from where I sat and saw all the possibility in the world. My cousin evoking a dance long buried. From those child's eyes she was the most incredible person I knew. I wondered how it was that she salvaged the dance? I wondered, had she read about it, had someone whispered it to her, did she time travel to find the moves, did the ancestors visit her in her dreams? Would they visit me too?

*

Second, looking down, is the street. Childhood in my mind is that street seen from a bird's-eye view. I recognise the Pizza Hut roof, back and front yards, wire squares of clotheslines, identical tin letter-boxes. Perhaps I remember it this way, looking down, because it's too hard to stand there at the front steps and peer through the flyscreen door. In the 1980s children wore fluorescent-coloured clothing; you couldn't miss us. From high up I can see the town pervert who lived opposite our house; I can see me in fluorescent pink bike shorts; I'm sat on the steps at my place, number 15, licking a lemonade ice-block during the time when summer was an entire childhood. If I looked across the road to where he was sitting on his elderly parents' front step, his legs would be wide, his shorts loose, no underwear beneath. He'd often be hidden in the dunes, watching girls and women, and only his arm moving with the lap of tide. I might see the lady who lived next door, and knitted dolls, in her backyard where she picked chokos from the shared vine. I might see the single mother on the other side who cried a lot and tried to befriend my mother, who never wanted friends. Next to the pervert was the girl's house; her mother was alone too, and was bubbly and bronzed; she might be working in the garden. The other house, diagonally from my front steps, was where the drug dealers lived. I can't remember the kids' names; their mother yelled a lot, yet most people yelled. Fights spilt into front yards like the broken toys waiting all year for the town council's rub-bish pick-up. Scavengers who drove the streets at that time, looking for thrown-out solid furniture and working electronics, didn't check our kerbside rubbish for bargains; they knew on our street there lay only broken things, bent hopes.

On the street there were bicycles everywhere. The smell of salt outside, inside: cigarette smoke and fly spray in the air. The sound of waves some nights, or cars doing burnouts and night-time argu-ments. It was night-time when adults made all their loud-voiced *money trouble a*rguments, fights that clapped like firecrackers at sunset. Looking down at the cruel intersection, I wonder what it was exactly that the neighbours noticed about us at number 15. Was it class I felt so keenly summed up by, or race? Or both?

At school we learnt explorers. In tablets of milk chocolate, kids could collect an entire set of explorer trading cards. For a brief moment in history class we were presented with archival drawings of

Indigenous men, standing one-legged, their rude parts red-clothed, spears in hand; the women were savage and noble, never dressed. *That's all?* I thought. *Well, that's not me*, I realised. We wore jeans, and lived in the commission house, not a humpy. I grew up with a brother, whose father is Torres Strait Islander; a sister, whose mother is my father's sister and is Wiradjuri and whose father is Barkindji; and another brother, who is my cousin. They are darker than me. They are more Indigenous than me. I think I saw life through the lens of a writer from a young age: I never knew how I felt, but wondered how it felt for them. Race was the paradigm that I didn't fit. But we were proud. We are still proud.

I'm still looking down, and I want to yell out to the young girl with bucked teeth, in fluorescent bike shorts; I want her to *look up*! Let me count the ways I love thee. Count the ways I was Aboriginal even if no one is playing AFL on our NSW street. Count the ways you belong somewhere. I'd get dropped off at the Aboriginal Medical Centre for teeth pulling, cavity filling, for painting workshops in the old garage shed out back. I have friends there; it's where I completed my first dot painting, experienced my first kiss, smoked that first cigarette. We got to go on Aboriginal camp once a year, celebrated NAIDOC day annually. Sometimes it feels as if I don't remember anything. I remember almost nothing. Memories are cryptic, translucent blimps rising and bursting, a slice of a life without the details coloured in.

Salvage . . . I'm standing with Dad at the little shop manned by no one at the local garbage dump – we'll find treasures there. Dad worked one year as a bricklayer for the botanic gardens' pond; there is a photograph of him somewhere – my mum turned up and brought him lunch perhaps, caught him mid-work or had him pose and laugh for the camera; there are rhododendron flowers in bloom. He's giving me lifts to the beach during his smoko another year when he's a taxi driver. The beach owned us, but the street owned us more. I can see everyone on the street, but we aren't neighbourly. The neighbours argued, our parents argued. I pleaded to have the surf-brand schoolbag, to invite my friends over in the afternoon. I still feel guilty for wanting more than my parents could offer. We went bushwalking. Dad went away working in the bush – he brought back gifts. We went to Lightning Ridge, slept in tents, mattresses beside the fire pits. Those were our holidays.

Salvage ... There are no artefacts. Not a *guluman* or *coolaman*, not the one that my grandmother bought on a bus trip to Alice Springs. Her souvenir is at my aunt's house, the last time I saw it she had the *guluman* in the kitchen, high on a shelf. She took it down for me: it used to be in our house growing up; its design was for carrying babies, or collecting berries, or for digging at tuber roots, but this one was a souvenir that was now collecting dust. Quiet truths, unspoken history, that's what lurks growing up, that's what's never dredged up straight from the mouths of rivers. No one is dancing except my cousin.

*

Third, in some middle distance, some certainty, something to look forward to when you're young, is the confluence. The junction of those two rivers, the gush of an estuary. Past and possibility and the knowledge that, if nothing else, I could make my own dance.

And then I left as quick as I'd grown: out into the wide highways, the yonder and blue, all not as brutal as they warned. I was seventeen, high school dropout, wannabe poet, professional hitchhiker. I left because all life is risk; if I stayed, surely that was the bigger risk? I wanted to get to where my sister and cousin were, I wanted to send postcards, to map my country and then the world and figure out exactly how I fit in it all. I think I learnt something early on: that I belonged and didn't belong everywhere. That I was from the world and of the world, and I could move, I could make that extinct dance anywhere, any way I wanted.

Recently my mother left Australia on holiday for the first time. Together we sat in a bed and breakfast in Brittany, France, and watched the TV. *Eurovision* was on, and framed by the screen was a young Aboriginal singer, representing Australia. He didn't win that night, but between where I sat at the end of the bed and the TV is where my daughter sat, a fist raised in the centre of the room. She'll inherit the world, and that place, that *long time ago* place, where her grandfather comes from. I knew then that she too would interpret her own dance, salvage our dance from the wreckage.

*

Fourth, there is the future.

The Aboriginal equation

Tamika Worrell

'What percent Aboriginal are you?'
'You don't look like an Aborigine.'
'You've done really well for an Aboriginal.'
'You're not like those other ones – you're one of the good ones.'
'You wouldn't have had it hard growing up.'
'I'm darker than you are.'
'Are you really Aboriginal?'
'So do you get all the benefits?'
'All Aborigines are angry.'
'Get over it, it happened two hundred years ago. No one alive today was there.'
'I'm not racist, I have an Aboriginal friend.'

These are the phrases I hear constantly. I'm an Aboriginal woman, I'm a Koori woman. I'm not a percentage, I'm not part Aboriginal and I'm not an Aborigine. My skin colour does not dictate my connection to country, my attachment to culture or my understanding of who I am. I'm not your ever-available resource to learn about culture, but being sick of ignorance I'll probably be inclined to share what I know. I'm not an expert. I know my life, my mob and my stories, but I don't speak for the diversity of Aboriginal Australia. I do get all the benefits, if you're referring to belonging to the longest-living culture in the world, a culture of beauty and wonder that has guided my identity in every facet of the world. But, no, I don't get more Centrelink study allowance than you. I haven't done well *for an Aborigine*: I've done well for any twenty-two-year-old who has overcome hardship.

I have spent my life defending my identity. At times it was a struggle: in high school I felt almost embarrassed of being Aboriginal. I was treated as if I must be dumb because I'm Aboriginal, which is challenging for a teenager to comprehend. I remember pleading my case, being told I needed a tutor when I was second in English in a cohort of two hundred; the school's response: 'We know you don't like to wave the Aboriginal flag.' That phrase still cuts me to this day; if I was as confident as I am now my response would have been different, rather than feeling anxious and blocking everyone out.

High school made me see being Aboriginal as a bad thing. I am now a secondary teacher because I don't want any Indigenous students to go through what I did, to constantly be bombarded with a 'deficit model'. We also need Aboriginal teachers to ensure whitewashed history is not being taught and our diverse voices are being heard.

Growing up in my household meant eating devon sandwiches, and listening to Mum's stories and making her cups of tea. We understood that things were really hard for Mum because she was taken from her family so young. As a child I made no connection between the Stolen Generations and my mum's stories; it was just what we knew and how things were: that we didn't have a big family around us, just scattered remnants of relationships that were torn apart by government policy. As I got older I realised how these things added up and why they were the way they were; why there was so much pain and trauma in the family, why addiction and violence were prevalent, but also how I can acknowledge them and avoid them in my future.

University provided me with a space to understand myself and learn that everything I believed was actually shared by many strong Aboriginal men and women. My tiddas are so important in my finding strength as an adult, in being able to vent about – and compare – what we are going through.

University also means walking in two worlds. It is knowing that my experience has been different from non-Indigenous students.

It is feeling hyper-aware of the lack of knowledge that adults have when it comes to Indigenous people. I'm continually shocked by those who are studying to be educators who have asked me: 'Are you *really* Aboriginal?' and 'Like, what percent are you?' It's disheartening to know these people will be educating others, including teaching Aboriginal and Torres Strait Islander histories and cultures, as well as teaching Indigenous students. This usually means I'm going above and beyond in order to share my experiences, and to hope others can learn from them.

Walking in these two worlds also requires acknowledging that being a fair-skinned, or 'white-passing' Aboriginal woman means being vulnerable when sharing culture, and acknowledging that by being fair-skinned I have privilege that other mob don't have. I deal with constant, casual racism. It's listening to people tell racist jokes, or rant on about myths and stereotypes about Indigenous people. From my experiences, lots of non-Indigenous people don't seem to understand that Aboriginality is not tied to skin colour, and it's not my job to help them come to terms with my heritage, or overcome their white guilt. I'm not your expert, and I'm not your token Aboriginal person and I'm not an equation or percentage for you to work out. It's none of your business which parents of mine are Aboriginal or how 'far back' my Aboriginality goes or, god forbid, if any of my relatives are 'full' Aboriginal.

It's because of this I have developed a thick skin – I will not sit quietly while my identity is questioned. It doesn't matter how many times you say you didn't mean to be offensive, that doesn't dictate whether or not I'm offended. So, yes, I'm an angry Aboriginal woman. But wouldn't anyone be if they were questioned day in and day out about their heritage?

Aboriginality for me is a journey, a journey I've come a long way on, but there's still a long way to go. I will forever be learning about myself and my heritage. For now, it's knowing who I am, and knowing what's important in life, and having hope that I will live to see a future that is less ignorant, less racist and at least somewhat decolonised. Until then, I'll continue to be an angry Koori woman, educating those who don't understand and those who choose not to.

Notes on Contributors

SUSIE AND ALICE ANDERSON are Wergaia women who grew up on nearby Wotjobulok country in Horsham, Victoria. Susie (27) is a writer and producer, currently living in Sydney, who has been published in *The Lifted Brow*, *Australian Book Review* and *Voiceworks*. Alice (22) is a singer–songwriter who has performed with the likes of Archie Roach and Dan Sultan. Her first album is soon to be released through CAAMA.

EVELYN ARALUEN is a poet and teacher researching Indigenous literatures at the University of Sydney, where she is completing her PhD. She coordinates Black Rhymes Aboriginal Poetry Nights in Redfern and is a founding member of Students Support Aboriginal Communities, a grassroots organisation based in Sydney. Born and raised in Dharug country, she is a descendant of the Bundjalung nation.

BEBE BACKHOUSE is a Bardi man from Western Australia. With a background in classical music as a concert pianist, repetiteur and teacher, his educational work with Indigenous and non-Indigenous youth in the Kimberley led him to win 'Western Australian Young Person of the Year in the Arts' at twenty-one. He now lives in Melbourne where he designs and produces creative high-profile festivals and events for that city's diverse communities.

ALICIA BATES is a twenty-eight-year-old Gunditjmara, Kirrae Whurrong woman living in south-west Victoria. She is an early childhood teacher, foster carer for both Aboriginal and non-Aboriginal children, and a previous director of the Gunditjmara Co-Op board. Alicia has degrees in both education and psychology. Alicia shares her story in the hope of dispelling pre-conceived negative views about Aboriginal people.

DON BEMROSE is a Gungarri man and Australia's foremost male Aboriginal classical opera singer. In professional productions, he has sung four leads of which three were in world premieres: *Pecan Summer* for Short Black Opera Company; *From a Black Sky* for The Street Theatre; *Cloudstreet* for State Opera of South Australia. Don currently works for the ACT Government within the Education Directorate at a Bilingual Italian Primary School while contributing to the local and national arts sector as a speaker, trainer and performer.

TONY BIRCH is the author of *Ghost River*, which won the 2016 Victorian Premier's Literary Award for Indigenous Writing, and *Blood*, which was shortlisted for the Miles Franklin Literary Award. He is also the author of *Shadowboxing*, and three short story collections – *Father's Day*, *The Promise* and *Common People*. Tony is a frequent contributor to ABC local and national radio, and a regular guest at writers' festivals. He lives in Melbourne and is a Senior Research Fellow at Victoria University.

NORLEEN WITH HER LONG-LOST RELATIVE ALAN MEEKS

NORLEEN BRINKWORTH was born in 1947 in Yarrabah mission, Queensland, where her grandparents were placed as young children at the beginning of the twentieth century. She later went to school in Cairns, where her parents moved with their six children. Opting to do factory work to help supplement her family's finances, Norleen let her secondary schooling lapse but returned later, as a mature student and mother with two children, and obtained a tertiary degree. She worked in the judicial system until retirement seventeen years later.

KATIE BRYAN's great-great-grandmother was born on Jackie White's station, near Naracoorte, in 1855. She was the first light-skinned girl born in the district and, at the age of two, she was taken from her mother and sent to Blackford mission at Murrabinna. Katie is the first generation of her family to grow up without language, culture and connection to kin and country. Her family have been assimilated; she is the only one who remembers their origins.

Deborah Cheetham is a Yorta Yorta woman, soprano, composer and educator, who has been a leader and pioneer in the Australian arts landscape for more than twenty-five years. She was appointed as an Officer of the Order of Australia (AO) in 2013. In 2009 Deborah established Short Black Opera, a national not-for-profit opera company devoted to the development of Indigenous singers. The following year she produced the company's first opera, *Pecan Summer*, Australia's first-ever Indigenous opera, which has been performed around the country, and in 2016 became the first Indigenous opera to be presented at the Sydney Opera House.

Natalie Cromb is a mother, legal professional, writer and activist. Belonging to the Gamilaraay people of Burra Bee Dee Aboriginal Reserve, she enjoyed a childhood on country despite being born and raised two hours away in Tamworth. Natalie now lives and works in Sydney and returns home to country and family whenever possible. She is a determined advocate of change and reform for her people, a responsibility instilled in her by her grandfather (a Gamilaraay elder) from a very young age. She is a founding member of the Gomeroi/Gamilaraay Sovereign Peoples, advocates for Treaty and structural reform of our political and justice systems.

KAREN DAVIS is a Mamu–Kuku Yalanji woman who grew up in a family of six in Far North Queensland during the 1970s and 1980s amongst a backdrop of crystal-clear swimming holes, monsoonal rains, sugar cane burn-offs and tropical cyclones. She now lives in Melbourne, works in the tertiary education sector and volunteers for community radio.

IAN DUDLEY lives on Wirangu *manda* (land) on the west coast of South Australia, but his roots could be from just about anywhere. He has three young daughters and, when he's not running around after them, he splits his time between teaching, helping revegetate a run-down old station back into the she-oak forest it would have been 200 years ago and trying to catch a few waves in peace.

ALICE EATHER was a bilingual school teacher, activist, poet and leader. Born in 1988 in Brisbane, she completed primary, secondary and tertiary education in Queensland before moving in 2010 to live in Maningrida to pursue educational and community projects. In 2014 Alice became the first Ndjebbana-speaking Aboriginal teacher to graduate from the Remote Indigenous Teacher Education program in Maningrida though Charles Darwin University. That same year she also won the NT Young Achievers Environment Award for her work establishing 'Protect Arnhem Land', a community campaign against coal-seam gas-fracking on the coast of Arnhem Land. Alice took her own life in June 2017, but her family hopes her work and messages will remain as a legacy to inspire others.

SHANNON FOSTER is a D'harawal saltwater knowledge keeper, educator and artist who was born, raised and is still living on country in Sydney's Tucoerah (Georges River). She has been teaching her family's stories and knowledges for over twenty years to a range of audiences, including at venues such as Sydney Olympic Park, Taronga Zoo and the Australia Museum, and in various universities. Shannon is currently undertaking her PhD in the Centre for the Advancement of Indigenous Knowledges at the University of Technology, Sydney.

Jason Goninan is a Gunditjmara man from his mother's side, who was born and raised in Sydney's eastern suburbs. During the day, Jason works for the NSW Government to support Aboriginal communities realise their dreams and aspirations; and by night, he and his wife look after their three beautiful children. He has the world's biggest sweet tooth and has been known to inhale a tub of ice cream in one breath. He's also had to make the most of being tall by playing basketball.

Adam Goodes was born in South Australia and moved to Victoria as a young boy where he developed a passion for Australian Rules Football. He holds an elite place in AFL/VFL history as a dual Brownlow Medallist, dual premiership player, four-time All-Australian, member of the Indigenous Team of the Century and representative in the International Rules series. Adam was named the 2014 Australian of the Year in recognition of his community work aimed at empowering the next generation of Indigenous role models as well as his advocacy in the fight against racism. In 2009, Adam set up The Goodes–O'Loughlin Foundation (GO Foundation) with fellow Indigenous teammate Michael O'Loughlin. The GO Foundation's vision is to create a brighter future for Indigenous children through education.

JODI HAINES was born and raised in Hobart and is a valued member of the Tasmanian Aboriginal community. She is a Gomeroi woman, with her dad's family coming from Toomelah mission in northern NSW. Jodi currently lives in Hobart and works at the University of Tasmania as an Associate Lecturer at the Riawunna Centre. She has a background in sports, teaching and journalism and also as a singer–songwriter.

JOHN KARRANJAL HARTLEY was birthed on Cadigal homelands at Kogarah ('place of reeds') in 1956. He left school early to travel around country and spent time with First Nation Cree elders in Kanata and Anangu Pitjantjatjara–Yankunytjatjara of the western desert, finding ways of reclaiming ancestral values, beliefs and practices, and Yalanji language and storytelling. John has developed art-based presentations addressing the impacts and effects of colonial violence, and co-produced the documentary *Two Brothers Walking* and a bilingual animation promoting cultural understanding and maintenance.

DIANE MCDONALD

TERRI JANKE was born in Cairns in Far North Queensland and is of Wuthathi and Meriam heritage. Her family moved to Canberra in 1976, and she now lives in Sydney with her husband and two kids, where she runs a successful legal practice. The firm is well known for its work with Indigenous business and intellectual property. She is the author of the novel *Butterfly Song* and has also written many articles about Indigenous cultural and intellectual property. Terri believes in the power of stories to inspire, connect and heal. Her proudest moment was being awarded NAIDOC Person of the Year in 2011.

KEIRA JENKINS is a Gamilaroi woman from Moree in north-west New South Wales and spent many years growing up in Lismore, on the NSW north coast. She is a journalist and photographer who is passionate about telling the grassroots stories of her people and their achievements. She also has Norwegian and English heritage and is keen to tell stories of growing up walking between different worlds and cultures.

PATRICK JOHNSON is a Kaanju man from Far North Queensland who had a twelve-year career in elite sport, spent ten years working for the Department of Foreign Affairs, and has more than twenty years' experience in ambassador, mentoring and media roles. He was the Deadly Choices Ambassador for Danila Dilba promoting a healthier lifestyle, supports NT Athletics Remote Athletics program, and works as a sports presenter for ABC Grandstand. His personal experience of having family members pass away due to chronic diseases, such as asthma, diabetes, heart disease and obesity, has strengthened his resolve to develop leadership in Aboriginal health.

SCOTT KENNEDY is a Ngiyampaa man from Condobolin in New South Wales, who was born in the 1970s and was settling into his childhood when his family moved to Mount Druitt. Growing up Scott's life was hard as part of a single-parent family that lived in poverty and experienced violence. Later, as a Kings Cross kid, he turned to drugs, which led to him ending up in prison in his youth. In his mid-twenties, he moved to Adelaide, got off drugs, and worked in construction, bands and stand-up comedy. In 2017, unexpected circumstances led Scott back to prison where he is now writing a memoir of his childhood that he hopes to publish after his release in 2021.

SHARON KINGABY was born in 1960 in Brisbane and married at seventeen. She has three children and moved her family from Queensland to Victoria in 1994, where she's lived ever since. She works full-time in Aboriginal employment within a local council. She has been welcomed into the Aboriginal communities where she lives and works, supported by elders and respected leaders, and tries to give back as much as she can.

AMBELIN KWAYMULLINA is an Aboriginal writer, illustrator and law academic who comes from the Palyku people of the Pilbara region of Western Australia. She has written and illustrated multiple award-winning picture books as well as the dystopian young adult series *The Tribe*. Her books have been published in China, Korea and the United States. Ambelin is an expert commentator on diversity in Australian children's literature and works across the literature, business and tertiary sectors to promote ethical best-practice engagement with Indigenous peoples and Indigenous stories.

JACK LATIMORE is a Goori writer and journalist living in Melbourne. His work regularly appears in *IndigenousX*, *The Guardian*, *Overland* and *Koori Mail*. He has also been published by *Inside Story*, SBS, NITV and *Crikey*. He is the daily editor of *IndigenousX*.

CELESTE LIDDLE is an Arrernte woman, an opinion writer, a trade unionist and public speaker, who currently works as the National Aboriginal and Torres Strait Islander Organiser of the National Tertiary Education Union. She launched her blog, *Rantings of an Aboriginal Feminist*, in June 2012 and now writes for a number of publications, including *Daily Life*, *The Guardian*, *New Matilda* and *Tracker Magazine*.

MATHEW LILLYST belongs to the Gunditjmara people of south-west Victoria and the Bunitj people of north-west Arnhem land, but was born and raised in Melbourne. He is the youngest of six kids and the uncle to eight beautiful nieces and nephews. Over the past few years he has worked as a high school teacher in Victoria, the ACT and the Northern Territory. Currently, he teaches English at Muswellbrook High School in the Hunter Valley in NSW.

TARYN LITTLE is thirteen years old and lives with her mum and dad and pet dog Manny in the inner-western suburbs of Sydney. Her dream job would be to backpack around South America soaking up the local culture and sharing her experiences on a travel blog. Her family comes from Gilgandra, which is just north of Dubbo in New South Wales, and she is a member of the Wiradjuri tribe.

Amy McQuire is a Darumbal and South Sea Islander journalist who lives and works in Rockhampton. She has more than ten years experience in Aboriginal journalism and has previously worked at the *National Indigenous Times*, *Tracker Magazine*, NITV and *New Matilda*. She is currently the Indigenous Affairs reporter for *Buzzfeed*.

Melanie Munumggurr-Williams is a Djapu, Irish and Scottish woman. She is married and has a son. She has a love of writing poetry and has recently started writing spoken-word pieces. She lives in Darwin and works with Indigenous teenage girls.

DOREEN NELSON is a Noongar woman who was born in a town called Kellerberrin in the central wheat-belt area of Western Australia in 1947, a time when life was very hard for Aboriginal people. She has travelled extensively throughout Australia, living and working in remote areas with her people. She has lived in Perth for the past twenty years and is a respected elder in the community. She has four children, eleven grandchildren and eleven great-grandchildren.

SHARON PAYNE is a Wonnamutta elder of the Badjula from K'gari (Fraser Island). She grew up in Queensland before moving to Ngunnawal country (Canberra) in 1986 where she still resides. In 1974 Sharon became the first Aboriginal student at the University of Queensland and, since then, has completed a Bachelor of Law and Diploma of Neuroscience. Professionally she has been a senior public servant and CEO of legal services in Darwin and NSW. Currently Sharon is a member of the Galambany Circle Sentencing Court, and is working on her PhD thesis on the neuroscience underlying Aboriginal incarceration.

Zachary Penrith-Puchalski was born in 1990 and is from the Yorta Yorta and Dja Dja Wurrung tribes. His grandfather, Burnum Burnum, was an Indigenous rights activist best known for planting the Aboriginal flag on the White Cliffs of Dover in England in 1988. Zachary currently lives in Melbourne and studies criminology and psychology at RMIT University, and plans to work in the justice and community services sector. He has appeared on ABC TV's *You Can't Ask That* and works to support Indigenous and LGBTQIA+ Australians through various organisations, as well as providing workshops on identity for young people.

Carol Pettersen was born at Gnowangerup Mission and raised in the bush at Jerramungup in a family of seventeen, but has spent most of her life on her traditional 'country' of Albany, Western Australia. She identifies as a Traditional Owner with the Menang and Gnudju peoples of the south coast of Western Australia. She loves writing and it has been a form of escape and a way of relieving painful episodes in her life. She has long been involved in Indigenous Affairs and been appointed to many federal and state government advisory bodies, in addition to being awarded National NAIDOC Female Elder of the Year in 2008.

TODD PHILLIPS is a Bundjalung and Gumbaynggirr man from the north coast of New South Wales. He has three degrees in education from Queensland University of Technology and ten diploma-level qualifications. Todd is leading Macquarie University's Indigenous Connected Curriculum Project, an Australian-first, university-led educational framework that has been designed and developed by Walanga Muru, the university's Indigenous peoples' unit, which is applying the embedding of Indigenous values, philosophies and knowledges across all educational faculties and departments.

KERRY REED-GILBERT is a Wiradjuri woman from central New South Wales who has performed and conducted writing workshops nationally and internationally. She was the inaugural Chairperson of the First Nations Australia Writers Network (FNAWN) from 2012 to 2015 and continues today as a Director. Kerry is a former member of the Aboriginal Studies Press Advisory Committee, and her poetry and prose have been published in many journals and anthologies nationally and internationally, including in the *Macquarie PEN Anthology of Australian Literature*.

WILLIAM RUSSELL was born in 1949. His poetry and writing have appeared on education curricula in many countries and at all levels, from primary through to university. He is blind, with significant hearing loss and other scars from service in the armed forces. His vast breadth of life experience and wide travel, in addition to his military service, his disabilities and his deep cultural roots, give his poetry and short stories a broad palette that defies pigeonholing.

MARLEE SILVA is a 21-year-old Kamilaroi and Dunghutti woman who was born and raised on Dharrawal country in the Sutherland Shire, south of Sydney. She is completing a double degree at the University of Wollongong, and has also worked with Aboriginal and Torres Strait Islander high school kids through an Aboriginal non-profit called AIME Mentoring. In 2016 she spent twelve months as the organisation's Co-CEO, which allowed her to travel across the country speaking to hundreds of Aboriginal kids and showed her that while the experiences we face are diverse, rich and complex, we all seem to have an unfaltering resilience in common.

LIZA-MARE SYRON is a teacher, theatre maker and academic, whose father's family is from the Birripi nation of New South Wales. She is a founding member and Co-Artistic Director of Sydney-based company Moogahlin Performing Arts. She has published widely in the areas of First Peoples actor training, theatre practice and intercultural performance. Liza-Mare has a Doctor of Arts and has received a number of awards for her research.

FRANK SZEKELY is from Port Augusta and currently finishing Year 12 at Sacred Heart College. His hopes and dreams for the future are to be drafted to an AFL club, but if that doesn't work out he intends to find a job as a carpenter.

JOHNNY DIAZ NICOLAIDIS

MIRANDA TAPSELL is an actor best known for her roles in the multi-award-winning feature film *The Sapphires* and for the phenomenally successful TV series *Love Child*. Her recent work includes *Newton's Law*, *Secret City*, *Redfern Now*, *Wolf Creek*, *Cleverman*, *Get Krack!n* and *Play School*. Miranda has appeared in the Sydney Theatre Company's *Secret River* and *Gallipoli*, Griffin Theatre's *The Literati*, Sydney Festival's *I Am Eora*, Riverside Theatre's *Rainbow's End*, Yirra Yakin's *Mother's Tongue*, and played the lead in Belvoir Street's *Yibiyung*.

JARED THOMAS was born in Port Augusta in 1976. Both his parents have Aboriginal heritage, and he identifies as Nukunu due to being raised on Nukunu land and with Nukunu culture. He has published many books and his writing explores the power of belonging and culture. In 2015 his novel *Calypso Summer* joined the 2015 International Youth Library White Raven list of books that deserve worldwide attention because of their universal themes and exceptional artistic and literary style. His recent releases include *Songs That Sound Like Blood* and the *Game Day* series written with NBA player Patty Mills.

CEANE G. TOWERS is a Dang–Wiradjuri–Gamilaraay woman. She is a visual artist and has studied, performed and taught Aboriginal dance for over twenty-five years. She is a practising Aboriginal medicine woman who initiates healing in others. She has a Bachelor's of Education and a Master's degree in Social Policy, specialising in Indigenous issues, and works in her local communities. Ceane is the mother of five children and has two grandchildren.

AILEEN MARWUNG WALSH is Pila Nguru (Spinifex People) and Noongar. Her life since the age of twenty-four has been a combination of raising four children, study and work, hence her children are very familiar with universities and have fond memories of their childhoods associated with them. She is now an Assistant Professor at the University of Western Australia where she teaches Aboriginal history, Indigenous research and Indigenous knowledge. Her research interests include the naming histories of Aboriginal people.

SHAHNI WELLINGTON – or, as her dad would call her when she was younger and causing trouble, *Shahni-Eva-Marlene-Wellington-You-Get-Here-Right-Now!* – is a Jerrinja woman from the south coast of New South Wales, now living on Larrakia country in Darwin. Since she was little she wanted to be a storyteller. She's currently a journalist by day, and an over-eater and sports fiend by night.

ALEXIS WEST is a proud Birri Gubba, Wakka Wakka, Kanak, Caucasian writer, poet, director, performer, artist, collaborator and facilitator. She is currently the co-curator of the Australian Theatre Forum 2017. She has collaborated to create theatre with No Strings Theatre of Disability, and co-written *Sista Girl* for the State Theatre of South Australia.

ALISON WHITTAKER is a Gomeroi poet and scholar. She is author of the award-winning poetry collection *Lemons in the Chicken Wire* and a Fulbright scholar at Harvard Law School. Her second collection, *blakwork*, will be published by Magabala.

JOHN WILLIAMS-MOZLEY was adopted at seven months old to a non-Aboriginal family in New South Wales. He was reunited with his birth mother when he was twenty-seven years old and learnt that he was the eldest of eight siblings and had roughly 700 Western Arrernte family members. John pursued a lifelong aspiration to join the police after being told at a tender age that his grandfather was a 'policeman' in the Northern Territory. After twenty-six years of service as a police officer and criminal investigator, John pursued an academic career before taking up positions as the Director of Indigenous Education at Charles Sturt University and, subsequently, at the University of Southern Queensland.

TARA JUNE WINCH is a Wiradjuri writer living between Australia and France. Her first novel, *Swallow the Air*, won numerous literary awards, including the Dobbie Award and the Victorian Premier's Award for Indigenous Literature. In 2009 she was awarded the International Rolex Mentor and Protégé Award that saw her work under the guidance of Nobel Laureate Wole Soyinka. She is also the author of a collection of short fiction, *After the Carnage*.

TAMIKA WORRELL is a proud Kamilaroi woman, who grew up and was educated on Dharug country. She is a trained secondary English and Society and Culture teacher, who undertook her studies at Macquarie University. Her passion is to promote equitable education for all, and to ensure students appreciate the diversity and value of Aboriginal and Torres Strait Islander histories and cultures.